Tarot & Oracle Card Reading

by Charles Harrington

for
dummies®
A Wiley Brand

Tarot & Oracle Card Reading For Dummies®

Contents at a Glance

Table of Contents

Introduction

When considering the future and wondering what decisions they should make, people have tried quite a few things: gazing at the stars, tracing the lines of their palms, and peering closely at sheep's livers (yikes). However, one of the most beautiful and versatile methods for asking questions is the reading of cards.

Not too long ago, the only places you'd see tarot cards were horror movies, where they'd predict the hero's imminent demise, or late-night TV commercials, where they promised to reveal the identity of your one true love. And you never saw oracle cards at all! But today, the art of reading the cards is widely embraced by people around the world who appreciate their universal wisdom and amazing artwork.

Card reading doesn't necessarily require you to believe in fate, destiny, or even the ability to make predictions about the future at all. A growing number of readers appreciate the cards' function as a psychological tool to assist in creative thinking. But for those who do want to explore their mystical side, the cards can be an ideal partner for sharpening your intuition and communing with the divine.

I've read tarot and oracle cards for nearly 30 years. They've opened my eyes to worlds of possibilities and made me *very* popular at parties. I'm excited to share the techniques I've learned with new readers of all ages and backgrounds.

About This Book

Tarot & Oracle Card Reading For Dummies introduces you to the art of, well, reading tarot and oracle cards! It gives you lots of simple, fun exercises to try with your deck(s). I include many skills that experienced readers employ to go beyond the basic information and techniques used behind the scenes when designing new decks. Above all, my aim is to make this *esoteric* (obscure) art accessible to anyone interested in beginning their journey as a reader.

You can read the chapters in any order and jump around the text as you please. To make your life easier as you master the art of card reading, I've divided the book into five parts:

>> **Part 1: Getting Started with Tarot and Oracle Reading:** This part gives you the lay of the land, with some fascinating history (but not too much), an overview of the tarot's structure and traditions, and some considerations for new readers.

>> **Part 2: Mastering Card Reading Basics:** Discover how to prepare for a reading, techniques for taking the cards further, and the ins and outs of spreads.

>> **Part 3: Exploring What Tarot Cards Mean:** This part is your resource for traditional card meanings and techniques to discover your own associations for the cards.

>> **Part 4: Embracing Oracle Cards:** In this part, you explore the rapidly evolving world of oracle cards and find ways to take your readings further.

>> **Part 5: The Part of Tens:** I finish with insights I've gleaned from three decades as a reader.

The card illustrations in this book come from high-quality scans of the very first printing of the Rider-Waite Tarot (today, usually referred to as the Rider-Waite-Smith or RWS), specifically a *Pam A* (the first of four printings of the original edition). This deck, originally published in 1909, has become something of a sacred text for readers and is the basis for most decks on the market today. But you have thousands of decks to choose from for your practice.

Note: A tarot card can describe a person of any gender. A calculating man may be a Queen of Swords, for example, and an adventurous woman may be a Knight of Wands. When describing the figures who appear on a card, however, I use *she* and *he* as it applies. When I refer to the real person the card describes, I say *they*. That person can be the querent (whether you're reading for yourself or for another person) or someone in the querent's life.

Foolish Assumptions

I've written this book with a few assumptions in mind:

>> You're interested in reading tarot and oracle cards for yourself and possibly others.

>> You're looking for a guide that's accessible, straightforward, and interactive and that doesn't require you to already be familiar with any esoteric symbolism or concepts.

>> You own a deck (or several) or are on the verge of acquiring one. You do need your own deck to try out all the exercises in the book.

>> You may or may not have done some readings already. Regardless, I start from the beginning and run through all the basics, taking you step-by-step through the process of performing readings.

>> You're looking forward to having fun! Card reading is a safe and exciting experience available to everyone.

I make zero assumptions about your personal beliefs with regard to fate, destiny, free will, fortune-telling, or what you may refer to as "the divine." Card readers hold a wide spectrum of beliefs, from those who use the cards to make predictions to those who prefer to see their decks as tools for exploring their psyches. Readers of all viewpoints can use the techniques I describe in this book.

Icons Used in This Book

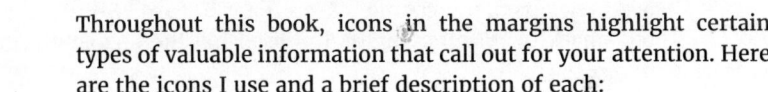

Throughout this book, icons in the margins highlight certain types of valuable information that call out for your attention. Here are the icons I use and a brief description of each:

TIP

This icon marks suggestions and shortcuts that you can use to make your reading experience easier.

REMEMBER

Remember icons highlight information that's especially important for you to hang onto for the future.

IT'S IN THE CARDS

This icon points to hands-on exercises for you to try with (or sometimes without) your cards.

WARNING

Warnings tell you to watch out! They flag important information that will keep you from getting yourself into trouble.

Beyond the Book

In addition to the abundance of information and guidance related to tarot and oracle card reading that I provide in this book, you can find even more help and info online. Check out this book's online Cheat Sheet: Just go to www.dummies.com and search for "Tarot and Oracle Card Reading For Dummies Cheat Sheet."

Where to Go from Here

Card reading is a fairly nonlinear practice, and you can explore the chapters in this book in any order. But if you're the type who likes to start from square one, then you can begin with an overview of the practice of card reading in Chapter 1 and then go straight to Chapter 2 to travel back in time for some history.

If you've done a reading and need further insights into what the cards are trying to tell you, head to Chapter 10 for an extensive overview of the meaning of each tarot card. Stick an extra bookmark in this chapter, as it's probably the one you'll return to most often.

If you'd prefer to start by going deeper with your oracle cards, this book begins to focus on them in depth in Chapter 11.

If you're itching to get going and play with your cards in new ways, scan through the book for the "It's in the cards" icon and you'll find plenty of fun exercises to try. You should also check out the collection of tarot card spreads in Chapter 7 and oracle card spreads in Chapter 13, which provide new layouts for you to sample.

Wherever you're at in your journey as a card reader, just remember to be patient with yourself. Like any undertaking, this requires time and practice for you to master. Fortunately, it's a whole lot of fun at every stage of the journey.

1

Getting Started with Tarot and Oracle Reading

Receive an overview of card reading's many forms and benefits and select your first deck.

Chart tarot's history from inventive playing card game in Renaissance Italy to one of the most beloved divinatory tools in the world.

Dive deep into tarot's structure and the nature of its five suits. Match numbers and court personalities with elemental correspondences in readings.

Reflect on your journey as a reader. Think through your goals and how to meet them, navigate ethical dilemmas, and explore techniques that will expand your skills.

Chapter **1**

Introducing Tarot and Oracle Card Reading

I n this chapter, I help you start your journey as a card reader at the very beginning with a quick discussion of terminology, a broad look at different viewpoints on card reading, and a few thoughts about which decks you may want to read with.

Defining Some Key Terms

For an exploration like this one, let me begin with a few definitions:

» **Cartomancy:** To give it its proper name, the technical term for card reading is *cartomancy*. *Carto* refers to cards, and the suffix *-mancy* means "divination by means of." For example, *necromancy* originally referred to divination by summoning the spirits of the dead (trust me, stick to the cards). As a person who reads cards, you are now a *cartomancer*. It's official!

Note: Cartomancy sounds very dignified, and you should feel free to use it, but through most of this book I stick to the more common term *card reading* to refer to using both tarot and oracle cards.

>> **Querent:** *Querent* is a fancy term used mainly by card readers and lawyers today. Of course, card readers are far more trustworthy. The querent is the person asking for a reading. If you're reading for yourself, you're the querent.

>> **Tarot cards:** A *tarot deck* consists of 78 cards separated into five suits, most commonly the Major Arcana (or trumps), wands, swords, cups, and pentacles. It was originally a card game developed in Italy in the 1400s (and is still played today). In the 1700s, occultists began to use the deck for divination. I briefly explore the complexity of tarot history in Chapter 2.

>> **Oracle cards:** *Oracle cards* are a broader category of deck specifically designed for use in divination and personal reflection. These decks have no set number of cards, and most of them are centered on a specific theme — for example, angels, animals, deities, and so on. Head to Chapter 11 for more on various types of oracle decks. Most of these decks include the word *oracle* in their title.

Recognizing the Unique Gifts of Tarot and Oracle Cards

What has kept people enchanted with card reading for more than two centuries? All systems have something to offer, but I think card reading has a few unique characteristics that have helped it grow exponentially in popularity.

Shuffling the fates

Cartomancy falls into a category of divination called *sortilege*, which means the answer is given by randomly selecting one or more items from a group. This idea suggests a view of the future that isn't set in stone. Your reading isn't a calculation; it's a shifting series of scenes that change their story each time you lay out the cards. One question naturally brings another to the surface, and you can layer a new reading onto the first.

Sparking your imagination

The first readers looked at the traditional images of the tarot playing cards and saw the secrets of the universe encoded within them. Their initial theories have proven to be untrue (I get to it in Chapter 2), but that's not important. What's important is the way the images spoke to them and got the wheels of their minds turning.

The cards have sets of traditional meanings, but the real magic happens when your sense of intuition comes into play and those meanings take on a new life as you see your own world reflected back to you. You'll discover new, personal meanings in the cards that the author and artist never imagined.

Telling stories

The cards are incredibly user-friendly. For more than 100 years, deck creators have found new and exciting ways to convey their ideas through beautiful and thought-provoking artwork. Card reading is filled with incredible mysteries and complexities, but at its core it's about finding the thread of your story in the pictures. Your brain is wired for narrative, which is why you can look up at a billboard and immediately understand the story the advertiser wants you to see.

IT'S IN THE CARDS

Ready to start playing with the cards? This technique — which allows you to tell a story with the cards — is one that I return to a few times throughout this book (and it's also a great way to become familiar with your cards):

1. **Shuffle your deck and lay out one card.**

   If you don't have a deck yet, for this exercise just turn to a random page in Chapter 10 and use the image you find there.

2. **Look at the card and start telling the story that comes to your mind based on what you see in the card's imagery.**

   This step works best if you say the story out loud or write it down. Don't worry about the "correct" meanings; just begin with "Once upon a time, there was a . . ." and say what you see in the scene.

3. **After you've told the first card's story to your satisfaction, lay down a card next to it and continue the story.**

4. **Place a third card and bring the tale to its conclusion.**

   If at any point you get stuck, pick a single object, animal, or other symbol on the card to focus on. Describe why that's important to the story and you'll be back on track.

Notice what surprised you about this experience. Perhaps small details in one card took on new significance when you saw a later card. Maybe you felt like some part of this story was really about what's going on in your own life. You just read a "three-card spread!" You'll find an exploration of that spread and others in Chapter 7.

Serving Diverse Definitions of Divination

Many definitions of *divination* insist on using the phrase *supernatural means*, but I define *divination* as "asking the universe a question and receiving an intelligible response."

This broader idea of divination fits better with the varied types of readings you can perform with the cards. In Chapter 4 you explore your personal worldview and how your ideas about the existence or nonexistence of divine beings will shape your practice. Here, I look at the range of ways you can seek answers with your cards.

Predicting outcomes

This is the fortune-telling side of the cards. In this mode, they answer the question "What happens next?"

This aspect of divination has been an essential pursuit for humanity since ancient times because

>> Uncertainty is stressful.

>> Decision-making can be crippling.

>> Having an idea about what's coming allows you to make choices in the here and now to prepare yourself.

Many people won't touch the cards because they're afraid to receive bad news, but forewarned is forearmed. Contained within every disappointing reading are directions for the best choices you can make. If it's going to rain tomorrow, try to find an umbrella.

Exploring your psyche

In this practice, the cards form a map of your life and your inner self for you to contemplate. They mirror the struggles and challenges you face and point to opportunities for healing and growth.

You'll find yourself responding to readings with new questions like these:

>> In what ways am I like this warrior on horseback?

>> What's in the cup I'm trying so hard to reach?

>> How can I wash away the pain of the past like this woman at a pool of water?

This sort of card reading relies more on your intuitive response to the images than the traditional meanings and keywords. However, those traditional meanings can be important because they help you push past personal biases that are ingrained in your worldview.

Kickstarting creativity

Here, the cards serve you as a symbol-rich brainstorming tool that helps you open yourself to new pathways of possibility. If you ever find yourself creatively blocked, the cards will help you by asking

>> What will bring more balance to this story?

>> What part of this project needs to die to give it new life and freedom?

>> How can I reclaim my throne?

This method of divination has been popular with artists, writers, and musicians looking to find new pathways, but increasingly engineers, project managers, marketers, and role-playing gamers are turning to the cards as a font of inspiration.

Pondering the mysteries

Philosophers, spiritual teachers, and mystics find a trove of inner wisdom in the images of the cards. Using this method, sometimes called *wisdom reading,* diviners wrestle with topics that have eternally confounded humanity. Weighty issues you can consider with the cards include the following:

>> What is the soul?

>> How do I find union with the divine?

>> What's the purpose of life?

WARNING

To be very clear: This method is intended to explore *your* answers to these questions and not to imagine you've uncovered *the* answers to them.

Choosing Your Deck(s)

All you need to get started as a reader is a deck of cards, a flat surface, and a healthy dose of curiosity. But which deck should you get?

When I started reading tarot in the mid-'90s, I remember my local game store had perhaps five or six different options to choose from. Today, readers are blessed with thousands of decks, from beloved classics to new releases by major publishers and indie creators alike. This wealth of options creates its own set of issues and a potential stumbling block for new readers.

TIP

Despite what you may have heard, you *can* purchase your own deck. I cover this myth in Chapter 5 but know that it's baseless; the deck you purchase will work just as well as one that's been gifted to you.

My formula for any new tarot reader is to start with two decks (I explain each in the upcoming sections):

>> The Rider-Waite-Smith

>> The deck you find most visually appealing

Considering the classic

If there's one deck every reader should have in their collection, it's the Rider-Waite-Smith (or RWS). Throughout this book, I use a reproduction of an RWS deck originally published in 1909 (as noted in the Introduction).

The RWS serves as the foundation for just about every deck in the English-speaking world. It's been beloved by readers for more than 100 years, and its images have stood the test of time for good reason.

Its artist, Pamela Colman Smith, was renowned for her work as an illustrator and a stage designer for the theater. Her clear and straightforward linework makes the details and rich symbolism easy to decipher. You can read more about the RWS deck in Chapter 2.

Because of this deck's pervasiveness, two tarot readers discussing the meaning of the Six of Swords likely will both picture Smith's image of a shrouded figure rowing a boat with upright swords in it — even if neither of the readers uses the RWS as their primary deck.

You don't have to own a copy of the RWS, but you want to be aware of its images. If the deck's artwork doesn't quite do it for you, the good news is that most decks in the tradition let you know they're Rider-Waite-Smith-based (usually on their back cover).

Responding to the art

REMEMBER

One of the clearest indicators of whether you can work with a deck is the impact the imagery has on you. Card art comes in myriad styles and mediums, from realistic to fantastical to surreal. If you find a deck drab, boring, or otherwise off-putting, it will be a struggle to read. Here are some artistic concepts to think about:

>> **Themes:** Most modern tarot and oracle decks are designed around a single theme. The sky is the limit here; you can find decks based on nature, magical and spiritual traditions, mythological creatures, and much more. If humans aren't your thing, you may prefer one of the many animal decks on the market. Many readers love cat-themed decks in particular but you can find decks featuring animals of all kinds.

If you're curious about a particular type of deck, quickly searching online for "[theme] tarot" will soon lead you to what's available.

TIP

To explore potential decks more fully, look for videos online where reviewers flip through each card in the deck. Your local metaphysical bookstore is likely to have samples of each of its decks for you to look through, too.

>> **Diversity:** Modern decks have come a long way in terms of representation, with the cards better showcasing humanity in its infinite variety. Many modern decks feature people of various races, body types, genders, and sexualities.

>> **Scenes:** For most intuitive tarot practices, you want to choose a deck with scenes on every card. Decks without scenes, called *pip decks,* show simple arrangements of suit symbols on the cards. This setup has become increasingly common with media tie-in decks based on popular films and television series. I offer guidance for reading pip decks in Chapter 8, but you'll get much more mileage from this book with scenic decks.

>> **Pop-culture tie-ins:** Decks based on popular films, movies, and games are a quickly growing trend for both tarot and oracles. These decks can make learning the cards easier for beginning readers whose prior knowledge of the characters and story lines help them make connections with the meanings. Many of these decks have non-scenic minors, or *pip cards* (see Chapter 8).

Observing oracle decks

Unlike tarot, oracle cards don't have a single foundational deck on which the rest are based. Many of these decks are similar enough that they blend well with one another, but each one contains its own unique structure.

I explore the world of oracle cards more fully in Chapter 11, but for starters I advise you to choose a single deck whose theme and artwork are inspiring to you.

Growing your collection

With such variety available and the influence of social media videos in which collectors show off their latest acquisitions, you may be tempted to run out and buy a boatload of decks to play with.

TIP

Your skill with the cards will grow more quickly if you become intimately familiar with just one or two decks at the beginning. This approach allows you to encounter the same characters in all sorts of different spreads and exercises, training your intuitive muscles to recognize certain patterns and combinations. Start small; your deck library will increase in time.

Chapter **2**

Tapping into (Just Enough) Tarot History

To fully appreciate tarot cards requires spending a little time on their unusual history and metamorphosis from card game to divination tool and beyond. Many new readers ask, "What are the original meanings of the cards?" Spoiler alert: There aren't any. To understand why that's the case, I need to take you on a trip back in time.

REMEMBER

I throw a lot of history your way in this chapter, so I want to be sure to underline the most important takeaway: The tarot's creators didn't have a set of divinatory meanings in mind when they developed the deck. They didn't even agree on which cards were in the trumps suit! Readers have developed systems of meanings over the years, and learning those systems is worthwhile, but no system stems from an original text that sets anything down in stone.

Dispensing with the Myths

The first few tarot guidebooks I read were decidedly mysterious regarding the deck's origins. In part, this murkiness happened because these books focused on divinatory interpretations. But I suspect the more significant reason for the mystery was a fear that if people understood the truth, they'd doubt the cards' ability to divine the future.

Understanding the value of a good story

Many people have a notion that for anything spiritual to be valid, it must be ancient. If it isn't, then some modern person just made it up. Giving the deck an impressive pedigree that stretched back into the misty, distant past was essential for the first occult tarot writers. In fact, a few of these writers likely actually believed these theories, imagining they'd solved a mystery buried for centuries.

Magically minded people have always had an interest in things exotic or antique. Something is undeniably romantic about feeling connected to spiritual practitioners from the past. You can close your eyes and imagine a priestess in ancient Egypt or a medieval Kabbalist spreading their deck of cards before them to uncover the secrets of the universe. (*Kabbalah* is a spiritual tradition within Jewish theology, and its practitioners seek a deeper, mystical connection with God.)

The true story of the cards doesn't diminish their usefulness as a tool for card readings.

REMEMBER

An essential quality of a divination tool is its ability to generate a random result. A whole host of different everyday objects has been used to glimpse the future over the ages, such as sheep's knucklebones, coins, shells, tea leaves, apple peels, passages from books, and more.

Cataloguing a few favorites

You hear many bold claims about tarot's origins. I highlight a few of my favorites in this list:

>> **A secret Kabbalistic text:** This theory launched tarot from an obscure playing card game to the premiere occult text. The idea is that each of the 22 cards of the Major Arcana corresponds to a letter of the Hebrew alphabet. The early decks didn't have a standard number of trump cards, so connecting the original imagery to Kabbalistic symbolism is a stretch. However, many modern decks have been designed to intentionally incorporate these symbols.

>> **An ancient Egyptian guide to initiation:** This legend claims that a secret library containing numerous scrolls and 22 columns was buried deep beneath the paws of the colossal Sphinx of Giza. On each of these columns was a gold plaque depicting one of the images from the Major Arcana (for some reason, the Minor Arcana never seems to feature in the ancient stories). The idea here is that the images from the Fool to the World depict the different stages of initiation into the Egyptian religious mystery traditions.

A few passages lie within the Sphinx, but no secret chamber with the Major Arcana has been found.

>> **Rescued by the Romani:** Further legends were created to suggest that the mysteries of the tarot were taken by Romani people from Egypt. This claim comes from both the mistaken belief that the Romani are themselves of Egyptian descent and the desire of some early readers to tie the creation of the deck to the Romani people.

REMEMBER

This legend and others that occultists dreamed up to make the tarot more exotic by tying its origins to the Romani are false. However, the Romani people indeed developed many fortune-telling traditions. Much of what we think about when we imagine a professional fortune-teller comes to us from the Romani, and modern readers owe much to their innovations.

>> **A record of lost Atlantis:** Pretty much every spiritual or metaphysical practice has been linked at some point to the lost continent of Atlantis. Mystical teachers like Helena Blavatsky and Edgar Cayce theorized that the Atlanteans had mastered the psychic arts, and that their wisdom was dispersed (along with the art of pyramid construction) throughout various ancient cultures. If such a place ever existed, it doesn't seem to have influenced the creation of playing card games, which was the first stop on tarot's journey.

>> **The poker deck's ancestor:** This one is slightly different from the others on the list. A few books I've seen claim that the 52-card playing deck used for most games descends from the tarot (and that the Joker card, which was added to playing card decks in the 1800s, is the evolution of the Fool). Poker and tarot share common ancestors in the earliest playing card games but neither is derived from the other.

The fact that none of these legends is a true history for the cards doesn't mean you can't have fun with them. Keep the baby; just ditch the bathwater. I own and enjoy decks that are designed to tap into Kabbalistic, Egyptian, and even Atlantean symbolism. The key is that these decks are clear about applying a theme to the tarot rather than renewing an ancient origin.

Tarot's structure makes it an incredible vehicle for artists, philosophers, mystics, and all sorts of people to explore any ideas or concepts that inspire them.

Exploring Tarot's Roots

To get to the beginnings of tarot as you know it, I need to set the dial on this time machine to way back before the tarot came onto the scene.

Meeting tarot's ancestors

Playing cards were invented in China sometime in the 1100s or 1200s. The earliest examples depict the possible numerical combinations you can get when rolling two six-sided dice. Later, decks were used and divided into several different suits.

Card games proved to be a popular pastime, and that popularity spread as international trade boomed following the Crusades and travelers brought their favorite games along their routes. Historians know that playing cards made their way into Europe sometime in the 1300s because you can find religious treatises on how their structure could be used to teach moral instruction and official bans prohibiting their use.

The decks themselves maintained a fairly consistent structure of 4 suits with 13 cards each, but the suit emblems varied widely depending on which country you were in. For example, German cards featured suits of bells, hearts, leaves, and acorns, and French decks had hearts, clovers, leaves, and pikes. The French system eventually evolved into the common suits of today: hearts, clubs, diamonds, and spades.

IT'S IN THE CARDS

If your humble poker deck is so similar to tarot cards, can you use it for divination? You can! Fortune-telling with playing cards has its own system with its own instructions and meanings. However, you can blend this system with tarot with a few substitutions:

Clubs = Wands

Spades = Swords

Hearts = Cups

Diamonds = Pentacles

Kings and queens stay the same, but you need to combine knights and pages into the Jack to represent someone with youthful or adventurous energy.

For the number cards, you can use the same associations that you'd use for a standard tarot deck or the suggestions for reading cards with *pips* (suit emblems) from Chapter 8.

With this system, you miss out on those big, exciting Major Arcana cards and their over-the-top energy, but you also have a stealthy way to perform a reading for someone who's uncomfortable with tarot cards or when you're in a place where tarot cards wouldn't be welcome. Many a young reader has gotten their start by using playing cards while their unsuspecting parents remained none the wiser.

The deck that most closely influenced the tarot's creation came from the Mamluk empire in Egypt in the 1300s. This deck, today known simply as *Mamluk cards,* featured suits of coins, cups, swords, and polo sticks (at least historians think they were supposed to be polo sticks). Each suit had three court cards: a king, a superior officer, and an inferior officer.

Bringing on the trumps

In these early days, trick-taking games were trendy for card players. When playing a *trick-taking* game, players place a card on the table in each round, and the person who plays the highest value card takes them all. Examples include bridge, whist, and spades (and, of course, French tarot is still played today).

In northern Italy, a new deck emerged in the 1400s, and a fifth suit was added to increase the game's complexity. This suit was *trionfi,* or triumphs. *Triumph parades* were a tradition of honoring victorious politicians and military leaders for their successes in which processions and floats would proclaim their status and success. Julius Caesar had four of these triumph parades in his lifetime.

The game was called trionfi and later *tarocchi,* which over time morphed into *tarot.* Historians believe one variation of the game was called *fancy tarocchi,* in which participants would compliment one another based on the trionfi cards that were played. For example, you may play the Chariot and congratulate your host on his impressive military career.

Doesn't fancy tarocchi sound like a fun, low-stakes way to familiarize yourself with the cards? Practice by pulling a card and finding something uplifting to say about a friend or family member. Because the game doesn't require any knowledge of the card's meaning, your non-tarot companions can also take part, pulling cards and using them to remark on some of your best traits. Pro tip: Pull all the scary or unhappy-looking cards out of your deck before trying this game.

In medieval and Renaissance Italy, the floats in triumph parades contained allegorical scenes depicting both classical Greek and Roman deities as well as scenes from Christian tradition. Many of the images in the tarot can be traced to the poem *I Trionfi* by Petrarch, including the Lovers, Temperance, the Wheel of Fortune, the Pope, the Emperor, the Empress, and the World. In these earliest decks, no single standard dictates how many trionfi cards a deck should have or in which order they should appear. Different cities like Ferrara, Milan, Bologna, and Florence developed their own traditions for which cards to include. Additionally, some decks had alternate arrangements of court cards, including female knights to complement the male ones.

Although decks used by ordinary people haven't stood the test of time, beautiful hand-painted and gilded tarot decks — created for members of the aristocracy — remain from this period. The oldest surviving deck was commissioned as a wedding gift for the members of two powerful ruling families, Bianca Maria Visconti and Francesco Sforza. Today, the deck is known as the Visconti-Sforza Tarot, and beautiful reproductions are available.

Heading to France

The game of tarocchi (see the preceding section) became wildly popular and spread throughout Europe in the 1600s and 1700s. As its popularity grew, the deck became more standardized with an agreed-upon set of trump cards whose names were now printed on them. At this point, the deck arrived at the official structure of

78 cards with 22 majors and four court cards per suit. Nearly every tarot deck you pick up today follows this formula.

In particular, the French city of Marseilles was famed for being a major playing card producer. Gone were the days when hand-painted decks were available only to the nobility. Advancements in woodcut printing technology meant that decks became more readily available for the everyday citizen and that the images on them would be more easily recognizable.

In the late 1800s, card readers began to collectively refer to these decks as the *Tarot de Marseille*. I describe this system more fully in Chapter 3. A significant number of these decks has survived to the present day, and reproductions of them are available.

"Discovering" Tarot's Secret Wisdom

The tarot may have remained a simple, somewhat obscure playing card deck if not for the intervention of three influential Frenchmen — Antoine Court de Gébelin; Louis-Raphaël-Lucrèce de Fayolle, comte de Mellet; and Etteilla — who forever altered its destiny.

Linking the tarot to the "primeval world"

Antoine Court de Gébelin was a Protestant pastor born in southern France in 1725. A lifelong scholar, Court de Gébelin was recognized during his lifetime for his pursuits in philosophy and linguistics. One of his chief passions was his theory of an enlightened prehistoric global civilization, which was the subject of a nine-volume series of books titled *The Primeval World, Analyzed and Compared to the Modern World*.

In volume eight of that series (in 1781), Court de Gébelin claimed he had met with some friends at a salon who were playing a game with tarot cards that he had never seen before. Instantly, he believed he recognized the art on the cards as Egyptian. At this time in history, Egypt was seen as the birthplace of all magical and spiritual wisdom. This event was ten years before the discovery of the Rosetta stone, and most theories formed at that time were wild speculations. Court de Gébelin believed that the cards were the remnants of a mystical text used by Egyptian priests and that the Romani people, whom Europeans thought descended from Egypt, must have smuggled the cards out of the country (as I mention in the "Cataloguing a few favorites" section, earlier in this chapter).

Louis-Raphaël-Lucrèce de Fayolle, comte de Mellet (a collaborator of Court de Gébelin; *compte* is French for "count") wrote an essay in which he suggested that the 22 cards of the trumps suit must be related to the 22 letters of the Hebrew alphabet as well as the 22 pathways found in the Kabbalistic symbol known as the Tree of Life. Court de Gébelin published the essay along with his own work even though this idea was different from his theories.

Meeting the first (known) tarot reader

The theory of an ancient origin for the tarot proved popular with students of esoteric (obscure) and occult subjects. They studied the cards with the hope that they'd reveal great mysteries if the student could unlock the puzzle of their meanings.

A few years after Court de Gébelin's theories were published (see the preceding section), the tarot evolved again thanks to French occultist and alchemist Etteilla's work. Etteilla was the pen name for Jean-Baptiste Alliette. He identified the tarot as pages from the Book of Thoth, gifted to humanity by the Egyptian god of writing and magic of the same name. In his view, the cards could be used to divine the future by following an operation he claimed to have learned from three Italian readers over several years.

Etteilla made a living telling fortunes with the tarot and teaching others his methods through correspondence courses and later at a school. He designed his own tarot deck, the first made with the intention of divining with it, and composed two meanings for each card, both upright and reversed — some readers assign special meaning to cards that appear upside down after shuffling. (I explain reading reversals in Chapter 8.) His text for reading the cards was preserved by his devoted students and is still in use today.

Thriving among the magicians

Throughout the 1800s, the tarot became a focus of intense study for anyone interested in the magical arts. Numerous writers devoted themselves to uncovering its secrets, designing their own decks to fit their theories.

One prominent group that rigorously studied the cards was the Hermetic Order of the Golden Dawn (often referred to simply as the Golden Dawn), a secret order based in Britain and dedicated to studying magic and metaphysics from around the world. The Golden Dawn outlined its own set of Kabbalistic and astrological correspondences for the tarot in a text titled *Book T* and required members to draw their own tarot decks by hand, strictly following the group's system. This new system proved to be quite influential; most readers still use it today because it serves as the foundation for two of the world's most popular tarot decks.

Rebirthing Tarot for the Modern Age

At the dawn of the 1900s, the tarot was poised to make its next massive leap in evolution, and it would continue to grow and become more accessible as new thinkers, writers, and artists became involved with the cards.

The Rider-Waite-Smith (RWS)

Nearly all decks created before 1900 paid most of the attention to the exciting trump cards with their mythical and larger-than-life characters. The decks depicted the numbered cards simply (if attractively) with the appropriate number of emblems: A Four of Cups would contain four cups and nothing else to work from. This approach required the reader to memorize meanings, either a long list of different keywords as in Etteilla's writings or exceedingly complex and convoluted ones as in the Golden Dawn guidebook. Head to the earlier section "'Discovering' Tarot's Secret Wisdom" for more on both of these important tarot figures.

The Rider-Waite-Smith tarot (RWS), named for Rider and sons (publisher), Arthur Edward Waite (author), and Pamela Colman Smith (artist), changed this tradition forever. The deck contains simple but evocative artwork (see Figure 2-1) on the Minor Arcana cards that tell relatable and human stories.

Take a moment to look at the scene in the Four of Cups image shown in Figure 2-1. Try to imagine what the person is thinking and feeling in this moment. No official story explains what's happening in that card; you're allowed to speculate about what has happened. Make up your own story for what led this person to this moment beneath a tree with all these cups. Think about a time when you felt like the person on this card. What had happened to you, and what did you do in response to it? What advice would you give to someone who found themselves in a similar situation?

Pamela Colman Smith/Wikimedia Commons/Public Domain

FIGURE 2-1: The Four of Cups as featured in the RWS.

This process illustrates the significant contribution that Smith's fully scenic suit cards made to the tarot. Her scenes take the Golden Dawn's concepts about the cards and make them more easily understandable.

REMEMBER

The RWS's other significant contribution to the history of tarot was its change of the suit emblems to wands, swords, cups, and pentacles; I explore this shift further in Chapter 3.

The Book of Thoth

Another alumnus of the Golden Dawn who left his mark on the world of tarot was Aleister Crowley. Crowley felt that the Golden Dawn had botched its system of correspondences, and he came up with his own astrological and Kabbalistic associations for the cards. He published his thoughts in a guidebook also titled *The Book of Thoth* (once again connecting the cards to the Egyptian god of magic). You can read more about the original Book of Thoth as it relates to tarot in the earlier section "Meeting the first (known) tarot reader." Crowley also renamed several trump cards to fit his ideology and assigned new titles and a new order to his court cards.

He undertook the project in collaboration with one of his students, Lady Frieda Harris, who corresponded with him and painted each card following his ideas. Although his guidebook was published in 1944, the deck itself wasn't published until 1969, after both Crowley and Harris had passed away.

Thanks to Crowley's prominence (and notoriety) in occult circles, the deck is still beloved by many readers all around the world. I cover the Thoth system briefly in Chapter 3.

Expanding the scope of tarot

In the second half of the 20th century, things really started to take off for the tarot, thanks to the efforts of three incredible women who breathed life into the deck and introduced it to new generations.

Eden Gray

A prominent actress who was a star of stage and screen, Eden Gray was an avid student of Eastern and Western spirituality. In particular, she was a proponent of the *New Thought* movement, which emphasized the power of the human mind and positive thinking to manifest desired change in the real world. In the 1950s, she opened a metaphysical bookstore where she taught classes and sold decks (a rarity at the time). Gray soon discovered that most of her students found the guidebooks available then to be impenetrable, loaded up with complex, esoteric information that made readers heads spin when they tried to read them.

Gray resolved to change this situation by self-publishing her first book, *Tarot Revealed: A Modern Guide to Reading the Tarot Cards*. The book took a straightforward, conversational approach (imagine that!) to the meaning of the cards. Additionally, Gray incorporated her New Thought perspective into the text to address the problems and challenges readers can create when they scare their *querents* (the people getting the readings). She emphasized an approach to the cards that avoided doom and gloom and empowered the reader to make positive changes in their life based on their reading. In her lifetime, she published two more guides to the tarot, which remain bestsellers today.

Mary Greer and Rachel Pollack

All the way up through the 1970s, the focus for tarot readings remained squarely on prediction and fortune-telling. Authors Mary Greer and Rachel Pollack helped usher in a new age with their first books on the subject. *Tarot for Your Self* (Greer) and *78 Degrees of Wisdom* (Pollack) both advanced the art of card reading in two significant ways:

>> Encouraging the reader to explore personal psychological and spiritual topics with the cards

>> Emphasizing an intuitive approach to reading the cards that emphasizes your insights and impressions when you react to a card in a reading

These shifts had an incredible impact on the world of tarot, opening the practice up to people who don't believe in or aren't interested in prediction. They set aside the idea of an original or universal set of meanings for the tarot and put the power in the reader's hand to use the cards as creatively as they liked.

Thanks to the rise of the Internet, the beginning of the 21st century brought on a more profound sense of connection between tarot readers, and conferences and symposiums started cropping up all around the world. You could usually find one or both of these women headlining the programming.

Chapter **3**

Touring the Tarot

A great question beginner tarot readers ask is "Are all tarot decks the same?" Each deck has its unique art style and personality, but they mostly share a standard structure. This chapter takes you under the hood to see what makes a deck of cards a tarot deck and how the parts of the deck differ.

Understanding Tarot's Structure

As I explain in Chapter 2, tarot was created as a playing card game called *tarocchi.* Just like modern playing cards, the tarot decks are divided into suits:

» The Major Arcana (22 cards in one suit)

» The Minor Arcana (56 cards in four suits)

- Wands

- Swords

- Cups

- Pentacles

This section provides a quick introduction to these suits. See Chapter 10 for a card-by-card exploration of a complete tarot deck.

The Major Arcana

The suit that sets the tarot apart from all the other playing cards is referred to today as *the Major Arcana*. Sounds spooky, right? *Arcana* means "mystery" — not the kind of mystery that involves detectives and clues, mind you. In this case, *mystery* refers to the secrets of the universe that the reader can explore through a study of the cards.

Originally, this suit was simply known as the *trumps* (today, they're often referred to collectively as the *majors*) and depicted characters and scenes that would've appeared in *triumph* parades in Renaissance Italy in celebration of important leaders, as I discuss in Chapter 2. Many of these images and symbols are taken from Christian spiritual tradition, such as, the Pope, the virtues of Justice, Fortitude, Temperance, the Devil, and even the Last Judgement.

The pictures on the Major Arcana cards are mysterious and exciting, depicting larger-than-life characters and scenes. For this reason, they've become the most iconic images connected with tarot, and they're the cards you see most often in movies and TV shows when the hero gets a reading as the fortune teller mutters about Death and the Lovers.

The Major Arcana from 0 to XXI

The cards of the Major Arcana run from 0 to XXI in Roman numerals. Though a little bit of variety sneaks into their naming and numbering conventions, this list shows the most common titles and order for them today:

0 – The Fool	VII – The Chariot
I – The Magician	VIII – Strength
II – The High Priestess	IX – The Hermit
III – The Empress	X – The Wheel of Fortune
IV – The Emperor	XI – Justice
V – The Hierophant	XII – The Hanged Man
VI – The Lovers	XIII – Death

XIV – Temperance	XVIII – The Moon
XV – The Devil	XIX – The Sun
XVI – The Tower	XX – Judgement
XVII – The Star	XXI – The World

REMEMBER

The order and titles here come from the Rider–Waite–Smith (RWS) system (more on systems later in "Recognizing the Three Big Schools of Tarot"). You occasionally see different orders for the cards; for example, the numbers for Strength and Justice are often switched. This discrepancy doesn't mean that the deck's creator doesn't know what they're doing; it just means they have a different system.

You sometimes see the order of the Major Arcana referred to as *the Fool's Journey,* a concept adapted from mythology expert Joseph Campbell's model of the Hero's Journey. In this view, the cards show an allegory for human growth in which the innocent Fool sets out into the world and experiences a series of trials and tribulations, culminating in their ultimate victory in card XXI, the World. This sequence can be a valuable model for learning about the majors. Still, in readings the cards appear in random order, and you interpret them individually.

The Major Arcana in a tarot reading

Simply put, the Major Arcana cards point to the "big stuff" happening in your life. They indicate moments of dramatic transformation, powerful forces influencing you, and opportunities for explosive achievement.

Every card in a tarot reading is important and deserves due consideration. If you lay out the cards and see a lot of majors, however, know that life may be intense for you. But this added drama and dimension in your life is likely to result in profound and significant growth and development for you. You may want to spend more time thinking through how these mythical archetypes are present in your life and how you can rise up to their example.

No majors present? Don't sweat it; that's not a bad sign. It just means that you can resolve what you're facing with practical, everyday solutions.

The Minor Arcana

If the Major Arcana cards (see the earlier section "The Major Arcana") are the gods or superheroes of the tarot, with larger-than-life personas and capabilities, then the *Minor Arcana* cards are the average citizens going about their business in conventional ways.

The four suits

As I discuss in Chapter 2, the creators of the first tarot decks (which were used for gaming) took a great deal of inspiration from the playing cards that had made their way to Europe from Asia and the Middle East. One of the most influential decks was divided into suits — swords, coins, cups, and polo sticks — for gameplay purposes. In the tarot, polo sticks were swapped out for batons, but the rest remained the same.

In modern tarot decks used for readings, the suits you most commonly find are wands, swords, cups, and pentacles. The suits' emblems relate to the four primary elemental tools ceremonial magicians use, so batons became wands and coins became pentacles. Each suit was assigned to one of the four elements of Western (European) magic: air, fire, water, and earth (see Table 3-1). I know that you won't find those listed on the periodic table of elements. These elements are metaphors for different forces that exist in a model of the universe.

TABLE 3-1 **The Suits and Their Elements**

Suit	Element	What it represents
Wands	Fire	Vitality, passion, energy, sexuality
Swords	Air	Intellect, strategy, strife, conflict
Cups	Water	Emotion, relationships, dreams, healing
Pentacles	Earth	Resources, the body, labor, manifestation

In the following sections, I explore each of the suits and the types of energy or meanings that have become associated with them.

Wands

The suit of *wands* is associated with the element of fire. Fire represents the vital energy that powers all living things in the universe. This force is the energy that gives you the drive to get up and go each day.

Think of it in terms of a car. The element of fire represents the fuel in the car's tank and also the excitement some people experience when driving down the open road.

Wands cards are typically

>> Passionate

>> Exciting

>> Action-oriented

Seeing a lot of wands in a reading may indicate life is getting pretty intense with plenty of activity and movement.

Generally speaking, wands cards advise you to

>> Take risks and make bold choices

>> Inspire others with your charisma

>> Look at how you're spending your energy

Swords

The suit of *swords* is associated with the element of air. Air represents the powers of thought and intellect — the ability to think things through and make smart choices.

If you're thinking about it in terms of a car, air represents the engineering wizardry that makes a car work, from the efficiency and functionality of its design to the way its parts seamlessly work together.

Swords also have the dubious distinction of being the suit with some of the most unpleasant cards in the Minor Arcana. This design makes some sense because swords are weapons that can do a great deal of damage.

REMEMBER

The imagery on swords cards in many modern decks can be bleak and intimidating. It can be enough to make you want to finish the reading and pack up the deck. But fear not! Each of these cards contains the key to overcoming and transforming negative situations. Take heart and consider the cards' meanings to determine how to best proceed.

Swords cards are usually

>> Cerebral

>> Challenging

>> Aloof

If you see a lot of swords in a reading, that may indicate that times are tough and require careful planning.

Broadly, sword cards suggest that you

>> Make decisions with your head and not your heart

>> Strive to see the reality of any situation

>> Take decisive action to solve problems

Cups

The suit of *cups* is associated with the element of water. Water represents the emotional aspect of life as well as dreams and creativity. It also suggests the vast depths of the psyche and the different but harmonious parts of your personality.

In a car analogy, water represents all the aesthetic choices of the carmaker (like its unique shape and color), the feeling you have when you reflect on your fondest memories of driving, and even the way you can form a relationship with your car as if it's a human being.

Cups cards are typically

>> Emotional

>> Social

>> Passive

In a reading with many cups cards present, you may find that how you feel about your situation is more important than practical concerns.

Generally, cups cards advise you to

>> Make decisions with your heart and not your head

>> Connect with others

>> Look deeply at anything you have bottled up inside

Pentacles

The suit of *pentacles* is associated with the element of earth. Earth represents the material world and all things real and tangible. It's the suit most strongly connected to money and finances as well as to the human body.

If all the elements correspond to aspects of a car, earth represents all of the physical materials that make up the parts of your car, the significant cost of buying one, and the regular maintenance needed to keep it in good shape.

Pentacles cards are typically

>> Practical

>> Grounded

>> Slow-moving

In a reading with lots of pentacles, you'd likely benefit from setting aside the ideas and feelings associated with your situation, getting down to the brass tacks, and making real change.

By and large, pentacles cards suggest that you

>> Work hard and follow the rules

>> Establish a strong foundation for growth

>> Pay attention to your health and well-being

WARNING

When someone unfamiliar with tarot looks at your deck and sees any of the cards from the suit of pentacles, they may well assume that the five-pointed star in a circle is the symbol of devil worship. Thanks to horror movies, the pentacle symbol has become strongly associated with evil and black magic. Just do your best to reassure them about the pentacles' gentle and earthy nature.

The court cards

When tarot's designers modeled their new game on the playing cards that had made their way to Europe, a tradition they maintained was including a set of royal cards. In poker decks, you have a jack, queen, and king. Tarot has four ranks to its royals: page, knight, queen, and king.

Differing aspects

In a reading, these noble characters tend to represent one of two things:

>> People involved in your situation

>> Aspects of yourself

For example, the Queen of Cups is often considered a kind and compassionate figure who's excellent at listening to others. So in a tarot reading about how to progress in your career, the Queen of Cups can represent various things, such as the following:

>> **A benevolent person who may be helpful to you — perhaps someone you can share any doubts or fears with or who can help you soothe your stress levels:** That person may have knowledge of a job opening, resources, or even some advice you can benefit from.

>> **A need for you to tap into your own sense of kindness and compassion to get ahead:** Maybe you need to listen more carefully to other people's concerns. Or maybe you're being way too hard on yourself, and the added anxiety that stress is causing is getting in your way.

Well, which is it? Those are two completely different approaches; how are you supposed to figure out which one to take? Like many things in tarot, the answer requires you to trust your intuition, consider the context of the card's position in the spread, and think about what you already know in the situation. For that last one, if you're reading for someone else, please feel free to ask them directly.

TIP

If you're still feeling stuck, my advice is to decide whether court cards will represent people or aspects of yourself *before* you shuffle the cards, and then trust that your deck is complying. Some readers have a rule about the courts representing people in *predictive* readings, in which you ask about what will happen in the future, and aspects of self when doing *self-help* readings, in which you're asking for advice about what you can do to improve your situation.

Gendering the court cards

More than any other cards, readers tend to strongly assign genders to the courts. For a long time, the standard approach was this:

Pages = young women

Knights = young men

Queens = mature women

Kings = mature men

But the images on tarot cards are *symbolic*. When you see a card showing a knight holding a sword in your future, that doesn't mean an actual blade-wielding person is about to step into your life. The same is true for gender. A tarot court card usually describes a *type* of person. A young woman starting an exciting new adventure may show up as the Knight of Wands, and a man who is in the position of caregiver may be who the Queen of Pentacles is referring to.

REMEMBER

The deck you're reading with may depict a person of a different gender than is traditional, and the person you're reading for may be of a different gender than the person seen on the card. When I describe figures on a card, I generally use *she* and *he* as it applies. When I refer to the real person the card describes, however, I say *they* because that person may be the querent (whether you're reading for yourself or for another person) or someone in the querent's life.

REMEMBER

Plenty of people don't identify with the gender they were assigned at birth or don't identify exclusively as either male or female. You can't assume you know all the details of a person who appears in a reading.

Ranking the Courts

In the following list, I go through the tarot courts one level at a time. These ranks refer to a card's level of mastery of their suit element. Though a king has a higher degree of mastery than a page, that doesn't mean that being a king is always better. When you need to be a bit more maverick in your approach, tarot will drop a knight into your reading.

>> **Pages:** *Pages* represent someone dipping their toes into their suit's element. They're typically inexperienced but curious and eager for more. They're also often cautious.

When your deck asks you to be more page-like, you have an excellent opportunity to embody the student mindset and learn new skills. Take small steps and see how things go.

>> **Knights:** *Knights* are ready to put their knowledge to the test. They're usually interested in direct experience and taking action, and their attitudes tend to be confident (sometimes too confident).

When your deck thinks it's time for your knighthood, you're ready to go out into the world, take risks, and move things forward.

>> **Queens:** *Queens* have attained personal mastery of their suit element. They can draw on their vast body of experience to make decisions. They tend to be supportive, sharing their wisdom with others.

When your deck tells you to say, "Yaaasss, queen!", it's time to listen to your own council and act instinctively.

>> **Kings:** *Kings* have attained an outer mastery of their suit element, and their achievements give them a degree of authority. They're interested in making lasting changes and establishing strong foundations. Kings tend to be measured and grounded in their actions.

When your deck reminds you how good being the king is, you're empowered to take charge of the situation and lead others by your example.

Assigning significators

Sometimes the tarot spread you're using asks you to "assign a significator to a position" (for example, the Crossroads, Horseshoe, and Celtic Cross spreads in Chapter 7 all include significators).

A *significator* is a card that represents you (or the querent, if you're reading for someone else) in the reading. Court cards can make ideal significators.

WARNING

Some older traditions about choosing a particular card based on the person's age, hair, and eye color feel outdated. (Three-quarters of the court cards would refer only to Caucasian people.) As modern decks include depictions of more diverse characters, it's less important that your significator literally looks like you.

Instead, you can choose a court card that feels like a good match for the subject of the reading based on their personality and the question they're asking. You may select a cups card for someone asking a romantic question or a pentacles card for someone interested in business.

TIP

If you're feeling at all unsure about which card to pick as a significator for a reading, just let the tarot decide. Draw a card randomly from the deck and place it in the significator position. This approach may reveal something about your querent that surprises you — especially if it's a reading for you!

Recognizing the Three Big Schools of Tarot

Alas, a tarot school has nothing to do with a magical castle like Hogwarts where wizened readers teach you everything you need to know. *Tarot schools* represent different schools of thought in our approach to tarot.

As readers throughout the ages have considered how to use this playing card deck for divination, they've shaped their decks to match their philosophies. Understanding the differences in those philosophies is a good idea for new readers as they form their own approaches to tarot.

REMEMBER

You're never locked into using only one school of tarot and its associated decks. You can learn all of them (I have!) and switch back and forth depending on the kind of reading you want to do or even just the mood you're in.

The Tarot de Marseille school

This school skips any of the decks created after the 1700s. Instead, it employs beautiful reproductions of historical decks used for gaming across Europe. Some of these are absolutely faithful in every detail (including the centuries of wear and tear the decks have suffered), while others clean things up a bit to present the cards as they may have looked when they were new. The decks in this school tend to be named after the master card makers who first printed them, such as the Nicolas Conver Tarot, the Jean Noblet Tarot, and the Jean Dodal Tarot.

REMEMBER

Not all historical decks are technically a part of the Tarot de Marseille tradition of card making. For example, the Visconti-Sforza Tarot, the oldest deck historians have a copy of, predates the Marseille decks by hundreds of years, but people who read with it tend to use the same techniques as the Tarot de Marseille tradition. To any Tarot de Marseille enthusiasts offended by my painting with a broad brush, *je m'excuse.*

If you look through one of these decks, you immediately notice that the numbered cards of the Minor Arcana are *nonscenic.* This designation means that the Four of Cups has four cups arranged attractively on the card but doesn't have any people to give you clues to its meaning. These cards are often called *pip cards* because the suit emblems on them are referred to as *pips.*

The greatest benefit to this approach is how neutral it makes the interpretation of the pip cards. Having characters and scenes on a card tends to narrow its interpretation — especially when those characters seem to be either happy or sad. You can find out more about how to interpret pip-style cards in Chapter 8.

The Tarot de Marseille school is for you if

>> You're inspired by the beauty of the Renaissance art style and woodcuts.

>> You want to read with a "purer" deck that hasn't been overtly influenced by later writers.

>> You prefer a more open reading style, less concerned with specificity, that you can interpret more freely or solve like a puzzle.

The Rider-Waite-Smith school (RWS)

This school is named after the publisher Rider Company, the author Arthur Edward Waite, and the artist Pamela Colman Smith. When it was published in 1909, their creation was originally titled the Rider-Waite Tarot, but the -*Smith* has been added in recent years to pay long-overdue respects to the woman who illustrated the cards and whose artwork is the key to its longevity.

Although nearly all previous decks featured pip cards, as I explain in the preceding section, the RWS changed things up by depicting a scene on each Minor Arcana card that gave the reader keys to its meaning. This innovation instantly made tarot more accessible to the masses. Readers no longer needed to rely solely on the very complex and *esoteric* (obscure) guidebooks available at the time and could let the interplay of the scenes tell the story of the reading.

Today, the Rider-Waite-Smith is itself the most popular tarot deck in the world, and nearly all other decks available on the market are based on it. Even though most modern decks have their own unique theme, their imagery is a nod to the RWS (for example, you usually find a boat on the Six of Swords because the RWS version has one). For this reason, the tarot card images in this book are from the RWS.

If any of the following are true, the Rider-Waite-Smith School is for you:

>> You want scenes on your cards to help communicate their message.

>> You want the versatility to be able to read with a wide variety of decks.

>> You want to participate in the wider tarot community, where the RWS is something of a shared language.

The Crowley Thoth Tarot (Thoth)

This school is dedicated almost exclusively to a single deck painted by Lady Frieda Harris based on a text by Aleister Crowley, a rather infamous figure in magical circles. Crowley was an expert on many spiritual and metaphysical subjects, and that variety is displayed in the deck. Crowley's guide to the deck is called *The Book of Thoth* (named after the Egyptian god of writing and magic).

The Thoth is esoteric in the extreme, and its symbolism is drawn from both Eastern and Western forms of mysticism, including astrology, Kabbalah, and tantra. Although it doesn't feature scenes with people in them on the Minor Arcana, Harris's imagery is evocative and powerful, and her arrangements (accompanied by the cards' keywords) go a long way toward communicating the divinatory meanings.

Crowley's Book of Thoth can be intimidating for a beginner, but in recent years, a number of other writers have explored the deck and given their own interpretations of the cards.

The Thoth school is for you if

>> You're interested in complex and layered symbolism.

>> You're interested in learning more about astrology and Kabbalah and want the tarot to be a tool to help you.

>> You prefer a more mystical or philosophical approach to the cards rather than the more straightforward prediction.

The fourth school: No school at all

The three schools of tarot in the preceding sections cover a lot of ground, but of course, artists and writers have forged new paths and created decks based on their own ideas. Most of the principles and techniques in this book will serve you well as you read with these decks, but I encourage you to refer to their accompanying guidebooks to understand the specifics that make those decks unique.

Chapter **4**

Becoming a Reader

Sometimes, you hear people say that to be a diviner, you need to be born with fantastic psychic abilities passed down to you from your grandmother's grandmother. It's not true. Card readers are made, not born, and their practices reflect their individual tastes and beliefs. In this chapter, I help you get inside your head for a moment, look at what you hope to get out of this art, and figure out how to achieve that.

Knowing Yourself Is the Key to Success

In the ancient world, the most respected voice in divining the future was the Oracle of Delphi. People from all over the world visited the Pythia, a priestess of the god Apollo, with their questions about commerce, marriage, warfare, and even details of their newly drafted democratic constitutions.

When these dignitaries entered the Temple of Apollo, they encountered a few wise sayings written on the doorway above them; the most well-known is *Gnothi Seauton* or "know thyself." Before you can benefit from or act on any other wisdom, you must first understand your own inner workings and who you truly are.

Predicting the future . . . or not

There's no one belief about divination to which all readers must subscribe to benefit from tarot reading. Devoutly religious people and affirmed atheists alike read the cards every single day.

Let me head straight for the elephant in the room: Can you predict the future by using tarot or oracle cards? Here's a range of views held by many readers:

1. Future events are set in stone, and you can learn about them ahead of time.

2. The current trajectory of the future can be understood, but you can take action to alter its course.

3. The future can't be known, but you can learn what actions you should take for your benefit in the present.

4. The future (or even the present) can't be known, but you can look at tarot cards, and the creative power of your brain will help you consider possibilities.

I'm currently in camp 2, and many of my experiences have supported this view. Even among the true believers, I've never met any who claim to be 100 percent accurate 100 percent of the time. But I'm very happy to share in the wider tarot community with people of all beliefs.

REMEMBER

Note that I said *beliefs.* If I can caution you against one thing in this chapter, it's approaching the tarot with absolute certainty in any direction. Try to keep an open mind, give different techniques a shot, and let experience be your teacher.

Understanding the source of information

When you ask the cards a question, who's on the other end of the line?

Voicing divine wisdom

When visitors asked their questions in the oracle's chamber at the Temple of Apollo at Delphi and the priestess responded, it was understood that it was Apollo and not the woman sitting on the tripod who was speaking. Similarly, many religious traditions speak of prophets who transmitted the words of their deities to the faithful.

But the gods didn't always dial direct. At oracle shrines through-out the ancient world, when a person consulted their deities or departed ancestors, the answer came from a roll of the dice, the casting of shells or bones, the flight of birds, the innards of an animal (very messy), or the sound of the wind in the trees.

REMEMBER

What these approaches all have in common is their ability to pro-duce random results. Tarot cards (and regular playing cards) were invented to be an entertaining game, but because you can shuffle them and create (seemingly) different patterns, they can give dif-ferent answers.

In the mystical view of divination, you have the ability to ask a question to your conception of the Divine — be that a deity, guides, or the universe itself — and receive an intelligible answer. Here are a few ideas about how that answer arrives:

>> **Direct response:** You shuffle the cards, and the Divine intervenes to place them in a specific order that speaks directly to your question.

>> **Inner sight:** The process activates your psychic or intuitive abilities, and the answer to your question comes to you as you explore the images on the cards.

>> **Synchronicity:** All things are intimately connected, all time is now, and seemingly random events can be understood when you look for patterns around you and use your psychic talents.

CLAIR-ING THE AIR ABOUT "PSYCHIC"

The word *psychic* can be very uncomfortable for people. Partially because they connect it with scam artists pretending to be diviners, and partially because the only type of psychic gift that many people are familiar with is *clairvoyance,* which means "clear seeing." Think of the Wicked Witch of the West from *The Wizard of Oz* looking into her crystal ball and seeing full scenes play out before her eyes. But several other *clairs* exist; the one tarot readers most experience is *claircognizance,* or "clear knowing." This state is having a solid hunch about what's hap-pening or will happen; you may know it more simply as *intuition.*

Making room for the skeptics

When outlining the different views of readers in the earlier section "Predicting the future . . . or not," I note that some of them don't believe in any form of the divine or supernatural beings and still work with the cards. Can they be correct? Is tarot readers' success at prediction a mixture of creative problem-solving and confirmation bias? They may be right! I've had enough weird stuff happen with my readings that I'm comfortable with my position, but I do consider that this stuff may all just be made up . . . and it still works!

If you're pretty certain that predicting the future is pure mumbo-jumbo, you can benefit from reading tarot cards by thinking about how you can disrupt your normal thinking patterns.

People tend to go about their activities in the same way over and over again. If something works, you keep at it. When it stops working, you can feel stuck in a rut and unsure of what to do because your experience has dug a deep groove into your psyche that's hard to get out of.

Imagine you're in conflict with someone. Your normal approach is to explain the logic of the situation until the other person is convinced, but this time it's not working. Your deck of choice tells you that the answer to your problem is . . . this picture of a sailboat! The gears of your mind start working, and you may come to a few different conclusions, such as the following:

>> **Thinking about how sailors *change tack* by adjusting the sails in the opposite direction to catch the wind:** The expression *changing tack* also means taking a drastically different approach. In this case, that may be listening rather than explaining or coming at the problem from an emotional angle rather than a logical one.

>> **Concluding that this argument isn't one you can win and that you need to *sail past it* and leave this entire situation behind.**

>> **Noticing how nice the day looks in the picture and taking the person you're arguing with out for some fun, possibly in nature, to change the vibe.**

>> **Thinking it's time to call in other *members of your crew* to support you:** For example, who is the captain, navigator, or lookout in your situation?

In a similar way, the images of the tarot and oracle cards and the traditions of meanings associated with these decks can stir up new ideas for you and alter your approach to any project or problem you face.

Without any belief in someone or something on the other end of the conversation, you can ask your question to the cards and mull over the best way to apply the images or message to your situation. Cards are ideal for thinking outside the box.

Playing nice

No one can be absolutely certain about matters of the existence or nonexistence of supernatural beings or whether people have psychic abilities. Both the mystical and nonmystical views of card reading are valid and accepted within the community. Furthermore, as long as you have a practice that works for you, what other people get up to really isn't any of your business.

WARNING

For this reason, all readers should try their best to avoid any browbeating or name-calling and simply recognize each other's shared love for this practice.

Identifying your divinatory goals

Where do you want your journey with the cards to take you? Do you just want to have some spooky fun at your upcoming Halloween party? Do you want to become well-versed enough in the cards to read them without the need to look up their meanings each time? Do you want to go all in, collecting many decks and learning to read every system you come across? The following sections offer a few different approaches to the cards and strategies to help you achieve them.

REMEMBER

These paths aren't exclusive, and you can explore each of them whenever you desire for as long as you want. Divination is a diverse field, and each person's practice is unique to them in some way.

Dabbling with divination

REMEMBER

Most of the people reading tarot or oracles today do so with the guidebook open, looking up each card as they go along. You only have so much time in the week to divide among your interests, and making tarot a fun hobby you work with now and again is absolutely okay. You can still have profound experiences as you perform readings that speak significantly to your soul.

Your strategies as a dabbler may include the following:

>> Becoming familiar with the ins and outs of your deck(s) and trying out different techniques to find ones you enjoy.

>> Giving readings to family and friends who understand that you're still learning and share their feedback with you about the experience.

>> Finding a cadence for your readings that you can stick to and that keeps you connected to the cards. Perhaps you read every Monday or on the night of the full moon — whatever works for you.

Leaning into intuition

Your decks can help you in the process of building up your psychic and intuitive muscles. Rich traditions of meanings are associated with the cards (and you can tap into them when you feel stuck), but your path will focus more on quieting the conscious mind and letting the images speak to you directly.

If you want to use tarot intuitively, consider these strategies:

>> Using meditation and creative visualization to connect more deeply with the inner voice, sometimes referred to as the *higher self,* that perceives what the waking mind can't

>> Learning to trust the flashes of insight you receive both in readings and from the omens that pop up unexpectedly in your everyday life and discerning which insights come from an authentic place and which are based on hopes and fears

>> Maintaining a "beginner's mindset" to approach readings with a fairly blank slate and receive fresh perspectives on the cards in each session

Adding tarot to your creativity toolbox

Reading tarot and oracle cards is a fantastic way to bring an out-side perspective to any undertaking. Their multifaceted structure speaks to just about every part of the human experience and can jolt you out of any rut you find yourself in.

Strategies for using tarot in creative pursuits include these:

>> Making a habit to begin any new project or endeavor with a reading so that right from the outset you're thinking expansively.

>> Finding playful ways to interact with your deck and looking at readings as a puzzle that you can solve when your brain finds the hidden pattern in how the images interact.

>> Letting your cards take the wheel when a decision freezes you and you feel that you can go either way. Pro tip: Start with restaurant menus.

Mastering cartomancy

Cartomancy (a fancy word for card reading) is an expansive practice with no limit to how much you can discover and experience. Becoming intimately familiar with your cards, and the many techniques for using them, is an empowering experience and makes you a more confident and versatile diviner ready to meet the future come what may.

Your strategies for becoming a cartomancy master may include the following:

>> Working to memorize the meanings of the cards in one or more schools (I give an overview of tarot schools in Chapter 3). Becoming conversant with your deck brings both familiarity and ease to the process.

>> Connecting with the wider cartomancy community to share your own knowledge and benefit from the insights of others.

>> Diversifying the tools and techniques you work with. Learning the wisdom of many decks and other forms of divination adds to your bag of tricks and vocabulary when returning to your more familiar tools.

Going pro

For some, card reading is their true calling, going from a hobby or personal tool to a significant stream of income (whether as their main profession or a side hustle). As long as human beings need to make decisions, they'll turn to diviners.

If professional tarot reading is your goal, consider these strategies:

>> Getting a significant amount of practice reading for others to help you understand the complex dynamics between reader and querent.

>> Learning to read clearly *fast*. Most of your clients will expect you to get to the point and provide answers they can retain long after they've left your table.

WARNING

>> Becoming very familiar with smart small business practices as well as the laws regarding fortune-telling where you live. Cities can have vastly different regulations, and you don't want to be surprised.

Tackling Troublesome Topics

Learning to read the cards can be both fun and inspiring, and when you're new, most of your focus is on the how-to elements (techniques, spreads, meanings, and so on). After you're in the thick of things, a few tricky areas can trip you up. I explore some of them in the following sections because, as any diviner can tell you, forewarned is forearmed.

Dealing with ethical dilemmas

For better or for worse, no governing body hands out decrees for card reading do's and don'ts. That's mostly for the better, but it means each reader must form their own code of ethics. Having one in place makes things much easier in the moment when you're confronted with various issues.

You'll certainly encounter other issues, but the following are some of the most common situations readers find themselves faced with. Thinking through these sticky questions in advance can help you make good choices in the heat of the moment.

Minding your business/performing third-party readings

Is performing a card reading about another person the same thing as spying on them or reading their journal without permission? Other people's feelings and decisions often have a significant impact on your life, and at some point, you're going to want to peek into someone else's psyche.

Do you feel that any information you can obtain from a reading is fair game?

On a related note, if you read for others, they may ask you to tell them what's going on with the people in their lives. Very often, this desire comes from a place of legitimate concern about the health and well-being of their loved ones.

Do you only read about the querent's situation, or are you willing to investigate the affairs of others on their behalf?

Becoming too reliant on readings

Readings are a wonderful tool for helping people plan for the future, but sometimes people can develop addictive behaviors around them. They may be afraid to make any decision without a reading and return to the cards to look at the same issue again and again. Professional readers sometimes run into clients who call back every single day to ask the same questions. Being afraid to make any decision without input from your cards may indicate you're engaging in obsessive thinking.

How much is too much?

Exploring uncomfortable questions

Some readers refuse to explore certain topics with the cards. These no-gos can range from whether people will be successful in having affairs or getting away with other deceptions to readings about the dead.

Where aren't you willing to go with a reading?

WARNING

Some questions are actually criminal to tackle. In most places, people aren't allowed to give legal advice or make medical diagnoses without having official certification. That doesn't mean you can never read about someone's health in general, but you must be clear about what you are and aren't qualified to speak to.

Reading for children

Some readers have a hard and fast rule about never reading for minors. Others may be willing to give the reading as long as a parent or guardian gives explicit consent or is present.

Do you read for kids?

Charging for a reading

The issue here is less about whether charging for readings is unethical (though some people feel that way) and more about whether you're ready to start making money from the practice. Something to consider is whether you'd be willing to pay for the quality of reading you're able to provide.

Are you ready for paid reading?

Addressing mental health issues

WARNING

This area is one where I'm willing to butt in and give my two cents. If you or someone you're reading for is contemplating self-harm or experiencing a mental health crisis, that's not a job that cards are suited to answer. The best course of action is for the querent (whether that's you or another person) to contact a crisis hotline.

Acknowledging biases and prejudices

Whether you believe the cards are in touch with a divine source of wisdom or are just helping your mind explore possibilities, the answers still pass through the filter of you. Your best results come when you can approach readings with a clear and open mind. No small task!

Detecting bias

One night, I was hired to read tarot at a large party, and a woman sat down and asked for a general reading. I turned over the cards and shared the message that it'd be all right for her to let go of a burden she'd been hanging onto for some time. Instantly, waves of relief washed over her. She told me that she was one semester away from a degree in accounting, but she'd come to realize she absolutely loathed the field and what she really wanted to do was pursue a career in the arts. She was excited because she felt the cards had given her permission to pursue that dream. As she walked away, I wanted to run after her and shout, "Wait a minute, let's think this through!" But remember, she hadn't come for *my* advice; her question was for the cards, and they answered.

REMEMBER

A major benefit of tarot and oracle cards is their ability to offer an outside perspective. Whether you're reading for yourself or someone else, your role is to deliver the message.

Perhaps you've heard the expression "When all you have is a hammer, everything looks like a nail." If your interpretations have a high degree of similarity, that may indicate your personal biases are sneaking into your readings. Being aware of your own biases is difficult, but you can identify potential patterns by asking yourself a few questions when you look at a series of readings:

>> Is the answer almost always that the querent needs to work hard and soldier on?

>> Do the cards usually seem to predict doom and gloom?

>> Are they always telling you, "Yes, go for it!"

>> Does every new romantic partner seem to be the One?

Giving an answer you wouldn't personally give without the cards is hard to do . . . which means you should definitely practice. Try it out with this exercise:

1. **Think of a topic that's very important to you.**

   It may be a project you've worked hard on, a close relationship, or anything at all that feels crucial.

2. **Imagine you want to receive a reading in which you ask for advice about what actions you should take regarding the chosen topic.**

3. **Look through your deck card by card and place them into three piles.**

   Divide your piles like this:

   a. Cards that look like they'd give the answer you hoped for

   b. Cards that seem neutral

   c. Cards that look like they'd tell you to do the opposite of what you want

4. **Put piles *a* and *b* back in the box; you won't be using them.**

   I'm so sorry, but this will be good for you, I promise.

5. **Now imagine that you're the card reader you went to for this very important reading.**

   You're an impartial party with no skin in the game.

6. **Lay out one to three cards at a time and interpret them out loud as if they came up in the reading.**

7. **When you're finished, reflect on how giving advice you find counterintuitive feels.**

8. Eat a comforting snack to help you feel better after this ordeal.

Uncovering prejudices about querents

I was giving readings at a bar I'd never been to before when the members of a motorcycle club showed up clad in spikes and leather. The toughest-looking member of the bunch came over and asked for a reading. Instantly, my mind went to work forming assumptions: "This is going to be rough." "I'm sure he doesn't believe in tarot." "He's gonna say I'm not making any sense." "He must be making fun of me." "He probably expects me to say X, Y, Z."

I was wrong! He was lovely, and the reading went smoothly.

When you meet someone, your mind starts telling you stories about them within the first few moments. The way they dress, the words they use, and their body language are going to send you signals, and you may find that you're adjusting what you say to fit with what you believe they want to hear. This tendency can really muddle a reading.

REMEMBER

Remind yourself: You don't know what you don't know about a person. Furthermore, you can't be sure of what they're hoping for unless they tell you. Not every young woman asking about her relationship with her boyfriend is hoping they'll get married, buy a house, and have 2.5 kids. For some, that may be the worst-case scenario.

Shaking these prejudices is hard. I may have seen the light about biker gangs, but when a business executive in an expensive suit sits down for a reading, some part of my mind assumes that they don't believe in tarot and think I'm a fraud. I'm not perfect! But in those moments, I *do* acknowledge the thought and do my best to imagine the querent is a blank slate and their beliefs about the cards aren't truly relevant to our interaction.

REMEMBER

If you identify as an intuitive or psychic reader, you may feel that you're picking up on the energy of the querent in the session. Focus on learning to tell the difference between a message from your higher self and a snap judgment based on stereotypes and assumptions. What does that inner voice sound like when it's speaking the truth? Notice the difference.

Defusing difficult readings

It'd sure be nice if the cards always told you that everything would be amazing and that all your dreams would come true. Alas, sometimes the answer is unpleasant. Even if you don't perform predictive readings, you may find that the cards' recommendation for you is exactly what you were hoping it wouldn't say.

Heeding the warning

Do you have a friend who is always asking for advice but never seems to follow it? Sometimes a reader is that friend to their tarot deck.

In my 20s, I was dating at a pace only available to the hopelessly romantic. When I started seeing someone new, I'd consult the cards to see how things were going to go. And no matter what they said, I'd twist the answer to mean "there's a chance." Fear of missing out (FOMO, as the cool kids say) meant I'd never listen to the cards' warning. Bad reading? I'd find a way to ask the question from a slightly different angle until I got a reading that made me feel better. And things would go miserably.

One day when chatting with a potential match, I shuffled the cards and got a "stand down" from them. And. I. Listened. I didn't plan the date and, to my extreme surprise, I didn't feel one iota of regret. I'd put in enough reps with my cards to trust them.

REMEMBER

What's the point of asking the question if you're not going to accept the answer for what it is?

TIP

Some people aren't looking for a reading, they just want a confirmation. If a querent pushes back on you, look at the cards and see if anything could reasonably support the answer they're looking for. If yes, give them that POV. If not, do your best to let them down gently. If they say you're not a good reader, just know they weren't truly open to other answers.

Here's a personal example: After a bad breakup in my youth, I called a reader to tell me it was gonna be all right. When she said we weren't getting back together, I started to ask, "But what if . . ." She stopped me cold with, "I can be your best friend and tell you what you want to hear. But that's not what I do, and it's not what you paid for."

What if you can redirect all the time, energy, and money you waste on things that don't work out elsewhere? This benefit is one of the values of getting a "no" from your cards.

Curing toxic positivity

A term that's making the rounds in the card reading community is *toxic positivity.* In this state, people are only allowed to project happy emotions, and all negativity and conflict must be ignored. In some households and workplaces, people are shunned or sidelined if their doubts or attempts to point out problems make others feel uncomfortable.

In a card reading, toxic positivity takes the form of sharing a positive message only, no matter what the cards indicate. You may feel guilty about giving someone bad news or feel that hearing that they face significant obstacles to achieving their goals may be harmful to them.

WARNING

In spiritual circles, some people espouse the belief that everyone can have anything they desire if they want it enough and believe in themselves. This mindset makes people blame themselves for any setbacks and feel like they don't achieve their aims because they're unworthy. If you could get anything by wishing hard enough for it, you wouldn't need to get card readings!

Imagine that you went to your doctor, and they saw an issue in your test results. Because they didn't want to bum you out, they let you know that you just had to keep on keepin' on and you'd be fine. Thankfully, the medical field doesn't operate that way (no pun intended). What they do instead is start by addressing the problem and then talk you through their plan for treatment.

Finding the silver lining

In the movies, the card reader tells the hero that doom is upon them, and nothing they can do will prevent their imminent death or transformation into a werewolf. And that's the reading!

Fortunately, that's not how it works in real life. For every unpleasant tarot card, a strategy for what you can do to make the most of your situation is available.

IT'S IN THE CARDS

Get ready to engage your intuition for some creative problem-solving. Since the fives of each suit are notoriously difficult cards, look through your deck and remove the fives from the Minor Arcana. Figure 4-1 shows them from the Rider-Waite-Smith: Five of Wands, Five of Swords, Five of Cups, Five of Pentacles. (More on the Minor Arcana in Chapter 3 and the Rider-Waite-Smith deck in Chapter 2.)

Pamela Colman Smith/Wikimedia Commons/Public Domain

FIGURE 4-1: Examining the fives can help to sharpen your intuition.

Imagine that you walked into any of these scenes. What might you say to the people who are suffering in these images? Think it through.

What did you come up with? My one piece of advice is to begin by acknowledging the person's pain. As a card reader, you want to quickly solve the problem, but sitting with the pain for a moment is okay. It makes a world of difference, and that moment of recognition helps grease the wheels of the exit strategy.

TIP

When the cards seem particularly heinous, read through the traditional interpretations of the cards in Chapter 10 to get some ideas for how to proceed.

Finding the silver lining doesn't mean you can have everything you want if you can find the right strategy. For example, in dismal romance readings, you have no control over the other person's agency. You can, however, reinvest your time and energy in someone else.

Practicing Is the Other Key to Success

Just like learning to play an instrument, drive a car, or paint a picture, your first forays into reading cards are likely to be clunky, confusing, and a little embarrassing when you look back years from now. Even if you have a natural talent for card reading, the way you become truly adept is to practice.

Reading as often as you can

I begin every day by drawing a card, making a good guess at what it signals, and writing it down. Okay, *almost* every day; I'm human!

But if the cards have meanings, why does practice matter? Even though cards do have many traditional meanings, getting your reading reps in

>> Familiarizes you with every card in your deck so that you're clued in to their nuances

>> Provides the context you need to take the lists of a card's many meanings and apply the correct ones to the question

>> Gives you the opportunity to see how the cards interact with each other

>> Introduces questions and topics you'd never come up with on your own when you read for others

>> Teaches you valuable lessons as you get it right *and* get it wrong

But what happens when you run out of questions? You've already asked about all the issues you have going on at the moment. What else is there?

First, check out the various spreads in Chapter 7 for the tarot and Chapter 12 for oracle cards and take the ones you haven't tried before out for a spin. When using a new spread, ask a low stakes question like, "How will I feel about my dinner tonight?" You'll be less tense as you work through the meaning. Offer your close friends and family members readings as well — with the caveat that you've still got your training wheels on and you'll likely need to look up the meanings.

IT'S IN THE CARDS

Here's a very fun way to find topics to practice with:

1. **Go to the grocery store and pick up a trashy tabloid magazine filled with celebrity gossip.**

   If those rags repel you, you can get a serious news magazine instead.

2. **For each article, imagine you've been hired by the subject to perform a reading about the new movie, romance, or breakup.**

   If you're using a serious news magazine, your fantasy client is any of the people involved in the story.

3. **Perform the reading as if the subject were sitting in front of you.**

   A friend of mine uses her teddy bear as a stand-in. Speak out loud and go card by card, giving full details.

WARNING

I'd be remiss if I didn't point out that this exercise is intended to be a fun way to practice; don't imagine you've received insights into the actual celebrities' lives.

Recording your readings

The Venn diagram of people who like to read cards and people who like to buy very fancy journals is nearly a perfect circle. Start putting those notebooks to use by beginning your tarot journal.

TIP

If paper and pens aren't your thing, you have plenty of digital options to choose from. Whatever app or software you use, just make a new entry for each reading. The electronic route has the added benefit of making your readings easier to search for.

Each time you do a reading, create a new entry in your journal in which you record the following:

>> The date

>> Your question

>> The deck you used (if you have multiple that you work with)

>> The name of the spread (if you use different ones)

>> Each card in the reading, followed by your interpretation

If you're feeling pressed for time, you can skip going card by card and just write a single entry for the whole spread, but when you're learning, taking the more robust approach is best.

This process helps you in a few ways:

>> **It forces you to give yourself a complete reading.** It's easy to just scan a spread and think of a quick sum-up, but much more is revealed as you explore each card and articulate its meaning in this moment for your question.

>> **It allows you to return to your reading for further insights.** Instead of performing a new reading because you forgot what the cards said last week, you can lay them out again and see what jumps out at you this time.

>> **It both makes you feel very psychic when you get it right and allows you to learn from your errors when you get it wrong.** More on mistakes in the next section.

About those fancy journals: They don't actually need to be fancy. My first tarot journal was a composition book I bought at a drug-store for a couple of dollars. Starting with a cheap notebook can actually be a great way to work out your preferred note-taking system without feeling like you're messing up a good journal.

TIP

A lot of readers have a hard time "ruining" their expensive leather-bound books with their imperfect handwriting. One trick to help get past this hurdle is to begin by numbering all the pages.

Many readers keep two separate tarot journals: one with their readings and another with all their notes on card meanings, spreads, and anything else they learn. You can take that route or opt for a single book; it's up to you. If you go for the electronic option, all you need to do is have separate folders or tabs for each section.

Learning from mistakes

Whether you read predictively or not, sometimes you're gonna get it wrong. For some people, that first majorly botched reading is enough to make them decide that card reading is a load of malarky. As I mention earlier in the chapter, that's certainly possible. However, experience has shown me that reading errors are usually my own.

The first step to examining your mistakes is to return to the tarot journal and see what couple-of-weeks-ago-you actually wrote down for each card interpretation. Note which parts of the reading, if any, did turn out to be correct.

As you review, keep a lookout for the two biggest culprits in card reading errors: hope and fear. I'm not saying you can't be hopeful or fearful, but those two states of mind can really throw you off your game and tell you what you want to hear. Some readers feel that extreme hope and fear can even cause the wrong cards to turn up based on their firm beliefs about what will happen. I don't subscribe to that way of thinking myself. With misinterpretation, I usually find it's a case of user error.

Now zoom in on the cards that you feel you really missed the mark. Consider what actually happened in your situation and see whether you can come up with a reasonable angle to interpret the card to match what took place. Perhaps the person you thought would help was meant to be a hindrance. Don't worry if you can't find the answer now; perhaps in a future reading it'll all make sense.

Another thing to consider is a matter of scale. You can easily over-read a card. For example, the Tower (shown on the left in Figure 4-2) is a card that notoriously seems to say that a disaster will take place. But people don't usually have too many disasters in any given week, and the Tower's energy tends to manifest as a rough patch, setback, or unexpected moment. On the opposite end of the spectrum, the Four of Wands (shown on the right in Figure 4-2) can sometimes mean a wedding, but it's more often going to appear as a nice date where you have a good time.

FIGURE 4-2: These two cards have very different energies.

TIP

When someone considers the reading you gave them a failure, it can feel debilitating. You may even feel the urge to be defensive. Thank the person for the feedback and commit to learning from it. What about when they've clearly misinterpreted what you said? Your best bet is to avoid arguing; just take the feedback as helpful information.

Divinatory ambiguity

Legend has it that the Pythia at the Oracle of Delphi once told a king that if he invaded another country, he'd destroy a great empire. (Flip to the earlier section "Knowing Yourself Is the Key to Success" for info on Delphi.) The king invaded — and it was his kingdom that was destroyed.

Modern readers look at this story and assume that all the priestess's prophecies were completely ambiguous and could be interpreted to mean anything after the fact. (This kind of ambiguity is known as a *Delphic answer*.) But the historical record shows that most of the Pythia's prophecies were straightforward.

As for the ruined king, the ancient Greeks didn't interpret this story as a con. Instead, they saw it as a comeuppance for the king's hubris. If Delphi didn't have a strong record of success, it wouldn't have remained a prominent institution for centuries.

I bring this point up just in case the previous section, "Learning from mistakes," sounds like I'm saying that card readings are all ambiguous and can mean anything when reviewed after the fact. Please know that if my readings only panned out some of the time, I'd have packed my decks away years ago.

However, being willing to give failed readings a thorough review is a great way to grow in your practice.

Trying new techniques

One of my favorite things about card reading is its infinite variety. Keep your practice fresh and vibrant by continually adding new techniques to your bag of tricks.

IT'S IN THE CARDS

To get things started, consider a few ways to jazz up your readings:

>> **Make up a fictional fortune teller and read your cards in their voice.** Be as extreme as you want with your interpretations and have as much fun with it as you can.

>> **Give a friend a reading in which you respond to their question with questions of your own.** (If you've ever taken an improv class, you may be familiar with this game). If the Emperor comes up, ask them whether they need to act with more authority. For a page, ask them what they want to learn.

>> **Hold a card to your heart without looking at it and try to listen for it to share its message with you psychically.** Then look at it and see how you connect the message with the card.

>> **Try all the spreads in Chapter 7 of this book and then make up a few of your own.**

>> **Draw a card and then try to emulate one of the characters in it for the rest of the day.** Pose like them, dress similarly to them, and speak as you imagine they might.

>> **Blend oracle and tarot cards together in a reading,
seeing where they complement one another.**

>> **If you don't believe in predictive reading, give it a whirl
and see how you do.**

>> **For a card that's getting you stuck, see what it looks like
in a variety of other decks.** An online search can introduce
you to many new versions.

>> **Read for your pets and other animals.** Prepare for slobber
if you let them pick the cards.

2
Mastering Card Reading Basics

Understand practical and metaphysical aspects of working with the cards and how to identify unhelpful superstitions. Discover the value of stepping out of the ordinary in a reading and set the mood for divination. Consider the care and feeding of your querents.

Get an overview of each element within a reading from crafting the right questions to shuffling the cards.

Think through the structure of tarot spreads and how to use them for maximum benefit in your readings.

Chapter **5**

Shaping Your Practice

The only thing you need to read the cards is a deck and a flat surface (and occasionally I've even improvised the flat surface when riding the bus). Oh, and this book; you *must* own a copy of this book, or it won't work! How fortunate for you, discerning reader. With a deck in hand and a place to set the cards down, you're ready to begin. But in this chapter, you get practical and mystical advice about how you can further enhance your experience.

Caring for Your Deck

Your decks are your working partners in this practice, and treating them with respect is a great idea. In the following sections, I run through some old wives' tales about how to properly treat cards, a few actual tips for keeping your deck in tip-top shape, and a few ideas for injecting more mojo (if you want to).

Discarding unhelpful superstitions

A surprising number of taboos about tarot decks are floating around that the community just can't shake. As I note in

Chapter 1, the earliest readers felt they needed to shroud the cards in mystery and made up false histories because no one would believe the cards could be used for divination if they were just regular playing cards. Creating a set of practices you implement for your deck can be empowering, but too many like the following are based on fear:

>> **You must be given your deck as a gift.** This question is one of the most common that beginners ask in tarot community spaces. I've bought decks and I've been gifted decks, and there's no difference in how well they work for me.

>> **You must steal your deck.** Just in case this point isn't obvious, you probably don't want to go around stealing things that you hold sacred. Don't steal decks.

>> **You must never use another reader's deck.** If you mean *without their permission,* then sure. A recent (very fun) horror movie made this myth the premise for unleashing evil spirits to attack the heroes who broke this rule. It's a great plot device, but it's not true. People sometimes wonder whether you can read with secondhand decks, and the answer is that you absolutely can. You may want to perform a small ceremony to cleanse their energy — or you may not!

>> **No one else may touch your deck.** Following from the preceding entry is the idea that anyone else's energy pollutes your cards. You can certainly choose to make this a rule for yourself, but generally speaking, I find that letting the querent shuffle and cut the deck involves them in the process in a positive way.

>> **You must wrap your deck in black silk and sleep with it under your pillow.** You may enjoy doing this, but it's not necessary. Just be careful about smooshing your cards.

>> **You can't read the cards for yourself.** Okay, this one isn't technically about your deck, but it's pervasive, so I want to address it here. You *can* read cards for yourself. Being as objective for yourself as you can be if you read for another person is challenging, but it's possible.

TIP

Have you noticed the pattern? If anyone tells you that you must *always* or should *never* do anything with your deck, they're likely quoting some taboo that has no basis in this practice.

Considering practical issues for your deck's well-being

Your deck is (in almost all cases) made of paper that has been treated with chemicals to help protect it. It may have a smooth linen finish like poker cards or a glossy finish that brings bold colors to life. All the rules about how to treat paper apply to your deck.

Over time, your deck will likely develop a slight bend as you read with it. Gentle shuffling can help avoid making this shape too severe, but often a very minor curve is the sign of a well-loved divinatory tool. It's a bit like the way owners of cast-iron skillets are proud of the way their pan is seasoned with use. A more extreme curve is the sign of overzealous shuffling, which I don't recommend.

Housing your deck

Most decks spend their lives in the same cardboard boxes they came in. This approach does a great job of helping maintain their shape, and it makes storing a large collection of decks on your shelf a lot easier.

If you plan to take your deck on the road, consider upgrading to a pouch to keep your cards in. More on pouches later in "A light scarf and deck pouch."

Keeping it clean

To keep your deck looking pristine, make sure everyone who touches it washes their hands first. Keep food and drinks away from the table because one small jolt can mean your cards are going to be the color of merlot. A spread cloth (see the later section "Spread cloth") also reduces the amount of grime that gets on your deck.

If you do manage to get some schmutz on your cards, wiping them with a slightly damp cloth, drying them, and then leaving them out to become totally dry before putting them back in their box takes care of the issue.

Trimming your cards

This topic is one that can give card collectors heart palpitations. In the past, some of the limitations of printing technology meant that cards had to have fairly thick borders. Otherwise, the printers ran the risk of cutting off part of the image. This necessity meant the already oversized cards became even bigger, which was an issue for anyone with small hands. Printing tech has improved, and more new decks are borderless, but you still find them in some cases.

In recent years, readers have been trimming their decks to remove the borders. Doing so tends to make the colors more vibrant and gives the deck a more personalized feel for the trimmer.

TIP

If you want to try trimming, I recommend getting a good paper cutter or a pair of sharp scissors from the craft store. You also want to get a corner rounder because newly trimmed cards are pointy, which doesn't feel good for your fingers.

The sides of your trimmed deck won't be as pretty as they were before. You can solve this problem by running a marker or a paint pen around the edge of each card. Choose a color that complements the color scheme of your deck. Take your time with this process.

TIP

The best advice I've ever received about trimming a deck is "If you need things to be flawless, don't trim your deck." I'll add to that: You may want to have a backup copy just in case.

Creating a Liminal Experience

You hear the word *liminal* thrown around a lot these days. It comes from the Latin word for "threshold" (the bottom of a door) and is associated with a transitory place, like a hallway or lobby, where you aren't meant to spend much time. These places can have an eerie quality and a sense of otherworldliness.

Many sacred or spiritual spaces have been designed to help create this sense of stepping out of your ordinary, mundane life. Gothic cathedrals draw parishioners' eyes toward the heavens with their vertical structure and high stained-glass windows.

By bringing in a touch of the sacred to your reading, you can help facilitate a liminal experience for both you and the querent (if you're reading for someone else). You more easily enter a head-space that's open to receiving wisdom from your reading.

TIP

It doesn't matter if you aren't religious or spiritual; your liminal experience can skip the supernatural entirely. Human beings find rituals can enhance experiences and make them more meaningful.

Experimenting with aesthetics

A few years back, I noticed that the big Halloween stores had added a special aisle dedicated to card reading. In that aisle, along with a few decks and Ouija boards, were spread cloths spangled with moons and stars, wall hangings featuring the signs of the zodiac, black lace shawls to help you channel your inner Stevie Nicks, and candles in glass holders decorated with eyes and pentagrams.

All that presents a fairly cookie-cutter version of "fortune teller parlor chic" (and I don't mind it), but what will be most beneficial for you is to create a space and experience that aligns with your idea of the divine, whatever that may be.

For example, a reader who focuses on angel oracle cards may want to skip all the goth accoutrements and instead fill their space with lighter colors, soft music, and imagery that can suggest wings. An energy healer may lean toward natural elements like plants and crystals and imagery associated with healing modalities like the chakras.

WARNING

Aesthetics are meant to help support you; they should be additions rather than pull focus from the reading itself. If your table is cluttered with too many candles and crystals, you don't have room for the cards. And no matter how cool and witchy your setup looks, it isn't a substitute for giving clear and helpful readings.

Engaging the senses

Aesthetics go beyond *stuff* for you to acquire. You can create an empowering ambiance for reading in a few other ways, as I explain in the following sections.

Sound

The right playlist blocks out distracting noises and provides a soothing soundscape. Your music depends on your tastes, but aim for something relaxing. I love Beethoven's "Ode to Joy," but I can't concentrate on the cards when it's playing. Smooth jazz, classical, *lo-fi* (an offshoot of the electronic genre), *chillhop* (lo-fi hip-hop), and new age are good options for me. Vocals are usually distracting unless they're in a language you don't speak.

Scent

Incense has long been burned to honor the divine and ward off negative energy. The choice of scent is personal, but sandalwood, rose, lotus, jasmine, and frankincense are believed to aid diviners in their work and dispel any bad vibes.

TIP

If you prefer to not have smoke in your space, aromatherapy oils are an appealing alternative. You can heat them in a diffuser or mix a few drops in a spray bottle filled with water and mist the space before your reading (just don't get any oil on your cards). Two blends I find effective are

>> **Lavender and lemon:** Great for uplifting your spirit and soothing your mood

>> **Rosemary and peppermint:** Brings a sense of clarity and focus to the mind

Sight

I love to begin a reading by lighting a candle. In a world of LED smart bulbs, candlelight is special, sacred, and intimate. Striking a match and lighting a wick signifies "the ritual has begun."

If you're worried about flames, or the fire code, battery-powered candles can help a little bit with ambiance.

REMEMBER

Generally, candlelight isn't enough to see your cards clearly. Soft light is best for the relaxed state you're aiming for.

Accessorizing the oracle

As I say earlier in the chapter, *all you need to read the cards is a deck and a flat surface.* But you may want to acquire a few other items at some point.

A light scarf and deck pouch

Wrapping your deck and storing it in a pouch protects it when you're on the go. Additionally, unwrapping and rewrapping before and after the reading sends the message to your brain and those around you that you're dealing with a sacred tool that's shown a high degree of deference and respect. As I mention in the earlier section "Discarding unhelpful superstitions," you don't need a black silk scarf. If you want to wrap your deck, choose whatever you prefer.

Spread cloth

You can put a *spread cloth* on your table to lay your cards out on. Doing so serves two purposes:

>> **It keeps your cards clean and safe from any liquid or other substance that can get on them.** This barrier is essential if you want to read in cafes or bars or out in nature.

>> **It helps visually contain the reading, making focusing on the cards easier.**

A heavier material is preferable for spread cloths because it doesn't move around too much as you lay out the cards. A darker color usually nicely sets off the card images.

A modern option you may want to consider are the playmats sold in game stores to be used with trading card games like Magic: The Gathering. These mats have a rubber backing to keep them in place, and you can find a wonderful variety of images to choose from.

Crystals

Any card readings you see on social media may give you the impression that the process requires a collection of crystals. If you work with crystals as a part of your spiritual practice, then they may benefit you; if you don't go in for that sort of thing, you don't need to have any just for show.

You can place crystals on your reading table, store them with your decks, wear them as jewelry, and even hold them while you interpret the cards. Some readers even have the querent hold a crystal to help them absorb the reading. You can find exhaustive guides to the many crystals available to you, but Table 5-1 identifies a few common stones readers work with.

TABLE 5-1 Stones Commonly Used in Tarot Readings

Name	Description	Meaning
Clear quartz	Colorless crystal	One of the most common minerals on earth; used for opening your mind and bringing clarity
Amethyst	Purple stone	Calming the mind and enhancing spiritual gifts
Citrine	Golden-yellow crystal	Clearing away negative energy
Rose quartz	Pale pink stone	Supports self-love and emotional healing
Labradorite	Blue-green stone	Protecting your aura from taking on others' negativity
Lapis lazuli	Dark blue rock	Contains a mixture of minerals; believed to help open you up to accessing your inner sight

Enacting rituals

The only ritual you absolutely need is the following (head to Chapter 9 for more details about this process):

1. **Mix the cards.**
2. **Lay them out.**
3. **Figure out what they mean.**
4. **Put them away.**

That's as much as most readers get up to.

If you want to go big and adopt a more formal procedure to enter a state of mind to help you focus, check out the suggestions in the following sections.

Breath

When you take a few moments to focus on your breath before a reading, you can release some stress and anxiety. This tactic can help you let go of strong attachments to results and read from a more neutral frame of mind.

A great method is the *fourfold breath*. It's very simple. As you breathe, count to four in your head at each step:

1. **Inhale through your nose for a count of four.**
2. **Hold your breath for a count of four.**
3. **Exhale through your mouth for a count of four.**
4. **Hold this fully exhaled state for a count of four.**

Repeat for a few rounds until you feel relaxed.

Actions and words

Lay out your spread cloth if you're using one, light any candles or incense, and place anything you want on the reading space. (Flip to the earlier section "Accessorizing the oracle" for more about decking out your reading space.) You can place the deck on the table in front of you or hold it to your chest over your heart. Spend a few heartbeats breathing and visualizing a connection between you and your deck.

If you connect with any divine beings or higher powers — deities, spirits, ancestors, guides, or the universe itself — as a part of your practice, you may petition them to aid you in your reading. If you prefer to keep it simple, you can speak a short prayer. It can be unique to your reading or one you use before every session. You can write one of your own or simply borrow mine:

> *Open my eyes so I might see.*
>
> *Open my heart so I might understand.*

Perform one or more readings with your deck, taking any notes in your journal if you're reading for yourself. (I cover tarot journaling in Chapter 4.)

Closing

After the session has come to an end, I like to verbalize this conclusion by simply stating the following:

> *That is the reading.*

In terms of ritual action, follow the magical rule of thumb of *going back the way you came in* by performing in reverse any preliminary steps you took (see the preceding section). If you called on divine beings, thank them. If you unwrapped your deck, rewrap it. If you lit candles, extinguish them (you can leave incense to burn out).

Striving for authenticity

Implementing aesthetics and procedures is intended to help you connect with your concept of the divine and enter a liminal state in which you're open to the wisdom of the cards. They can also be a lot of fun, and I do think card reading is best when it's fun.

REMEMBER

The most important factor in all these choices is that they're genuine to you. If these actions and words are flowing from an authentic place, they feel natural, connected, and real. If they're just theater, they feel hokey and distract you from the process.

Try things out, keep what works, and get rid of what doesn't.

Finding space, making time

If you're going to read cards, you need a space to read cards and enough dedicated time to do so. You don't need a shrine in your home dedicated solely to this practice (though that'd certainly be lovely). The only requirement is that it has a flat surface and enough space to place your cards. No matter where that is or when you do it, put away anything not conducive to supporting the reading so that you can focus.

If home isn't the ideal spot for you, take your cards on an oracular adventure and find a place to read. The local library is often a nice, quiet spot, usually with plenty of desks. Your favorite cafe is another option and has the added bonus of providing something tasty to sip while you read. If you find that you get more inspiration from nature and the weather is cooperating, head to a park with picnic tables.

TIP

If you're reading outdoors, the wind is *not* your friend. Many a card has been carried off by an unexpected gust. A few pocket crystals or loose change can weigh down the cards. Remain vigilant in case one makes a break for it.

Practice makes perfect, so carving out enough time to play with the cards each day is crucial. Pulling a single card to reflect on for the day can become a part of your morning routine. You can return to it before bed and consider how its energy manifested for you. A coffee or tea break is plenty of time to do a quick spread of cards. But if other members of your household tend to disrupt your me-time, you may need to wait for everyone else to be in bed.

Perhaps the biggest challenge in this wonderful world of smartphones and screens wherever you look is avoiding their distractions long enough to read the cards. Consider putting your device on airplane mode during a reading so you aren't tempted by each buzz or notification.

Divining for Others

Many practitioners read only for themselves, but many brave souls offer their services to family, friends, paying clients, and even thousands of followers on social media. You want to keep a few things in mind if you decide to pursue this path.

Caring for the querent

The most important reason to read for others is to be of service to them and answer their questions to the best of your ability. Getting paid is fine, but the well-being of the person on the other side of the table, phone, or computer should be your priority.

Beginning from a place of humility

The biggest saboteur for a reader is an overdeveloped ego. You lay the cards out, you feel like your intuition kicks into high gear, and suddenly you're an all-knowing, all-seeing sage who perceives exactly how to solve every one of their problems.

Remember that you're a fallible human being and that reading cards is an art, not a science. You'll make errors if you aren't careful.

TIP

When you're starting out, being clear about where you're at on your journey is a good idea. It's fine to look up the meanings of the cards when you're new.

Moving forward with confidence

Too much ego can be a problem (see the preceding section) but the other side of that coin is having enough faith in yourself, your abilities, and the process. Trust that the right cards will come up and then give your interpretation based on your understanding of their meanings and what the querent has shared about their situation.

If you sound like you find the whole prospect of reading cards dubious, your querent won't be compelled to take your advice seriously.

Sharing the cards' message (not yours)

You're one member of the querent's team. They have people in their lives they go to for common sense, sympathy, and so on; like most of us, they have trained professionals for the really important stuff. You're the oracle member of their team, and they come to you for the wisdom of the cards delivered in your style.

Your morals, past experiences, humor, and outlook on life absolutely flavor your recommendations. Your readings benefit from each of those aspects, but my experience has been that the readings where I got preachy or told people what I thought they wanted to hear tended to fall flat.

TIP

For those moments when you absolutely have to offer your two cents or you'll explode, just be sure to make it clear that this is your advice rather than the cards'.

Leaving the querent better than you found them

When delivering a difficult message, do your best to find some encouraging direction for the querent.

You don't have to find some miracle way for them to get what they want; you can simply tell them that, based on this reading, the time doesn't seem to be right for romance, career advancement, or whatever the case. Look to the troublesome cards' meanings for suggestions about how to avoid making things worse. Querents should leave the session feeling empowered, not doomed.

Releasing them back into the wild

After you've delivered your message, your job is done. You can't make your querent do anything they don't want to do. This area can be tricky, especially when you've read for someone who's really going through it. Do your best to wish them well and release them to continue on their journey.

When I've finished a session, I tend to say, "And that is the reading." Stating that the reading is over is a good idea because if you leave things ambiguous, some querents will keep asking for more and more information. Making a clear statement punctuates the process.

Recognizing challenging querent styles

Just about every person you ever read for will be lovely, and you'll have a pleasant experience. But over the years I've compiled my own rogues' gallery of tricky customers. Table 5-2 lists these challenging querents, along with ways to navigate the session with them.

TABLE 5-2 **The Rogues' Gallery**

Rogue	Dossier	Strategy
The Silent Stone	This person asks their question and then says almost nothing else during the session. (You usually have a bit of dialogue with the person you're reading for, and some readers really feed off of that back and forth.)	Some people are shy or feel that they aren't supposed to speak in the process. You can ask them a few direct questions to see whether they open up; otherwise, just perform the reading and let them sit in silence.
The Mythbuster	This person thinks card reading is a load of nonsense at best and genuinely dangerous at worst. They think that either you're running a scam or you've deluded yourself into believing in the utter quackery of divination. They may be antagonistic or challenge you at each step.	I've never seen one of these people be converted by a thoughtful explanation of how the process works. If you feel disrespected, you have the right to end the session and cease any further discussion.
The Better Reader	A rogue similar to the Mythbuster is a person who's a seasoned expert at reading cards and tries to teach you by explaining how your methods or interpretations are incorrect.	Just smile and make it clear that you're happy with your process. Having a dialogue about cards is fine, but no one likes a know-it-all.

(continued)

TABLE 5-2 *(continued)*

Rogue	Dossier	Strategy
The Chatterbox	This person loves to talk, and talk, and talk. Everything you say sparks a new story for them or reminds them of something they'd love to tell you about.	These querents are usually fun and only pose a problem if you have a time constraint (for example, if you're reading at a party and must keep each reading brief). Just let them know you want to be sure to get through the full reading, and then cut back on your word count for your interpretations.
The Confirmer	This person firmly believes they know the answer to the question and your job is to tell them how right they are. A reader who has a differing interpretation clearly doesn't know what they're doing.	Stick to your principles, but, if possible, humor them by finding a card or two in the spread that can have an alternate interpretation that supports their thesis. You've delivered your message with a dash of hope on the side.
The Eternal Victim	Nothing ever goes right for this poor soul. If you suggest actions to take, they may tell you that what you're asking is impossible (and why). Everyone is out to get them. They may feel like your advice is a form of judging them.	Your job is to get to the final card in the session and share what you see. Have compassion for them and share your advice for what they can do. Avoid getting drawn into their web of perpetual misery.

IT'S IN THE CARDS

When I've hosted tarot meetups, one of the most popular activities I've done is to write the dossiers for my rogues' gallery on notecards and give one to each attendee. In pairs, each participant takes turns being a reader and a problem querent. After the "performance," all participants talk about what happened and how they might react in the situation.

WARNING

The challenging querent who isn't on the fun list is someone experiencing mental health issues. They're very rare, but if you do encounter them, you can recommend that they seek professional counseling if you think they're a danger to themselves. And remember: You have the right to end any session for any reason at all.

Chapter **6**

Nailing the Mechanics of a Reading

W hat to ask about, how to lay out the cards, and how to turn them over for maximum effect are all things to think about before you spread the cards for yourself or a querent. This chapter covers these issues to prepare you for tarot readings.

Forming Useful Questions

Every tarot reading begins with a question, and spending time putting together a thoughtful question makes your life much easier as you interpret the cards.

REMEMBER

It boils down to this: What do you most want to know? Do you simply want to find out where things are headed? Are you looking for advice on what you should do? Both?

TIP

Including a timing component with your question is a good idea. It allows you to focus on a specific period of time during which you can make meaningful changes that will impact your situation. For example, consider the difference between what you want to do in the next few months in your career versus across your lifetime.

Generally, I like to look at the next three months because to me that's a manageable timeframe. Adjust your timing to match the question you're asking.

Categorizing readings

Let me simplify things by breaking tarot readings into three categories — predictive, guidance, and wisdom — based on the kinds of questions they ask.

Predictive questions

A reading using *predictive questions* explores the current trajectory of your situation:

>> Where's my career headed?

>> What's my romantic future with this person?

>> What'll happen if I move?

The answers take the form of a snapshot of the future if things continue to proceed on this path.

Guidance questions

Guidance questions in a reading ask the tarot for advice about how you can best proceed toward achieving your goals:

>> What'll help me improve my career?

>> How can I find a romantic partner?

>> How do I resolve this conflict?

In this case, the answers are helpful actions you can take.

Wisdom questions

If you want to explore your own inner experiences as well as some of the "big questions" about the world around you, approach the reading with *wisdom questions:*

>> Where should I go next on my spiritual journey?

>> What'll bring me healing around this issue?

>> What's the meaning of my life?

The answers to wisdom questions appear as metaphors for you to contemplate and reflect on.

Blending styles

Some readers avoid asking the predictive questions I cover earlier because they worry definitive answers will be too stifling. An easy way to alleviate this problem is to use a spread that includes both predictive and guidance positions, like the one in the Foresight and Action spread in Chapter 7. That way you satisfy the need to know what's coming while still empowering the querent to take action. (Head to the later section "Mapping a Spread" for more on spreads.)

REMEMBER

Not all querents know your personal style as a reader. Suppose you don't do predictive readings and are asked a more fortune-telling-style question. In that case, you can gently let the querent know about your approach to tarot and ask whether they'll be satisfied if you modify the question to focus on what they can do to improve their situation.

Having no question

Sometimes, you just want to hear whatever message the universe has for you right now. In that case, you need only to ask the cards, "What do I most need to know right now?" and begin the reading.

With this style of question, you interpret the cards broadly (even vaguely); piecing together what situation they're referring to is up to the querent — whether that's you or another party. Often, a querent takes this more general approach when they're nervous about the possible outcome of a reading, and the tarot quickly speaks to that question they really wanted to ask had they been brave enough.

Being careful what you ask

As the old saying goes, "Don't ask the question if you don't want to hear the answer." In life, you don't always get what you want; if you know that a negative response to your question will devastate you, find a different question. Sometimes, knowing that what you want isn't likely to work out is empowering because you can focus your energy and efforts elsewhere. But you should be the one to decide whether you're ready to receive potential bad news.

Some questions set off your intuitive alarm bells, especially those that indicate a querent is experiencing severe mental health issues or contemplating self-harm. *Do not* engage with these questions; instead, direct them to reach out to resources like a crisis hotline where trained professionals can provide the support they need.

Mapping a Spread

A *tarot spread* is the arrangement you place the cards in for a reading. You're using a spread if you're looking at more than one card. They can be simple, like a comic strip or storyboard, or complex, like a mystical *sigil* or design.

Selecting a spread

After you know what you want to ask (as I explain in the earlier section "Forming Useful Questions"), you must select a tarot spread. I cover tarot spreads at length in Chapter 7 and oracle card spreads in Chapter 13. You'll find plenty of examples of each to work with, and you can easily find hundreds online.

Despite the huge volume of spreads available to choose from, when you're starting out, I recommend working with a small group of versatile spreads that have just a few cards to interpret.

Sticking with single cards

For oracle decks, pulling a single card is the norm. Most of these decks' guidebooks have been written with this assumption and give thorough advice about what to do in your situation. I explore this topic further in Chapter 13.

Single-card pulls are trickier with tarot cards. You can use this method effectively if you have a very specific question, particularly when the question is "What should I do?" A single-card tarot reading is great if you've got a low-stakes situation. For example, when I struggle with what to order from a menu, a single tarot card gives me all the information I need. "Temperance? Okay, I'll order the salad."

Single-card pulls are perfectly acceptable for the following:

>> Choices you need to make quickly

>> Moments when you need some creative direction

>> Highly specific decisions that you need to make in situations you're very familiar with

>> When that pushy friend who always wants a reading asks for another reading

Upgrading to a larger spread

The added information that a larger spread provides is valuable when your question is more complex. If you're debating which job offer to accept, for example, the Temperance card urges you to pick the more balanced option. But are you certain you know which job would be more balanced? A Crossroads spread gives you more insights about each option.

Similarly, if you're wondering what will improve your marriage and you pull Temperance, you may wonder whether the card is saying you or your spouse needs to be more balanced. Or both? The Relationship spread provides more context. You can find both of these spreads in Chapter 7.

TIP

Larger spreads are ideal for the following scenarios:

>> When you have a larger chunk of time to devote to the reading

>> When you face big life decisions where you want to consider multiple options

>> When you want to understand the underlying facets that influence a situation

>> When you're in situations involving several people

>> When you're reading for a friend for the first time and you want to impress them

Shuffling the Cards

Mixing and randomizing the cards by shuffling them is essential when you're performing a reading. Beginners often need help shuffling because tarot and oracle cards are much larger than cards in a poker deck. Still, with patience and practice, you'll become a pro.

What's the magic formula to use? The good and bad news is that it's entirely up to the reader. I cover a few of the most common methods in the following sections.

TIP

The most important thing to remember is to decide before you begin how you'll shuffle the cards, how many times you'll shuffle, and whether you'll read *reversals* (that is, whether you'll take into account the card's orientation as it comes out of the deck). If you feel unsure, use my method:

>> Shuffle the deck three times.

>> Cut it into three piles.

>> Choose one pile to place on top.

REMEMBER

If you read reversals (which I explain in Chapter 8), flip half the cards vertically each time you shuffle the deck. After a few shuffles like that, about half of the cards in a spread will be reversed.

Note: When you're reading for someone whom you've never seen shuffle cards, protect your deck by shuffling the cards yourself and let them choose from a fan as I describe in the later section "Drawing cards."

Riffle

Viva Las Vegas! *Riffle* is the method people most often use to shuffle playing cards. Cut the deck, bring both halves together, and use your thumbs to apply just enough pressure to release cards from both halves one at a time. After they're riffled, slide both halves together to form one stack. If you're working with an especially large deck, place both halves side by side, grip them by their side edges, and riffle together the top inside corners.

Riffle shuffling is an elegant way to mix the cards, but it also has the highest potential to damage them. Over time, your tarot deck will naturally develop a slight curve, but putting too much pressure on them can warp the cards significantly. Riffle as gently as you can.

Waterfall

The *waterfall* is a much gentler method than the riffle in the preceding section. Cut the deck, hold one half above the other, and use your thumbs to release a few cards at a time so they fall into the half in your other hand. It's quick and easy. The cards aren't as evenly mixed as with the riffle, so waterfall shuffle a few more times if you use this method until your intuition tells you the cards are well and truly mixed.

Be sure to let the cards gently fall onto the deck below; do not force (the correct term may be *smoosh*) them together at the edges; that can chip the edges of the cards.

Wash

The *wash* can be a very fun method to mix the cards. Spread all the cards out on your table and then use both hands to gently swirl them around and around, finally bringing them back into one stack. Repeat until you feel the deck has been mixed to your satisfaction. Watch out for jumpers that try to escape your table.

Drawing and Laying Out the Cards

After you've considered your questions and spread options, as I discuss earlier in the chapter, you're so close to getting to the juicy part of the process where you draw and interpret the cards! You just have a couple of considerations:

>> How do you want to draw the cards?

>> Do you place the cards on the table face up or face down?

Spoiler alert: There's no wrong answer here, but the following sections walk you through your options.

Drawing cards

After you've shuffled the deck and it's a single stack, begin drawing cards from the top and placing them into the spread positions. (Flip to the earlier section "Shuffling the Cards" for more on mixing.)

Alternatively, you can fan the cards by gently spreading them into a single line and then choosing cards from the fan based on your intuition.

IT'S IN THE
CARDS

If you're choosing cards from a fan, a fun technique is to first rub your hands together vigorously until your palms are warmed and your skin feels tingly. Slowly wave your hand over the fan of cards and sense the cards that seem to pull your hand down or lift it up. It's a great way to feel the energy of the cards. (I explore this technique further in Chapter 13, which features several spreads to use with your oracle cards.)

Observing the cards face up

Placing the cards face up allows you to see the entire reading immediately. You instantly get some ideas about patterns and themes. Because you know what comes later in the spread, you have a better idea about what the early cards are referring to.

This method makes summing up the entire reading in a sentence or two before you begin easy.

Creating focus and drama with cards face down

By turning over the cards one at a time as you read them, you avoid being distracted by intense cards that may appear later in the spread. You have the time you need to fully process a card's meaning before moving on to the next one.

When you're reading for someone else, this method builds a little more drama and heightens anticipation as each card is turned over. You also have the querent's attention on the card you're describing now rather than the one with all the stabby swords in it at the end of the reading.

Chapter **7**

Selecting a Tarot Spread

I f you think of the cards as ingredients, spreads are the recipes you can use to mix those ingredients together. They provide structure and pattern to the process, helping you translate the message of the cards. I start with a small amount of theory to help you see why spreads are useful and then devote most of the chapter to examples so you can play around with the cards. Most of the spreads in this chapter are designed for tarot cards; for spreads specifically made for oracle cards, see Chapter 13.

Understanding the Benefit of Using Spreads

If you spend time in the online tarot community, you'll see lots of posts from people requesting help interpreting a reading accompanied by a photo of a line of around five cards. When you ask them what spread they used, they often answer, "I'm not using a spread; I just pulled a few cards."

ESOTERIC OPERATIONS

Esoteric operations are generally large-scale spreads in which you use a complex mystical diagram. In theory, you can use them to ask a specific question, but they mostly provide a high-level overview of your whole life. The process of performing them can be a bit like a ritual in which you shuffle and cut the cards in a certain way and count your way through the deck to assign each card.

The simplest of these spreads may be an astrological spread in which you place 12 cards in a circle representing the signs of the zodiac or astrological houses. The 12 cards tell you how things are going in each of these areas of your life. A more complicated spread can be something like the Opening of the Key, which consists of five different readings, each of which uses about a dozen cards. It's a *lot*.

In the plus column, these spreads give you time for a lot of personal introspection. They're also satisfying to perform if you're in an especially mystical mood and want to try something complex and ritual-like.

If a picture is worth a thousand words, without some guardrails you'll be giving yourself and others 5,000-word readings that mostly sound like a mixture of frightening warnings and spiritual sensibilities.

REMEMBER

When you use a spread, each position tells you the lens to use for interpreting that card, making the message simple, direct, and concise. Hopefully.

In this chapter, I give you a quick overview of what I call fun-size spreads, but most of the chapter focuses on several tried-and-true spreads (the workhorses) you'll want in your repertoire.

Fiddling with Fun-Size Spreads

This category started to pop up when readers began congregating online. *Fun-size spreads* are generally short spreads consisting of three to five cards organized around a fun theme. These spreads serve two main functions for readers:

>> **Sometimes you want to play with your cards but don't have a particular question.** Fun-size spreads provide exercises you can do that may offer a bit of insight.

>> **They're fun to design.** You can make a spread about anything in the world and then share it with other readers who can also have fun playing with it. One spread was designed by an online tarot community because July 11 is National Blueberry Muffin Day in the United States.

That Blueberry Muffin spread lives rent-free in my head, by the way. Here are its positions:

>> **From Scratch:** What you can do by yourself

>> **From the Box:** What you can do with a little help

>> **Store Bought:** What to let others do for you

Make one of these fun-size spreads now:

1. **Think of your favorite TV series that features at least five recurring characters.**

2. **Pick five characters to work with and consider the unique qualities of those characters that make them stand out.**

3. **Assign each of those characters to a position and then write a one-sentence explanation about what that position means.**

   If you get stuck on this part, an easy method is to make each position a question.

Here's my take on a *Buffy the Vampire Slayer* (1997–2003) spread:

>> **Buffy:** What do I need to be brave about doing right now?

>> **Willow:** What do I need to learn to make this happen?

>> **Spike:** How might I get in my own way in the process?

>> **Giles:** How can I get support in accomplishing this?

>> **Xander:** How can I make all of this more fun?

Wielding the Workhorse Spreads

You can find hundreds of spreads out there to try, but the backbone of your practice will likely be a small collection of simple, versatile spreads that you'll become intimately familiar with. What I call *workhorse spreads* are very effective because of a couple of factors (which also makes them popular among card readers):

>> **Their positions are broad enough to answer just about any question.**

>> **The shape of the layout makes sense to the human brain.** Cards in a line show a progression, cards in a column show a hierarchy, cards in a wheel show several factors influencing a central figure, and cards in a square show several things in a balanced state.

Throughout this section, I highlight various workhorse spreads to keep in your card reading bag of tricks.

REMEMBER

Several of these spreads include a *significator,* which is the card that represents the subject of the reading (most often this is you). You can choose a significator intentionally, selecting a card with similar qualities to the person the reading is about or showing someone in a similar situation, or you can let your deck decide and pull a significator at random.

The Three-Card spread

This spread (see Figure 7-1) is the one that I recommend all readers start with. Its basis is humanity's most familiar narrative structure of beginning, middle, and end:

1. **The Past:** A significant event from the recent past impacting the situation.

2. **The Present:** What you're currently experiencing in this situation.

3. **The Future:** The direction your situation is headed in. If you don't make predictions, this position shows the actions you should take now to create the best future for yourself.

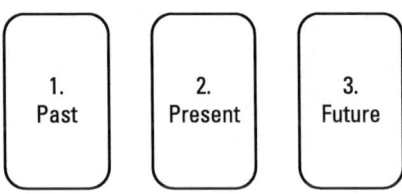

FIGURE 7-1: The Three-Card spread is a good spread to start with.

The Foresight and Action spread

This riff on the Three-Card spread from the preceding section addresses the two questions you always get asked after the reading: "What happens next?" and "What should I do?" Of course, non-predictors don't worry about the "what happens next?" part and can trim this spread to 1. Now and 2. Action.

Shown in Figure 7-2, this spread starts in the present because you (or the querent) already knows what happened in the past:

1. **Now:** How you're approaching this situation.

2. **Next:** Where things are headed in the short term (perhaps the next month or so).

3. **After That:** The long-term trajectory of this issue (perhaps three or more months from now).

4. **Action:** What you should do now to create the best possible future. If Card 3 looks great, this action will support that journey. If Card 3 is a nightmare, this action will help you avoid it.

The Crossroads spread

So many questions can be broken down into "Should you do X or Y?" Should you stay at your present job or find a new one? Should you move to this city or that one? Should Ingrid Bergman marry Humphrey Bogart or Paul Henreid in *Casablanca*?

That's where the Crossroads spread comes in (see Figure 7-3). It looks at two different paths and lets you evaluate them.

1. **Significator:** How you're approaching the situation

2 and 3. **Path A:** How things will go if you make this choice

4 and 5. **Path B:** How things will go if you make this choice

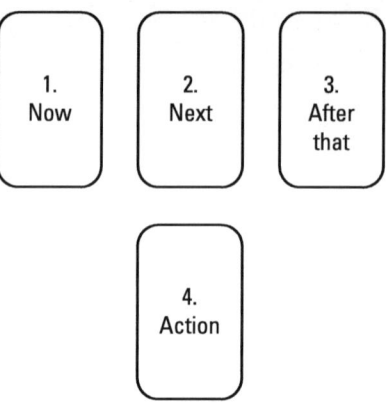

FIGURE 7-2: The Foresight and Action spread.

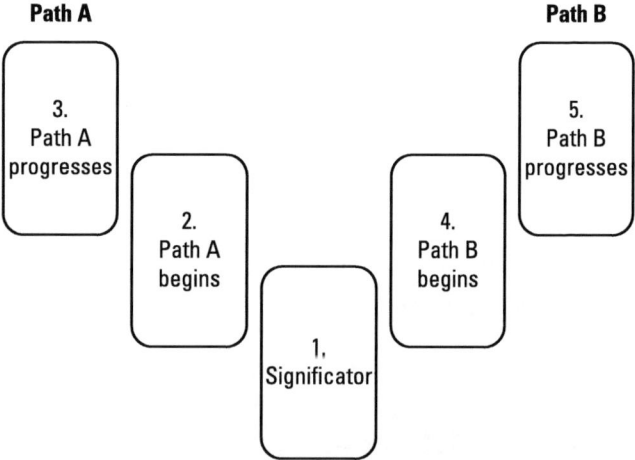

FIGURE 7-3: Evaluate two paths with the Crossroads spread.

If the cards on one path look more appealing, it's easy to make the call. Sometimes, the cards on both paths look about the same. I find that this means you're capable of succeeding at either choice. A good rule of thumb is to return to the significator and consider whether they'd be happier with either choice. A knight may want to choose the more dramatic or chaotic line, whereas the Hierophant would prefer something steady.

To help reduce bias when reading a Crossroads spread, write down the name of each choice on a separate slip of paper. Turn the slips face down and shuffle them. Perform the reading without knowing which set of cards apply to which option and then flip over the pieces of paper to reveal which path was which.

Asking "This or that?" creates a binary view of your situation. If neither path looks good to you, ask the cards what other options are out there.

The Relationship spread

Someone looking for a new relationship can use the Foresight and Action spread from earlier in the chapter. When you want to look at an existing relationship, which includes romances, friends, coworkers, and so on, use this spread instead (see Figure 7-4):

1. **You:** What you bring to the relationship

2. **Them:** What your partner brings to the relationship

3. **Your advice:** Changes you can make for the good of the relationship

4. **Their advice:** Changes you can ask your partner to make for the good of the relationship

5. **Relationship trajectory:** Where things are currently headed for you both.

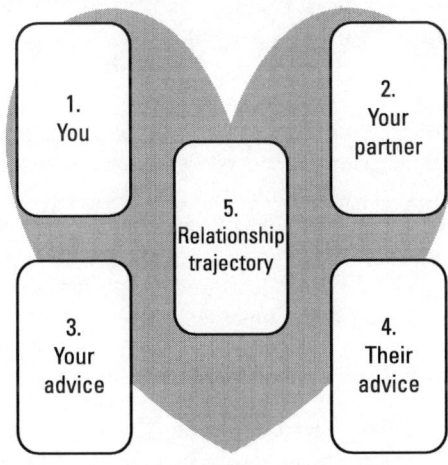

FIGURE 7-4: The Relationship spread is good for — surprise! — exploring relationships.

SEEKING WISDOM

Wisdom readings use a style of question that sets aside prediction and self-help entirely, using the cards to explore larger, more philosophical questions about life, the universe, and everything else. Crucially, the aim here isn't for you to uncover *the* answer to these questions. The purpose is to marinate on *your* answer to the questions with the aid of the wild card nature of divination (and perhaps a glass of wine) helping to push past preconceived notions. Ask whatever sort of question you may want to ask, such as

What is the purpose of life?

What happens after the end of the universe?

What is the essential nature of fear/love/faith?

You can pull a single card to contemplate or you can make the process even more thoughtful by creating a spread based on a sacred text or profound writing. A favorite tarot conference experience of mine was led by the greatest proponent of wisdom readings, the late tarot luminary Rachel Pollack, in which she explored the concept of beauty using a spread based on the traditional Navajo *Walk in Beauty* prayer. Pollack expands on the wisdom reading process in her book *A Walk through the Forest of Souls: A Tarot Journey to Spiritual Awakening* (Welser Books).

Think about what you consider to be your core values — empathy, freedom, creativity, honor, and so on — and pull a single card to get a deeper understanding of their nature. Or you can pull two cards, one to ask, "What is ____?" and one to ask, "What isn't ____?" Have fun!

Card 5 is optional. When a tarot spread has two columns, it creates a dramatic sense of tension between them, which can be very interesting. Querents will sometimes grab a card off the top of the deck and place it between the columns. This approach can help answer the question "Where's this thing headed?" If you'd rather not know the answer to that just now or you don't do predictive readings, feel free to leave it out.

The Hero's Journey spread

Here's an interesting narrative spread based on Joseph Campbell's model of the mythical hero's journey. It's fun to use when you have a major undertaking in your future. This spread uses six cards, as shown in Figure 7-5:

1. **Call to Adventure:** This card is the quest you're about to begin. It's the subject of your reading (it can just mean the next year or so).

2. **The Guide:** Forces that can help you on this journey. How you can prepare.

3. **Road of Trials:** External challenges you'll face on this journey.

4. **The Shadow:** The internal challenge you face; the part of yourself that gets in the way and acts as an antagonist.

5. **Reconciliation:** How to heal difficulties suggested in the Shadow position. What you need to do to accomplish your goal.

6. **The Journey Home:** How you'll finish this journey and how it'll impact both your life and those around you.

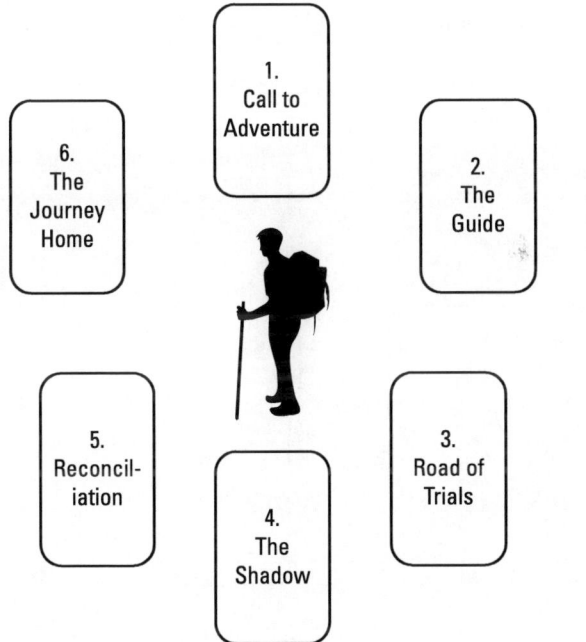

FIGURE 7-5: The Hero's Journey spread can help you navigate a new undertaking.

The Horseshoe spread

This option is basically an expanded version of the earlier Foresight and Action spread, offering both predictions and advice for actions to take (see Figure 7-6):

1. **Significator:** How you view this situation. You can pre-select this card or let the tarot decide.

2. **The Past:** Previous conditions influencing your situation.

3. **The Present:** Where things currently stand.

4. **The Future:** Where this situation is currently headed.

5. **Action:** The action you can take right now for your greatest and highest good.

6. **Environment:** The influence of other people on this situation.

7. **Challenge:** The thing you must achieve or overcome to succeed.

8. **Outcome:** How this situation will ultimately pan out in the long term.

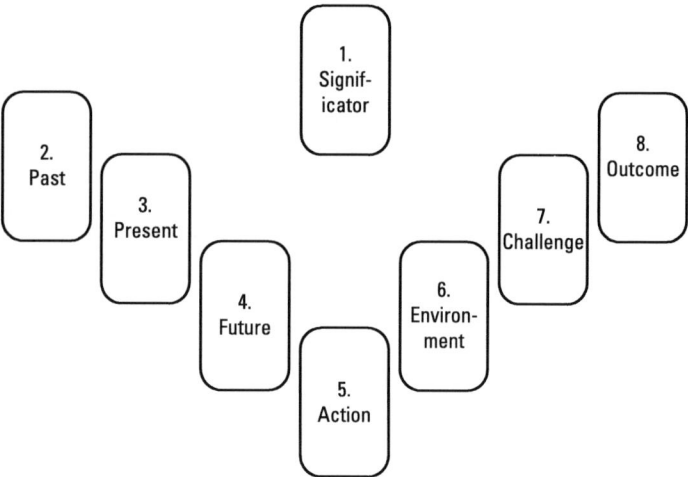

FIGURE 7-6: The Horseshoe spread offers predictions and action.

The Year Ahead spread

This layout, shown in Figure 7-7, is an excellent spread for New Year's Eve, birthdays, or any big moments of transition. Cards 1 through 12 represent what will happen in each month (or, if you prefer, the tarot's advice for that month), and card 13 shows the major theme for the year ahead:

1 through 12. **January through December:** Events or advice for each month

13. **Theme:** Reveals a significant focus for the journey ahead

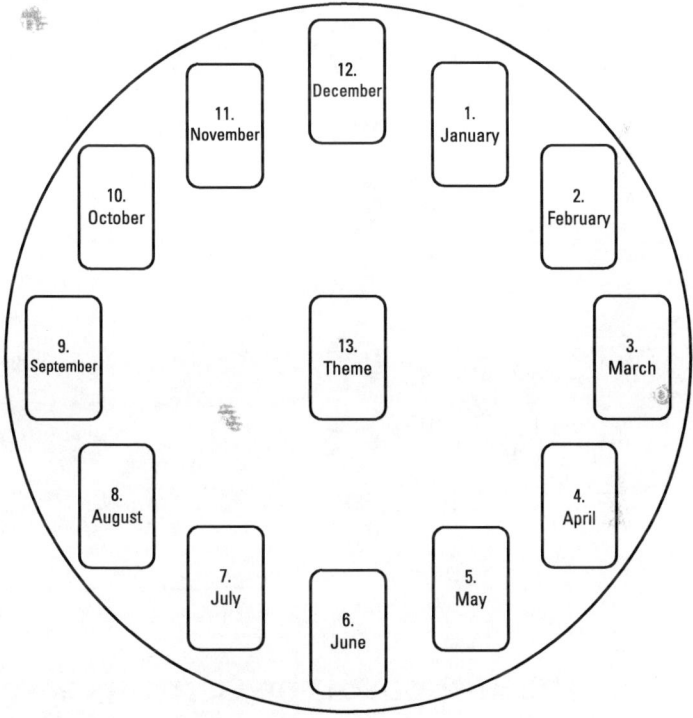

FIGURE 7-7: Use the Year Ahead spread to help you map out the coming year.

The Seven Chakras spread

The model of the Seven Chakras comes from Hindu spiritual tradition. In it, the *chakras* are psychic energy centers that connect to different parts of your life. Shown in Figure 7-8, this spread provides a full energetic diagnosis of your spiritual energy:

1. **Root:** Physical needs, stability, safety
2. **Sacral:** Instincts, primal emotions, sexuality, creativity
3. **Solar plexus:** Inner strength, vitality, identity
4. **Heart:** Love, empathy, and emotional expression
5. **Throat:** Communication and expression
6. **Third eye:** Intuition, psychic gifts
7. **Crown:** Connection to the divine, higher wisdom

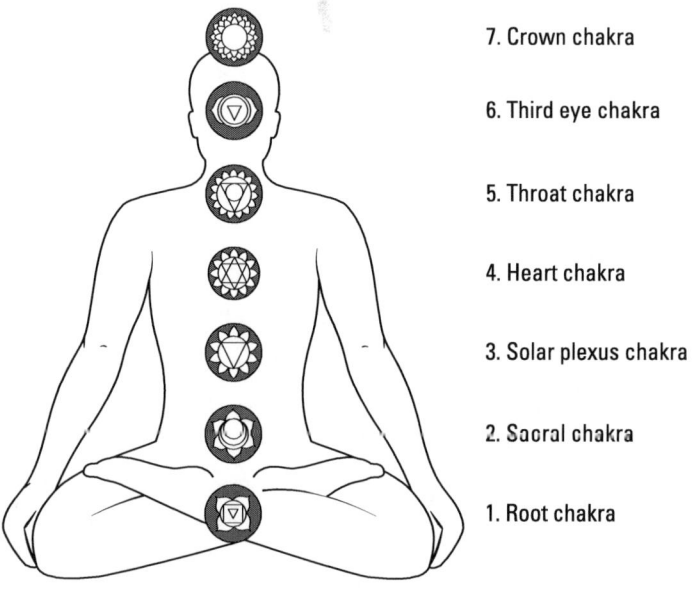

7. Crown chakra

6. Third eye chakra

5. Throat chakra

4. Heart chakra

3. Solar plexus chakra

2. Sacral chakra

1. Root chakra

FIGURE 7-8: Explore your spiritual energy with the Seven Chakras spread.

The Wisdom of the Elements spread

This spread brings you some advice from each corner of the tarot (see Figure 7-9). Separate your cards by suit into five piles: majors, swords, wands, cups, and pentacles. Shuffle each pile and pull one card to add to the spread:

1. **Major Arcana:** A spiritual or personal transformation you face
2. **Swords:** The strategy you should employ to overcome challenges

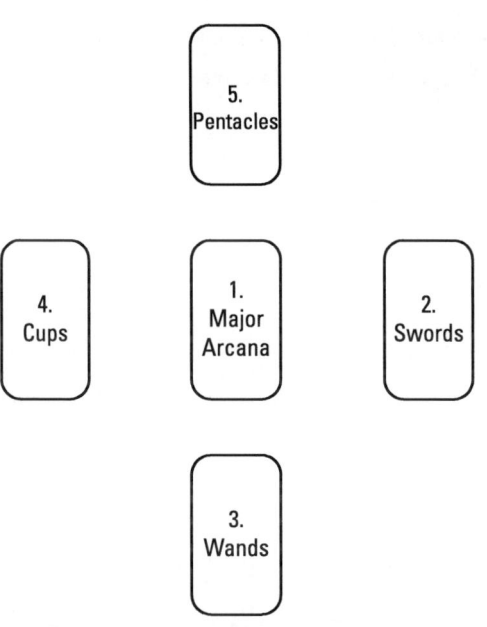

FIGURE 7-9: Seek advice from all corners of the tarot through the Wisdom of the Elements spread.

3. **Wands:** How to best channel your energy and passion

4. **Cups:** How to support your emotional needs and connections with others

5. **Pentacles:** How to manage your resources, including time, energy, and money

The Celtic Cross

This spread (shown in Figure 7-10) was included in the original guidebook for the Rider-Waite-Smith tarot, published in 1910, and was the most popular spread among readers for decades. It can be confusing for beginners, but this chapter would be incomplete without it. Here's what each position represents:

1. **This covers you:** The subject of the reading (as the significator, you can choose a card intentionally or at random)

2. **This crosses you:** Forces that can help or hinder you

3. **This is beneath you:** Foundations of the issue or what's beneath the surface

4. **This is behind you:** Recent events

5. This crowns you: What you aspire to

6. This is before you: The near future

7. The self: Your influence on the situation

8. The house: External influences

9. Hopes and fears: What propels you forward or holds you back

10. The outcome: Overall trajectory of the situation

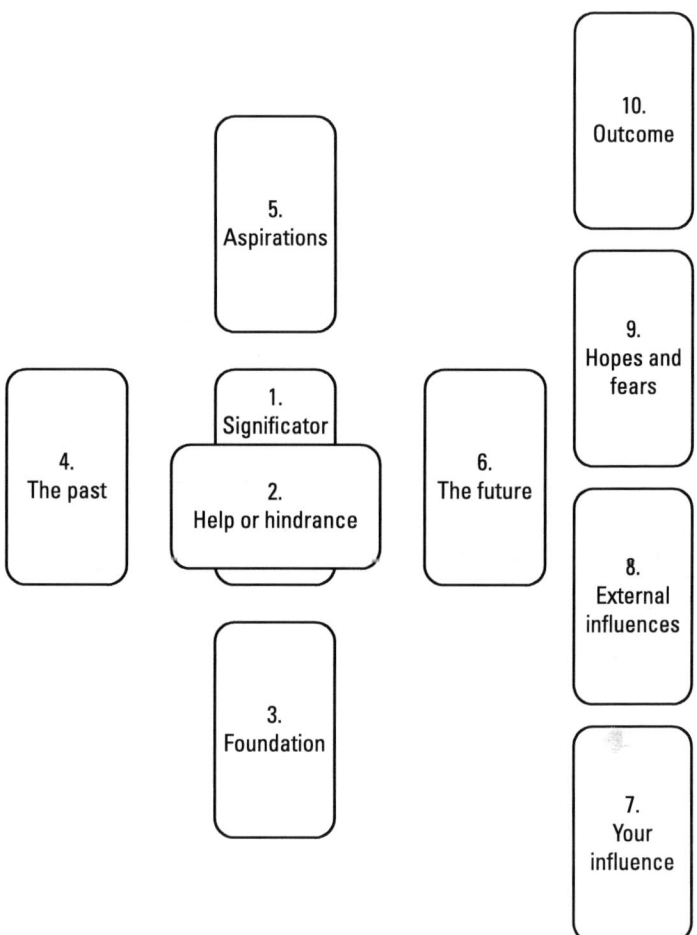

FIGURE 7-10: The Celtic Cross looks intimidating, but you can use it! Just practice.

Different sources feature slight variations of the positions. See Chapter 9 for a demo reading with the Celtic Cross.

Designing Your Own Spreads

Just like with the fun-size spreads earlier in the chapter, you can create your own workhorse spreads. These take a little more fore-thought, so here are a few tips to help you:

>> Think about an area, idea, or challenge you want to explore.

>> Consider all the critical information you need to know and assign positions to those items.

>> Play around with design until you find something that flows when you look from card to card.

IT'S IN THE
CARDS

Think about any sort of graph or model you've used at work or in school that stuck with you and try turning that into a tarot spread. Here's an example I made in college. When I heard of the marketing strategy of creating a SWOT (strengths, weaknesses, opportunities, threats) analysis, I thought, "That sounds like a tarot spread!" I made the four steps of the SWOT process posi-tions within the spread, as shown here and in Figure 7-11:

1. **Strengths** – Internal advantages you have over others

2. **Weaknesses** – Internal disadvantages relative to others

3. **Opportunities** – External elements that you can exploit or make use of

4. **Threats** – External elements that can make things difficult for you.

TIP

If you've ever presented a diagram to people to help you explain a concept, you have the makings of a tarot spread.

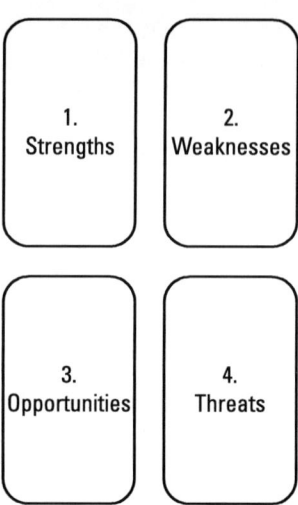

FIGURE 7-11: I made my own SWOT analysis tarot spread.

Exploring What Tarot Cards Mean

Hone your skills at bringing tradition and intuition together to arrive at useful and relatable meanings for cards in a reading. Make heads or tails of tarot reversals.

Walk through through several readings step by step to see how it all comes together, using both predictive and advisory spreads.

Find out about the traditional meanings associated with all 78 cards in a tarot deck.

Chapter **8**

Making Connections

O ne of the first questions a beginning reader generally asks is how long learning the cards' meanings takes. The accurate but unhelpful answer is that you never stop learning the cards' meanings. That's because the tarot is a living, breathing entity that speaks to you differently with every reading you perform. In this chapter, I show you how to dialogue with your deck to find relevant, valuable answers in any given reading.

Working with the Equation of Meaning

I distinctly remember coming home with my first tarot deck when I was in high school. It was finally here, the magic pack of cards that would allow me to see into the future and predict the fates and fortunes of myself and all my friends!

I shuffled the cards and laid them out, turned one over, opened the little white booklet (affectionately referred to as an LWB), and read the entry for the Three of Wands:

> Fruitful collaboration in business; also signifies enterprise, ingenuity, effort, and commerce.

Say what? What does that mean? I'm 15, and the deck wants me to launch a *business?*

Even if your LWB doesn't offer up just a handful of keywords, remember that no book can give you the exact interpretation of what a card means in answer to your question. When I interpret a card, the meaning comes from these factors, which I think of as the *equation of meaning:*

1. Your question
2. The card's position in the spread and whether it's upright or reversed
3. The official meaning and correspondences
4. Your intuitive response

Does that sound like way too much labor for a person in this economy trying to interpret a single card? The great news is that factors one and two come almost instantly, and three and four become easier the more you read the cards.

I run through these factors in the following sections.

Your Question

The interpretation of the card must relate to and contribute to answering your question.

Narrowing down possibilities

If you're doing a general *What does the tarot want to tell me today?* reading, then the possibilities can be pretty broad. But suppose you're asking about how to complete a complex project at work successfully, and you draw the Empress. In that case, you can discard the card's meanings about motherhood, physical nourishment, and sensuality. Instead, you focus on the aspects of the card that can relate to your question, like creativity, developing an abundant mindset, and possibly even self-care.

REMEMBER

No card relates only to a certain type of reading. I sometimes hear readers say that they asked about their marriage, and the cards that came up were telling them about their job. I believe this disconnect comes from a narrow view of what suits and cards can refer to. For example, the Lovers does indeed make querents smile when it shows up in a romance reading. Still, its general energy or essence can apply to issues around business, health, creative projects, what you should have for dinner, and everything else you ask about.

Asking for advice versus prediction

Keep in mind whether the question is asking for advice or a prediction. Many readers don't get into prediction. If you read for others, you can let a querent know that you prefer to change the question from "How will this go?" to "How can I make this go better?" if that's more your style.

This distinction also helps you narrow the card's meaning in a particular reading. For example, a tricky aspect of the court cards is how they can either represent a person in your life with the card's qualities or represent a need for you to embody that card's qualities. So when you ask about the future of your love life and the Knight of Cups shows up, you're highly likely to meet someone who is romantic, creative, and willing to make the first move. But if you're asking about what you can do to find a new relationship, the card is probably urging *you* to be more romantic, creative, and willing to make the first move.

The Card's Position

I've said it before, and I'll say it again: Using a spread cleans up a lot of the uncertainty you experience when reading cards. (Before you read through this section, I recommend looking at the spreads in Chapter 7.)

Taking direction

A card's position tells you *how* its energy is expressed in the reading. Each position within a spread has a different role in answering your question. Think of them as a team of specialists who each have a different point of view to share with you. The card's advice changes drastically depending on what area that specialist focuses on.

For example, the Eight of Wands (see Figure 8-1) is a card that speaks to fast movement, momentum, and enthusiasm. Here's how that same card reads in various positions:

>> **The near future:** "Things are about to really pick up speed in your life."

>> **Action you should take:** "It's time to mosey; if you're feeling uncertain about taking that leap forward, let go of that fear and trust that you're ready to run with this."

>> **Challenge/what to avoid:** "Whoa there! Slow down. Your current pace may be causing you to miss some crucial details."

>> **Environment:** "It looks like people around you in this situation are really moving right along. They may seem to be ignoring you, but they just don't have time now.

>> **Significator:** "You're looking for a solution that gives you freedom and empowers you to follow your dreams. Throughout the rest of this spread, watch for opportunities for adventurous choices that'll help you meet that goal."

The card itself carries the same energy throughout but is expressed differently.

IT'S IN THE CARDS

To test drive this idea, imagine a person who came to you who is single and looking to improve their love life. In particular, they want to date more. Perform the four-card spread shown in Figure 8-2 . . . using just one card! Pull a single card and consider how you'd interpret it in each position, starting with position 1. A type of person you should look for in a romantic match. As you move the same card into each position, think about how the advice you'd give changes as the card is viewed from a new angle.

TIP

If you're ever feeling stuck, use the language of the position like a writing prompt to help you vocalize the meaning: "The type of person you should date is _____," "When meeting new people, you should emphasize your _____," "A major red flag to look out for is _____," and "When you go on your first date with them, you should _____."

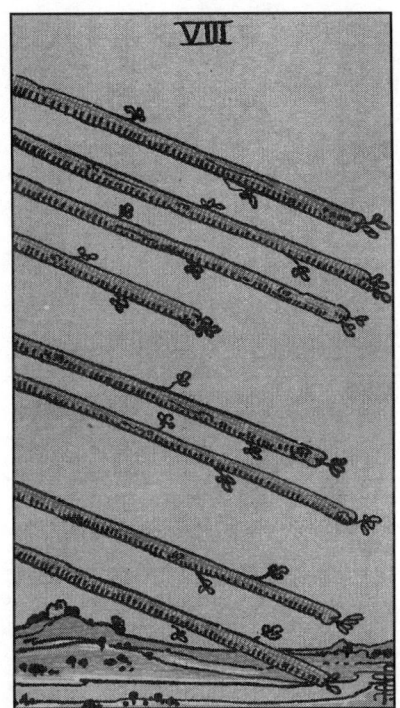

Pamela Colman Smith/Wikimedia Commons/Public Domain

FIGURE 8-1: The Eight of Wands is about fast movement, momentum, and enthusiasm.

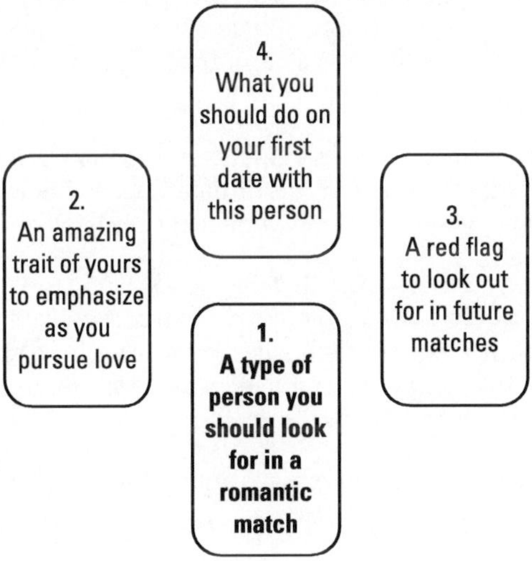

4.
What you should do on your first date with this person

2.
An amazing trait of yours to emphasize as you pursue love

3.
A red flag to look out for in future matches

1.
A type of person you should look for in a romantic match

FIGURE 8-2: Use one card to interpret a four-card spread.

Making sense of contradictions

Something that boggles the minds of tarot readers is finding a happy card in the "biggest challenge" position or a scary card in the "greatest strength" spot. Figuring out these square-peg-round-hole moments can make for very interesting sessions, but to help get you started, here's a handy set of suggested guidelines:

>> **Happy cards in negative positions** can indicate that trying to pursue or maintain the joy or success seen in the card creates difficulties.

>> **Unhappy cards in positive positions** can show how overcoming these adversities will help you.

Getting topsy-turvy with reversals

TIP

When reading for yourself, seeing which cards are reversed is easy — they're upside down when you look at them. If you read for someone else, just decide whether you prefer to have the cards face you or the other person, and when they shuffle, make that sure what's "upright" for them stays upright. In the movies, the cards always face the querent, but when you're learning it's easier to have them face you.

Divinatory meanings for reversed cards have been around since Etteilla published his first manual for reading the tarot in 1781. (More on him in Chapter 2.) Whether to read reversals can be a controversial topic with passionate voices on both sides of the fence. (Just like everyone else, tarot readers need something to be dramatic about, after all.)

Perhaps you were already finding the prospect of learning the different meanings of 78 cards a little daunting, and now I'm asking you to know 156 — what kind of monster am I?

Don't worry; it's not like that in my experience. When you're reading with reversals, the card's core essence remains the same, but the way it's expressed changes (similar to the way card positions take the same card and look at it from different points of view, as I explain earlier in the chapter).

Still, people give various reasons for not wanting to read with reversals:

>> They make readings too complex. Reversals absolutely do add a layer of complexity to a reading. You get double negatives that sound like "You shouldn't not do this."

>> Reversals are too negative. Although not every reversal means something negative, asking about your future and feeling like blockages and delays are ahead for you can feel a little dispiriting. It may be *accurate,* but it can make a reading feel less fun.

>> I don't want to look at the art upside down. Many readers like to look at cards purely intuitively and allow a story to form in their minds. This approach can become more difficult if about half the characters in your tale are standing on their heads.

>> I consider the many facets of a card already. Each card has its good days and its bad days, and some readers trust the spread and their intuition to identify which kind of day a card is having. You can look at the other cards in the spread to help you narrow that down. If a card can mean "boundaries," it can stand for healthy and unhealthy boundaries. If the other cards show things going smoothly, it's likely that "healthy boundaries" is the answer.

Have I scared you off reading reversals yet? I'm about to give my best arguments for incorporating them into your readings, but I want to clarify some things:

>> You don't have to read with reversals if you prefer not to.

>> Reading with reversals doesn't make you a better or smarter card reader.

In divination, you get to pick and choose the elements you make a part of your practice. I recommend trying a bit of everything to see what resonates with you and what doesn't.

TIP

I'll go so far as to say that if you're brand spanking new to card reading, you should probably hold off on reversals until you've gotten some practice in. Reversals aren't rocket science, but they're a bit more advanced. You'll likely have a better experience if you begin more simply. I imagine this is why kids learn to ride a tricycle before a bicycle.

Here's what reversals contribute to reading cards:

>> **They streamline a card's meanings.** Cards' meanings are broad, and reversals create a useful binary. If a card like the Six of Pentacles can represent "give and take," you can assign each of those to the upright or reversed position.

>> **They accurately convey the challenges of life.** Very often, people turn to card reading because they have some form of block or issue they must overcome.

>> **They can combat your biases.** Readers tend to lean toward reasonable, common-sense meanings for the cards, but haven't you had moments in life when the *insensible* plan is the one that worked? Reversals push you to give interpretations that are outside your comfort zone.

>> **They show the healing side of the more challenging cards.** Those swords stabbed in that person's back seem to be falling away, and the upside-down Hanged Man knows it's time to finally get right side up.

Picking a perspective

If reversed cards don't represent 78 brand new meanings, then what are you supposed to do when they turn up (turn down?) in your spread? Several perspectives suggest what reversals do to the card's energy.

TIP

I want to be sure to say this before running through all the examples: If you're going to read with reversals, decide *before* you begin the reading what they'll indicate in your spread. Having to consider each of these possibilities every time you do a reading would be exhausting. Hold the perspective you'll use in your mind and trust that the deck will cooperate.

With that out of the way, here are four possible perspectives cards can take in the reversed position. I follow up each option with an example based on the Ace of Wands:

>> **Opposites:** Perhaps the most common approach suggests that the situation normally indicated by the card heads in a different direction. A reward may be withheld or a crisis averted.

From this perspective, the Ace of Wands, which normally means an exciting new beginning, may indicate something coming to an end.

>> **Blocks and delays:** This perspective indicates that something in your situation keeps the energy in this card from fully manifesting or that things will take longer than you'd prefer. Looking at the rest of the spread, you'll probably see an indicator of what's causing the issue.

A reversed Ace of Wands may indicate that the beginning you hoped for won't start or you're not yet ready to begin this new path and should wait for more preparations.

>> **Too much or too little:** Some say that a person's greatest weakness is their greatest strength taken too far. This approach is an especially useful way to read the court cards, in which you see what happens when these big personalities take their natural inclinations to the extremes.

Because the Ace of Wands can indicate a passionate beginning, with this perspective you may say that your passion is over the top and may cause trouble as you begin this new journey. On the flip side, it can suggest that although you thought you wanted to start this new path, your heart just wasn't in it. Use your intuition to determine which.

>> **Inner experience:** With this perspective, an upright card represents something taking place externally in the "real world," and a reversed card points to something happening within you. This attitude indicates that you're reading the card from a more psychological or emotional standpoint.

With the Ace of Wands, this approach suggests a new passion has awoken within you, or you're feeling enflamed with energy.

Counting the reversals

When you lay out a spread with reversals, take a moment to consider the ratio of upright and reversed cards:

>> **About half the cards are reversed.** Typically, if you shuffle your deck to include reversals, you find half the cards are upside down in your spread. That's an indicator that the situation will proceed in a fairly normal way with some ups and downs.

>> **Most of the cards are reversed.** Have you ever felt like everything is upside down in your life? Seeing the bulk of the cards inverted can suggest that things are going to feel a little out of sorts. You may have a lot of blocks in your path or an unusually high number of delays.

>> **A few of the cards are reversed.** Things look especially stable and normal. That doesn't mean the reading itself is positive — there are plenty of upright bummer cards — but it means you're at least dealing with them without all the added blocks and delays.

Official Meanings

In this step, you consider the sorts of things a card generally means. Each card has a unique essence that can be expressed in many ways.

REMEMBER

You don't have to memorize the meaning of every card before you read tarot. Your deck probably came with a companion book, and Chapter 10 is a comprehensive guide to each card in the Rider–Waite–Smith (RWS) system. Looking up the answer isn't cheating; it's how you learn. You build a familiarity with the cards the more you practice.

Zoning in on the deck you're using

If you're reading with anything other than the RWS or one of its closest clones, you should pay special attention to how its author and illustrator depicted the card. Pay particular attention to the following:

>> **The theme:** In fantasy and science-fiction writing, you often hear the term *world-building*. This concept means the author has to think about all the ins and outs of the setting they're creating before they can start piecing together the plot. Creating a new tarot deck also requires a bit of world-building. The author and artist have to decide how magicians and high priestesses will show up in the deck's universe and how they represent the elemental energies of the four suits. The 78 cards all fit together in a shared framework.

>> **The specifics of the cards' scenes:** Sometimes, a reader turns over a card that diverges from the RWS and says, "I don't get it," or, "Well, the creator clearly doesn't understand the tarot." Ouch! One of the great joys of collecting lots of decks is seeing all the unique ways deck creators play around in the shared language of tarot.

When a card looks very different from the RWS, I always defer to what's happening on the card in front of me. My agreement with the tarot is that it'll use the deck in my hands to answer my question. It's just easier that way.

>> **The companion book:** Although the guide to the cards in Chapter 10 is top-notch, you gain new insights by reading the deck author's take on the card, which usually includes a rationale for what's happening in the scene. They've spent many hours with the images (I speak from experience).

Contemplating the traditional meaning

This part is very straightforward. Read the full entry for each card in Chapter 10. Note which of the various meanings for a card leap out at you as being relevant to your question.

Sometimes the right meaning seems obvious. For example, certain cards generally mean victory or defeat, so if you've asked how things are going, you probably have your answer right there. If none of the assigned meanings clicks right away, you need to lean into your intuition more.

Most cards have a few pieces of advice associated with them that tell you how to achieve what's happening in the card or how to absolutely avoid ending up like that. The advice has to be broad — because its shape changes with every question — but consider whether any of that advice seems to work right out of the box.

Puzzling over esoteric symbols

Many decks include sacred symbols such as astrological glyphs, Hebrew letters, runes, sigils, and the like. They add a mystical flare to any deck and can convey important information, but they're also a tad annoying for beginners.

In the RWS system, many of the cards' associations come from astrological correspondences, so you frequently see references to the planets and signs on the cards. For example, the Emperor is associated with Aries, and his throne is decorated with stylized rams' heads.

Including these symbols is all well and good if the creator is willing to explain what they're doing on the cards, but occultists like to use obscure symbols to encode hidden messages so that only the worthy and learned can perceive the wisdom. A guidebook also just doesn't have enough space to explain every tiny detail.

If your favorite decks include arcane symbols, make a point to explore their meanings. It'll be a fun treasure hunt that's likely to deepen your understanding of the deck.

Your Intuition

This factor in the equation of meaning is entirely up to you. No card in the deck means, "You'll have a nice date with a marketing executive." You're in charge of the specifics, and that's where your psychic senses and analytical skills come in.

Connecting the dots

You've read a card's various meanings, but now you must narrow them down. Look at the figures on the cards and ask yourself some questions:

» What was the first thing you thought when you turned the card over?

» What was your reaction to that first feeling? Were you encouraged by it, or did you try to talk yourself out of it? This clues you into potential biases.

» Does the spread contain a figure who seems to be the querent (whether that's you or someone else)?

» Considering the area of your question, when do you feel like the people or critters in this image?

Reading between the images

One of the most effective techniques for finding meaning is to see the spread as a story. If you're looking at a linear spread, let yourself wonder what actions and reactions took place between each card.

Notice whether any of the figures across the cards seem to be supportive of or at odds with one another. Imagine what happens when they get together. How do they get along?

Making the call

At this point, you sometimes feel like you have no idea what the card (or spread) means. Finally articulating the ultimate conclusion or advice of the reading is a lot of pressure — especially if you're reading for someone else. Sometimes, the reading seems to say, "You must do X," or, "You absolutely have to avoid doing X." It can feel that divergent. But at the end of the reading, take a risk and write down one final meaning in your tarot journal. (Check out Chapter 4 for more on journaling your tarot.)

IT'S IN THE CARDS

A technique that never fails in these situations when you feel you don't know the answer is to consider this question: "If you knew the answer, what would you say?" That may seem a little too easy, but I've used this question with many stuck readers in workshops, and in every case, they looked down, paused, looked up, and told me what the card meant. Having someone else ask you the question may help. Give it a try.

Making peace with uncertainty

Some days the answer is crystal clear, but often you have to take things on faith. Tarot isn't a foolproof system (it prominently contains a Fool), and you'll make the wrong call from time to time.

But I promise you that you'll get more out of the card reading experience if you can live with "a pretty good hunch." It's something you can explore and work with, which is a fine start.

And, of course, if your approach to reading cards is the purely psychological, creative problem-solving route, you don't have to worry! There's no wrong answer for you because there's no correct answer either. The reading got your mental processes to play around, and you arrived at your own conclusion. Yahtzee!

Something that gets in the way of people's intuitive gifts is the knowledge that an official meaning is out there and the belief that their intuitive response should match that meaning. Here's a fun way to start seeing things differently:

1. **Imagine that many images you come across have oracular messages.**

2. **Open a magazine to a random page, scroll quickly on your phone, or decide that the next time you see a picture with red, or someone wearing a hat, or whatever, it's a tarot or oracle card.**

3. **Decide whether it specifically has a message for you (or a phantom querent, if that makes you more comfortable).**

4. **Spend some time with the image.**

   Decide the following:

   ● What would the image mean if it were making a prediction?

   ● What advice do you think the image would give?

Because this system doesn't have a guidebook to correct you, you're the final word on the meaning of the message.

Deciphering the Pips

Throughout this book, I focus on the RWS system and decks that have characters and scenes on each card. But the pip deck is a category of tarot that's having a resurgence.

A *pip deck* is any deck in which Minor Arcana cards from ace through ten show a number of suit symbols rather than a scene (the emblems themselves are the *pips*). For example, the Six of Cups features six cups arranged artfully, possibly with some added decoration like flowers.

This category includes the historical reproductions of early decks like the Tarot de Marseille (see Chapter 3) and many modern decks that are media tie-ins featuring characters from beloved films and television series. Many readers who have trained themselves with Rider-Waite-Smith decks see the pip cards and go blank.

The lack of characters and scenes make pip decks much more open to the reader's individual interpretation, and this takes time to get used to. This style of reading can be a bit like putting puzzle pieces together. That neutral playing field of pip decks can be an advantage, though. For example, look at the Four of Cups as it appears in both the Rider-Waite-Smith (on the left in Figure 8-3) and the Tarot de Marseille (on the right).

FIGURE 8-3: The Four of Cups depicted in very different styles.

It's hard to look at the RWS version and not find it a little glum. Why would you want to be like this fellow? But suppose fours represent stability, and cups are emotions. (I share my number system in the following section.) In that case, emotional stability may sound pretty fantastic.

REMEMBER

You *can* read pip cards with the same meanings you use for an RWS deck. That misses some of the value of the pip system, but it's a perfectly reasonable way to use that fun media tie-in deck with pip minors or make a historical reproduction without having to reinvent the wheel.

If you want to use the pips differently, here are a few approaches.

Pairing number with suit

The most common method of reading the pips is to take the correspondences of numbers, marry them to the correspondences of the suits, and see what their blend produces. This list of number correspondences is a quick starting point for working with these systems:

>> **Aces** show new beginnings or the suit element (see Chapter 3) in its more primal state.

>> **Twos** show a desire for the suit's focus or a connection between things.

>> **Threes** show the first manifestation of the suit's focus in the world and how it takes shape.

>> **Fours** bring stability and balance.

>> **Fives** disrupt that stability with chaos, conflict, and lessons.

>> **Sixes** show the suit's focus being brought into a state of harmony.

>> **Sevens** show a suit's adaptability and how they pivot.

>> **Eights** show a deepening of the suit's focus or a moment of rebirth.

>> **Nines** bring the suit's focus to a climax.

>> **Tens** conclude a cycle.

Your number system may vary (I feel like lots of different theories about the sixes, sevens, and eights are floating around). If it does diverge, use your system. The important thing is for you to have some idea of what each number brings.

Slower, faster, less, and more

One of the easiest ways to look at the pips in a line of cards is to note how the number of pips increases or decreases. Consider this example (see Figure 8-4) featuring the Three of Swords, Four of Batons, Six of Swords.

That's an increase in the more active energy of swords and batons but a gradual one that'll be easier to manage.

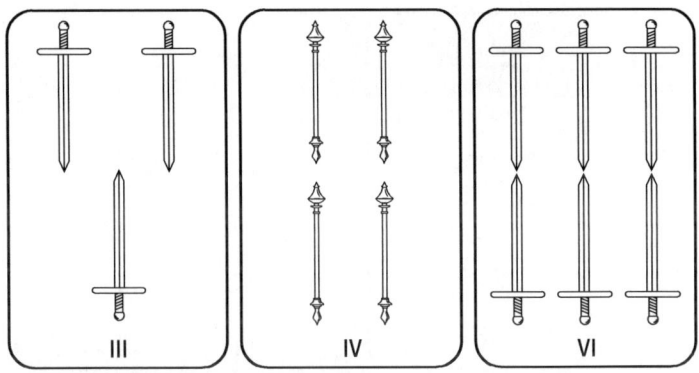

FIGURE 8-4: Swords and batons together designate active energy.

Whereas this spread — Two of Batons, Seven of Cups, Nine of Coins (see Figure 8-5) — jumps quite quickly from very little to a whole lot.

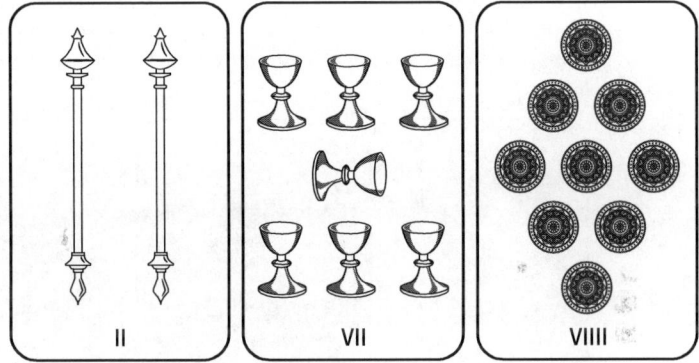

FIGURE 8-5: A spread showing batons, cups, and coins together.

A friend once asked about romance in her marriage, and the Tarot de Marseille gave me the easiest reading of my career: Eight of Cups, Three of Cups, Five of Cups (see Figure 8-6).

I skipped all the ideas about what the numbers of the cards meant individually. I simply said, "There used to be a lot of romance, and currently there's very little. There will be more in the future, but not at the same level as when you began." They're still together, by the way.

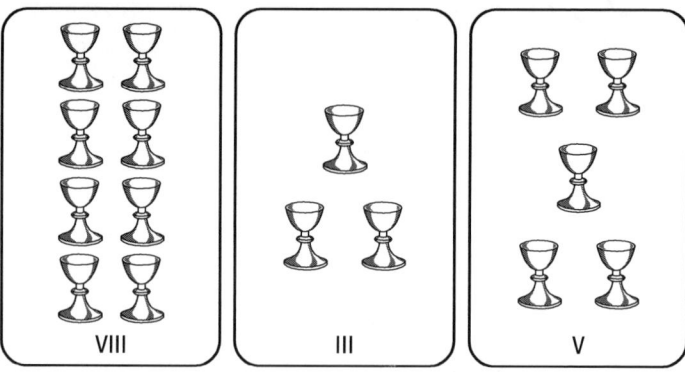

FIGURE 8-6: Cups cards in this spread can indicate waning romance.

The face cards rule the reading

I learned very early on when reading with pip decks that in a spread, the Major Arcana and court cards take on a special prominence. Additionally, some readers find great significance in the directions characters face in the cards. Consider the line shown in Figure 8-7: Seven of Wands, Three of Coins, Knight of Swords.

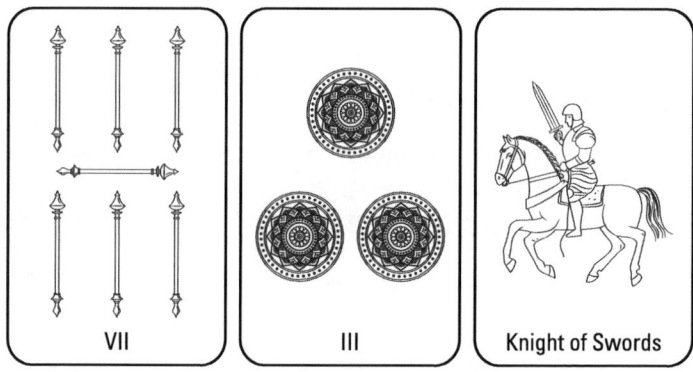

FIGURE 8-7: This reading flows from right to left, following the Knight's lead.

When I look at this line of cards, I can't help but focus on the Knight. They seem to be the most critical factor in the spread, and if you read directionally, you see what they're excited to get into. In this example, the reading flows from right to left because that's where the Knight's headed.

The suits

I cover these suit meanings in Chapter 3, but generally speaking, they go like this:

>> **Wands** represent vitality, passion, energy, and sexuality.

>> **Swords** represent the intellect, strategies, strife, and conflicts.

>> **Cups** represent emotions, relationships, dreams, and healing.

>> **Pentacles** represent resources, the body, labor, and manifestation.

The Marseille suits

If you're reading with a Tarot de Marseille deck, here are some unique correspondences that readers have assigned to the suits based on their earliest connotations:

>> **Batons** are associated with the peasant class because the sticks look like a weapon a commoner may wield. They suggest hard work and activity.

>> **Swords** are linked to members of the nobility and the military (the people who could afford swords). They're correlated with intellectual strategy; fighting with a sword takes more skill as well as pain and strife because swords are violent weapons.

>> **Cups** are associated with the clergy because they resemble religious chalices. They're connected to spirituality and relationships.

>> **Coins** go with members of the merchant class, who were the most actively involved in commerce. They symbolize wealth, resources, and ideas.

Using these as a guide, you may see a Two of Coins as a desire for money, a business transaction, a working partnership, or an exchange of ideas.

These are slightly different from the ones in previous sections, so try them all (or other associations you find) and use what works for you.

Pure intuition

A less common method of reading pip decks is to gaze upon the tableau of pip cards before you and let your intuitive skills run wild. Notice how the swirls of flowers in the background interact with the suit symbols. Consider why the character in one card longs to run toward or escape from another. Observe the interplay of order and chaos and see what message surfaces for you.

Chapter **9**
Doing Tarot Readings Step-by-Step

n this chapter, you can try your hand at performing a reading from start to finish. Here I include three sample readings: predictive and non-predictive, plus a hybrid version that includes reversals. Seeing these three attempts at tarot readings prepares you to begin doing your own if you haven't already. I focus on tarot cards in this chapter and oracle cards in Chapter 12.

Reading in a Nutshell

Here's an overview of the reading process. You don't need to include all these steps every single time, but familiarizing yourself with them is a good idea.

» **Form your question.** The question determines the type of reading you're doing: predictive, guidance, and so on.

» **Choose a spread.** Chapter 7 shows many spreads, but this chapter focuses on just three, including the classic Celtic Cross.

>> **Mix the cards and lay them out in a spread.** Shuffle the cards and put them out in your chosen spread.

>> **Note your first impressions.** You may have an immediate intuitive hit as to what the cards are saying or you may just be aware of a strong positive or negative emotional response to the cards that appear.

>> **Look for patterns.** Patterns may emerge with suits, numbers, or courts. (You can read more about these elements in Chapter 3.)

>> **Look up the meanings.** Check out what the traditional meanings are (see Chapter 10).

>> **Weave the answer.** Tie together the overall message and recommended action.

>> **Record the reading in your journal.** Having a record of readings enables you to learn from past readings. I cover tarot journaling in Chapter 4.

REMEMBER

If your conclusions about the cards' meanings in this chapter differ greatly from mine, don't sweat it. The point is to see how to conduct different styles of reading. Trust your skills with interpretation and be open to returning to past readings for a fresh take on the cards.

Sample Reading 1: Predicting with Tarot

Imagine you're someone who doesn't have much going on in your love life and wants to rectify that. You decide to get some insights from a tarot reading. Here's what that may look like.

Form your question.

After considering the question, you settle on "What does the future hold for my love life over the next few months?"

Choose a spread.

You pick the Foresight and Action spread from Chapter 7, shown in Figure 9-1.

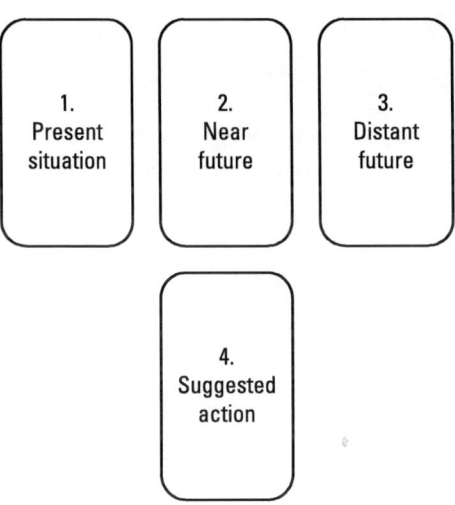

FIGURE 9-1: Use the Foresight and Action spread for this activity.

Note that cards 1, 2, and 3 are a narrative progression and card 4 is advice for the querent (in this case, you).

Mix the cards and lay them out in a spread.

At this point, you can go through any of the pre-reading activities I suggest in Chapter 5, from breathing to calling in the ancestors — whatever fits your practice. You can also just move right into shuffling and laying out the cards.

You shuffle the cards, cut them, and place them in the spread positions, and you get what's shown in Figure 9-2.

Note your first impressions.

Do you have a strong reaction to any cards in this spread?

Consider the vibe of this reading. Do things seem to get better, stay neutral, or get worse? To my mind that Eight of Pentacles looks like a downer in a love context, but then things get brighter with the dancing ladies in the Three of Cups. The Page of Cups seems to offer the ladies a drink. The Ace of Swords, on the other hand, looks pretty ominous. Swords can be kind of rough, can't they?

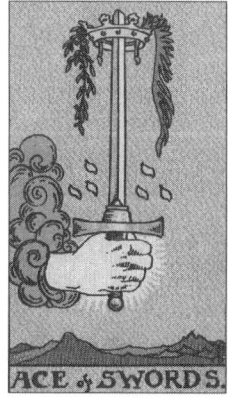

Pamela Colman Smith/Wikimedia Commons/Public Domain

FIGURE 9-2: The Eight of Pentacles, Three of Cups, Page of Cups, and Ace of Swords in the Foresight and Action spread.

Engaging your intuition, if you had to sum up the answer to the question "What does the future hold for my love life over the next few months?", what do you think the reading's answer is?

IT'S IN THE CARDS

You can take this stage of the journey a step further and make up a fairy tale about what you see in the cards. Don't try to match the story to the question; just roll with it and see what comes out. Mine may be this:

> Once upon a time, there was a craftsperson who made decorative plates for the people in their city. They were good at their job, but they were lonely. One day, they heard about a party in town and decided to attend to help their loneliness

and boredom. At the party, plenty of people were dancing, drinking, and having a good time. The craftsperson made their way to the refreshment table, where they met a nice person with a very fancy hat and started a conversation. The next day, the craftsperson went to their workshop and skipped the decorative plates, creating a sword and a crown instead. The end.

Do any points of the fairy tale you made up seem to be significant to the question at hand?

Now, repeat the story once more but swap out the craftsperson with "I," like this:

> I'm a craftsperson who makes decorative plates for people in my city. I'm good at my job but I'm lonely. One day, I heard about a party in town. . . ."

You may notice you get much more out of the exercise when you start telling the story again in first person.

Look for patterns.

Now think about the suits and numbers of the cards and consider what's there and what's missing (refer to Figure 9-2):

>> **Minor Arcana suits:** Pentacles, cups, swords. No wands at all, so your love life in the near future probably doesn't have much in the way of fiery passion or possibly sex.

>> **Major Arcana:** The reading has no majors at all. This status means you don't need more extraordinary personal transformation on the quest for love, and activities will be mundane.

>> **Court cards:** The spread shows one court card in the distant future position. That means that in the future you'll meet a person with a Page of Cups sort of personality *or* that to find love, you need to be Page of Cups–like in your approach.

>> **Numbers:** You can see a slight number pattern in the spread. The pages are the first card of the court, and the ace is the first card of the numerical cards. That suggests a theme of new beginnings.

Look up the meanings.

Before you look up the meanings, ask yourself what questions you have about the cards that appeared (refer to Figure 9-2). For this spread, that may include the following:

>> Is that sword good news or bad news?

>> How literal is the Three of Cups? Am I going to date three people?

>> Pentacles is a suit about work and careers; do pentacles mean something different in a love reading?

>> What's with the fish in that page's cup?

Now's the time to look up the meanings for each of the cards. As the wise purchaser of this fantastic guide to card reading, you need only to turn to Chapter 10.

REMEMBER

If you've done enough readings to be familiar with the cards, you can skip this step. However, if you feel stuck with an interpretation at any point, looking up the meaning to see whether something jumps out at you is always a good idea.

TIP

Why not just look up the meanings the moment you've placed all the cards? Because that ends up creating a very passive experience where your book becomes the reader. Noodling on the answer for a bit puts you in the driver's seat.

You can take a moment to read the entries for each of the cards. Here are a few concepts from each of them:

>> **Eight of Pentacles:** Repetitive action, hard work, improvement over time, drudgery

>> **Three of Cups:** Friendliness, celebration, support, joy, partying

>> **Page of Cups:** A person with youthful energy, creativity, a sense of wonder, artistic creation

>> **Ace of Swords:** A new beginning, truth, letting go, new perspective

Weave the answer.

As you can see, looking up the meanings gives you a pile of keywords that aren't connected to one another. Your intuition helps you find the links among the cards, their positions, and the question and come up with a useful answer. Try your hand at coming up with an overall answer to the question. If possible, distill each card down to just a few sentences.

Here's my take as though I'm the querent:

> The Eight of Pentacles is often about work, but this wasn't a work question. Instead, it seems to say I'm trying the same thing over and over with romance and it's not working. In the future, I'll have more fun with my approach and connect more with others. Maybe I'll go out with friends to bars or clubs or switch to dating apps. When I'm using apps, since I got cups but no wands, I'll want to focus on dating apps that that prioritize connections and conversations instead of hookup options. The Page of Cups could be me lightening up and being more curious, but I'm absolutely gonna keep my eyes open for a nice artsy type of person with a curious outlook on life. If I meet someone like that, it's a good chance they're my ticket to a relationship. Regarding the Ace of Swords as the action I should take, the cards say I need to start fresh with a new strategy. Forget about the people I have a crush on and the dating app I'm using. The Ace takes a realistic look at life and cuts away the things that don't work.

TIP

As compact as that interpretation is, I won't remember it word for word. To make a reading truly memorable, try to distill the whole reading down to a single statement of advice that'll live rent-free in your head. For this reading that may be something like the following:

>> Take the fun path.

>> Lighten up.

>> If it's not working, cut it loose.

>> Open minded, open hearted.

REMEMBER

Even readers within the same school or using the same deck have different insights into a reading. A good rule of thumb when dealing with prediction is to imagine that the cards turned up the way they did for the person reading them at that moment. Others can offer insight, but at the end of the day, trust your judgment and see how things pan out.

Record the reading.

This part is pretty straightforward. Your entry for this reading notes the date, question, spread, deck, cards, and a quick version of your interpretation. If you chose a sum-up statement, consider writing it in a different color pen or underlining it a few times so that it stands out.

Over the next couple of months, you may return to the entry. If you get curious about who the mysterious Page of Cups is, you can start a new reading about them with that card being the significator. (More info on significators in Chapter 3.)

Sample Reading 2: Guidance Reading

This reading example skips any ideas about prediction and focuses on looking to the cards for advice. For that reason, you consult the traditional meanings, but they take a back seat to impressions and intuition.

For this reading, imagine that you're thinking about your career. You've been in a holding pattern and want to move ahead, but you're not sure whether that means staying loyal to your company and trying to get a promotion or jumping ship and finding a job somewhere else.

Form your question.

Because you want to be action-oriented, ask *how* rather than *what.* The question is "How can I move forward in my career?"

Choose a spread.

This Do's and Don'ts spread is simple and gives you a clear strategy for what'll help and what'll hinder you; see Figure 9-3.

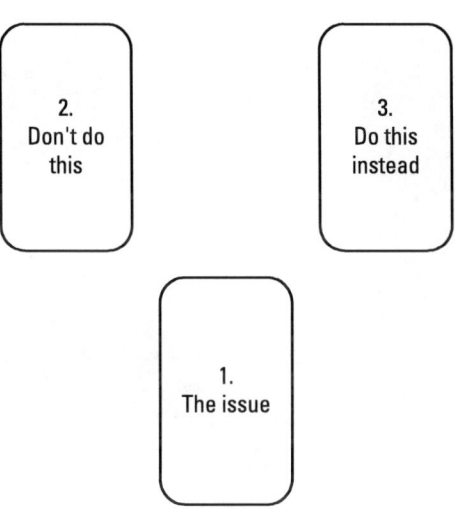

FIGURE 9-3: The Do's and Don'ts spread is simple and straightforward.

Mix the cards and lay them out in a spread.

You shuffle the cards, cut them, and place them in the spread positions. What comes up is shown in Figure 9-4.

Note your first impressions.

Do any cards in this spread inspire a strong reaction?

The question itself isn't explicitly about whether you should stay or leave; you left things a bit more open than that. But the energy of the Fool really stands out in this spread, leaping off the cliff and into adventure. In fact, each of the characters seems to be looking in a different direction; perhaps that'll play a part in the reading.

Look for patterns.

Think about the suits and numbers of the cards, noting what is and isn't there:

>> **Minor Arcana suits:** Well, it's just Pentacles. Pentacles are certainly associated with careers and finance. They're also on the slow side, being so centered and grounded in reality.

Pamela Colman Smith/Wikimedia Commons/Public Domain

FIGURE 9-4: The Queen of Pentacles, the Fool, and the Chariot in the Do's and Don'ts spread.

>> **Major Arcana:** Whoa! Two out of the three cards are majors. This lineup suggests you may be at a turning point in your career. This issue is bigger than just whether you can ask for a raise.

>> **Court cards:** The one court card may represent someone you work with, but — given this style of reading and the fact that it's in the *Don't* section — you're much more likely being told not to act very Queen of Pentacles–like at this time.

>> **Numbers:** You have a 7, Queen (technically 13), and 0. There doesn't seem to be a strong pattern with the numbers. Nothing seems to be escalating or de-escalating numerically.

Take a crack at interpretation.

I don't provide this activity for the predictive reading in the previous section. But generally, intuition plays a more significant part in a guidance reading. Looking at the cards (refer to Figure 9-4), you notice that movement versus standing still seems to be a theme. The Queen of Pentacles is seated on her throne, and her attention is drawn to a big, heavy pentacle in her lap. The earth and flowers also seem energetically heavy. In contrast, the Fool is a very dynamic image. He appears to leap forward — but you note that he's jumping off a cliff, and his dog seems agitated about that. The Chariot is literally a vehicle, but you see that it has no wheels. The sphinxes that are supposed to pull the cart are actually sitting down.

Continue the process despite this early interpretation, but the message about moving forward or moving on seems loud and clear.

IT'S IN THE CARDS

Here's an activity to further explore your feelings about these cards. Starting with card 1, say, "I'm like a chariot when I . . .," and let yourself speak or write down anything that comes to mind with this prompt. If you get stuck, just keep saying or writing, "I'm like a chariot when," until something comes to you. Do the same for card 2 by stating, "I'm like a queen when." (If you're already very familiar with the card meanings, you can absolutely specify Queen of Pentacles, but if you're new to the cards, you can take the more generic approach.) Repeat the process for the third card, the Fool. If you get a card with multiple people, pick the character you most relate to in the image and use them for the prompt.

Look up the meanings.

You probably have a strong sense of what the reading is saying at this point, but looking up the card meanings in Chapter 10 to consider additional insights that didn't occur to you is always wise. Here are a few tidbits for each card (refer to Figure 9-4):

>> **The Chariot:** Victory and conquest, uniting opposites, willpower, control

>> **Queen of Pentacles:** Caretaking, comfort, sensible

>> **The Fool:** New beginnings, recklessness, courage

Weave the answer.

A great way to connect meanings with position is to begin sentences with the language of the position. First, put together your interpretation of this spread.

If I were the phantom reader for this spread, I might come up with this:

> The issue is that I'm ready to move on, and I've proven myself, but I'm not going anywhere just yet. Regarding what not to do, the cards say, "Don't stay comfortable." I've settled in here, and it's time to break free. I also should avoid spending too much energy caring for others. I'm worried people will be unhappy if I leave, but I can't work for their comfort. The cards are saying, "Do take a risk." I should stop waiting for the right opportunity to fall into my lap and seek it out myself. I should be open to branching out of my current field. I'm ready to make a fresh start, either in a new position at my own company or somewhere else where I can try something new.

TIP

Pay attention to the *in a new position at my own company* line. You can make a change more than one way, but card readers sometimes leap straight to the most dramatic option. In this reading, the critical element is a fresh start.

A sum-up line for this reading may be something like any of the following:

>> Move up or move out.

>> Nothing ventured, nothing gained.

>> Don't put down roots just yet.

Record the reading.

Write down the date, question, spread, deck, cards, and a quick version of your interpretation.

Sample Reading 3: Hybrid Approach with Reversals

For this reading, I'm using a larger, more complex spread and adding *reversals* (cards that come out of the deck upside down) into the mix. I discuss reversals at length in Chapter 8 but in general they can represent blocks or inversions of the cards' meanings.

Form your question.

Imagine that you don't have a specific question in mind and want a general reading. A great question to ask is "What do I need to be aware of for my greatest and highest good?"

With a more general question, the meanings are a little more vague, and applying the meanings to their lives is up to the querents.

Choose a spread.

The Celtic Cross (see Figure 9-5) is a very traditional spread with a lot of history behind it. I suggest that new readers give it a whirl to see whether they like it.

Mix the cards and lay them out in a spread.

Traditionally, the Celtic Cross begins with the selection of a significator card to stand for the querent in position 1. As I explain in Chapter 3, you can pick a significator card or let the tarot choose for you. I go for the latter here.

You shuffle the cards, cut them, and draw them randomly to place in the spread positions, and you get what's shown in Figure 9-6.

Note your first impressions.

Do you have a strong reaction to any cards in this spread?

Right away, you may notice that this spread contains some very challenging-looking cards, several neutral cards, and only one or two positive cards (and one of those is reversed). This reading may be less cheery than the two in the preceding sections, but you can look for ways to improve your situation.

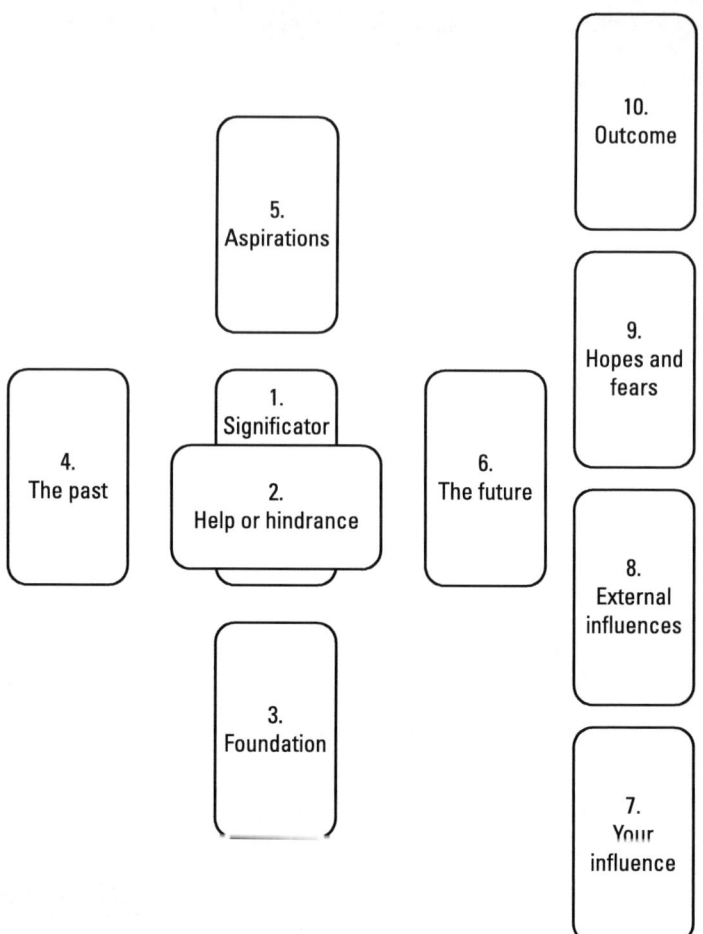

FIGURE 9-5: Give the Celtic Cross spread a try; you may like it!

Look for patterns.

Think about the suits and numbers of the cards, noting what's there and what's missing:

>> **Minor Arcana suits:** All the minor suits show up in this spread. You have one wand, two cups, three swords, and one pentacle. The prevalence of swords suggests trying times but also the need for clear thinking.

FIGURE 9-6: Take a few minutes to look at the cards and consider your reactions.

>> **Major Arcana:** Three majors are present in this ten-card spread. Mathematically, that's about what you'd expect, suggesting some big developments but not too overwhelming.

>> **Court cards:** You have three court cards in the spread, which means a few people will be involved or you'll engage with several aspects of your personality.

>> **Numbers:** The first and last card are both tens, and that suggests things are completing or coming to an end. You also see two sixes, the number of harmony and improvement — but they're reversed! Uh oh.

Note any reversals.

If you cut your deck evenly and reverse one of the stacks of cards to get reversals, then you expect to have about half of the cards be reversed. In this case, you have four (refer to Figure 9-6), which is roughly half the cards, so not too much is topsy-turvy for the querent.

TIP

Because there are multiple perspectives on how to read reversals (which I cover in Chapter 8), you should decide ahead of the reading how you'll interpret them. For this reading, I'm using reversals to indicate the inversion or opposite of a card's meaning.

Assign meanings.

Given the complexity of the Celtic Cross, I discuss the position meaning and my combined traditional and intuitive interpretation for each card (as though I'm the querent, unlike the readings in the preceding sections). Your mileage may vary. Refer to Figure 9-6 and consider these meanings and interpretations:

1. This covers you: Ten of Swords

- **Position meaning:** The subject of the reading.
- **Interpretation:** What an auspicious start! This reading is about recent setbacks I've had and the accompanying sense of overwhelm I feel. I'll be on the lookout for proposed solutions.

2. This crosses you: Strength

- **Position meaning:** Forces that can either help or hinder you.
- **Interpretation:** Strength suggests the power to withstand difficulty. When paired with the Ten of Swords, it indicates that personal restraint and self-control will help me get through these difficult times.

3. **This foundation: Six of Pentacles (reversed)**

- **Position meaning:** Things going on beneath the surface and/or in the subconscious affecting you.

- **Interpretation:** When upright, this card is about the need to give to restore balance. Reversed, it may mean it's time to receive help from others instead of giving. A major factor in my being overwhelmed may be a reluctance to ask for help.

4. **The past: Six of Cups (reversed)**

- **Position meaning:** Recent events affecting you.

- **Interpretation:** Normally, this one is a lovely card suggesting nostalgia and childlike joy. Reversed, it suggests I was wearing rose-colored glasses and ignoring how difficult things were becoming.

5. **This crowns you: Page of Swords**

- **Position meaning:** What you're working toward (whether you realize it or not).

- **Interpretation:** Courts represent either a person or an aspect of the querent's personality. Because this position is about aspirations, I lean toward aspect. Pages indicate starting a new path, and this one is interested in developing new strategies. I've accepted that things can't go on as they have been and I have to work smarter, not harder.

6. **This is before you: King of Wands**

- **Position meaning:** The near future.

- **Interpretation:** This king is a bold and charismatic leader. The trajectory of the spread, in which I seem to be starting fresh, suggests this figure is likely a separate person I'll meet. They may be a mentor or a new boss to help me on my path forward.

7. **The self: Five of Cups (reversed)**

- **Position meaning:** The influence you have on your situation. You may see this card as the advised action card.

- **Interpretation:** This card is all about grief and loss, but reversed it suggests that I'm ready to stop dwelling on past problems and move on.

8. The environment: Knight of Swords

- **Position meaning:** Sometimes called *the house;* indicates external forces impacting the situation.

- **Interpretation:** The position makes this one easy: The knight is someone in my life. This knight is a man of action, charging forward without much consideration. Someone is pushing me to move forward.

9. Hopes and fears: High Priestess (reversed)

- **Position meaning:** Shows what's drawing you toward your goal or holding you back (depending on how positive or negative the card is).

- **Interpretation:** The High Priestess is a keeper of secrets and mistress of intuition. Her reversed position suggests a profound lack of trust in my ability to read the situation. I may feel like I'm in the dark.

10. The outcome: Wheel of Fortune

- **Position meaning:** Points to where the whole situation is headed in the long term.

- **Interpretation:** The Wheel of Fortune begins a new cycle. Something ended with the Ten of Swords, but I'm moving out of this downturn and into something new and promising. Bonus: The upright Wheel often indicates good luck will be in my favor.

Weave the answer.

After going through so many cards (refer to Figure 9-6) and their complex meanings, you may feel like you're swimming in a sea of words and ideas with cards pointing in various directions. For that reason, simplify the reading by coming up with a few sentences of prediction and advice. For this reading, I may say this:

> Things are rough, but I have the power to move past the present difficulty and learn how to do things differently. I should be open to receiving the help of others, especially a mentor figure and someone with a lot of energy. An opportunity will present itself, and I should be ready to take it.

TIP

The Celtic Cross is a lot to take in. To make things a bit easier, break the reading down by pulling out groups of two or three cards and focusing on them:

>> **Read cards 4, 1, 6, and 10 as a past, present, near future, and distant future progression.**

>> **Look at cards 3, 1, and 5 as "above and below."** See how the lower card creates the middle card, which launches itself toward becoming the upper card.

>> **Place cards 2, 7, and 9 together.** The card in the middle gives advice about how to deal with your biggest challenges.

Always feel free to move the cards around on the table to better make sense of them.

Record the reading.

Record the pertinent info for posterity: the date, question, spread, deck, cards, and a summary of your interpretation.

IN SUPPORT OF RANDOM ORACULAR WISDOM

I was listening to an interview with a Nobel Prize–winning scientist talking about the significance of using random systems like a coin flip to make decisions. His main point was that the value of a coin flip is that your immediate emotional response to the result gives you the real answer to your question. Were you relieved or disappointed? Well, there's your answer! I've had several friends share this same wisdom with me since then, and I have to say that I absolutely disagree with this premise.

Assume for a moment that no magic forces are at work, guiding the coin as it arcs through the air, and that the result is truly random. Humans must make an astounding number of decisions every day. Increasingly, making the correct choice feels more critical than ever

(continued)

(continued)

lest you face the judgment of others. Your willingness to flip a coin for this decision suggests that the choice is inconsequential enough that either result will be acceptable. The value of this process is giving over a decision to the forces of blind chance so that it's out of your hands. If you make that toss and then decide to reject the answer, you're placing the weight of this decision back on your shoulders.

You can say the same about the process of cartomancy. You're releasing your uncertainty as you shuffle the cards. If you cast aside the result, then back comes the uncertainty. If you never let the deck make the call for you and always revert to doing what feels most comfortable, then you can't break free of the patterns you've established in your life. The cards give you permission to zag and break form, or they affirm that your decision to zig is correct and you should remain confident in your position.

Reading cards, whether you believe that destiny guides the process or that it's all up to your intuitive response, requires you to set your doubts aside and put your faith in your ability to adapt and flourish. I have faith in you.

Chapter **10**

A Treasury of Tarot Card Meanings

ere it is: the various meanings of the tarot cards within the Rider-Waite-Smith (RWS) school of tarot. This chapter is likely the one you'll turn to most often as a reference for the cards in your readings. (Flip to Chapter 3 for more on the RWS school, plus an introduction to the Major and Minor Arcana, suits, court cards, and the elements [earth, water, fire, and air].)

REMEMBER

A tarot card can refer to a person of any (or no) gender. The card descriptions use gendered pronouns to refer to the characters in images of the RWS deck but they/them when referring to the person the cards represent in a reading.

Unlocking the Cards' Meanings

In this chapter, I include the following for every tarot card:

» **Keywords:** Each card in the deck has various constellations of meaning. Keywords help open your mind to the cards' most essential meanings, creating pathways for you to explore.

» **Divinatory meaning:** I give a visual description plus a breakdown of the sorts of things a card (in its upright orientation) tends to mean within a reading. (Some of the cards' figures appear in the nude, not in a salacious way, but consider yourself warned.) This info includes both predictive meanings for the card as well as suggested actions to take when it turns up in a reading. These bits can serve as a jumping-off point for you.

>> **Reversed meaning:** Chapter 8 shows a few approaches to reversed cards. This category covers some of the more common ideas for them. If you don't read with reversals, I still recommend reading through this text to get an idea of a card's total range of meanings.

Making sense of the meanings

Throughout this chapter, I make frequent use of the words *possibly, may, could, can*, and so on. I'm not trying to be a weasel! Each card's essence can be expressed in a multitude of ways, and you need to select one of those expressions and apply it to your reading. For example, the Page of Wands can represent a bright, youthful person in your life, the need to explore an area you're excited about, or an important message — but it's not going to mean *all* those things. Trust your intuition and sense of discernment.

Tracing the history

What do I mean when I say a card *traditionally* means this or that? The RWS system began when A.E. Waite combined the ideas of past tarot writers with many of his own beliefs and penned *The Pictorial Key to the Tarot*, which was accompanied by Pamela Colman Smith's excellent artwork. Then, the system took on a life of its own. A succession of writers — especially Eden Gray, Mary Greer, Rachel Pollack, and Barbara Moore (this book's esteemed technical reviewer) — worked to make the system more accessible and to keep it relevant for the modern age. As you learn, the collection of the cards' meanings forms a deep reservoir from which you can draw in a reading. The cards are not static, and you'll fill this reservoir throughout your whole life. For this reason, you don't need to memorize these descriptions word for word. As you perform readings and become familiar with how the cards speak and interact, you'll discover what they mean to you.

Regarding the esoteric

These cards have many magical symbols, including astrological and Kabbalistic glyphs. You can find rich meaning in exploring those signs but covering it would weigh things down in a *For Dummies* text. If I tell you that the RWS High Priestess's pillars are named Jachin and Boaz but don't explain what those words mean, that info isn't very helpful. I point out some especially relevant ones and leave the rest to your continued exploration.

0 — The Fool

Keywords: Beginnings, impulse, innocence, foolishness

Divinatory meaning: A young man in garish clothes walks precariously close to a cliff while a small dog barks nearby. As the very first card of the Major Arcana, the Fool heralds a new quest or exciting opportunity. It's the dawn of a new day, or you're headed for a moment of rebirth in which you release attachment to old baggage to start anew. Sometimes, when your head is filled with too much information, you must let go of what you think you know and, like the Fool, see the world with fresh eyes.

The Fool is often compared to the very first stage of Joseph Campbell's Hero's Journey. Think Dorothy before she steps onto the Yellow Brick Road or Luke Skywalker before he takes up his father's lightsaber.

Pamela Colman Smith/Wikimedia Commons/Public Domain

You may fear the unknown that lies before you, but something is calling you to undertake an adventure. To the question "Should I?" the Fool enthusiastically answers, "Yes!"

The Fool is exceptional at the art of improvisation. Try things differently; zag instead of zigging. Fools travel light, with nothing more than whatever they've got in that little bag. Don't wait until you feel more prepared; you already have everything you need. Be ready to go with the flow and pivot when circumstances change unexpectedly. Above all else, try to have fun.

Don't let others put you in a box or keep you in your place. When this card appears, you're unstoppable.

Reversed: When reversed, this card points to the sort of foolishness that may land you in trouble. Here, you see recklessness and destructive tendencies. Keep an eye open for warning signs, like the little dog nipping at your heels telling you that you're about to step off a cliff. This is a time to play it safe, step back onto the path, color within the lines, and follow the rules to the letter.

I — The Magician

Keywords: Creation, skill, willpower, manipulation

Divinatory meaning: The Magician has had quite an evolution. The earliest versions of the card show a street conjurer performing tricks (and running scams), but in the 20th century, the Magician became a *magus,* a master of the most powerful mystical arts. The through line is manipulation — the ability to make things work skillfully and easily.

This card suggests that you use your considerable talents to direct this situation as you desire. Doing so requires visualization; you must be able to clearly see the end state you want in all its glory. Holding that vision in your mind, let every action move you closer to its realization. Be relentless; don't hold back after you know what you're after.

THE MAGICIAN.

Pamela Colman Smith/Wikimedia Commons/ Public Domain

On his table, you see the symbols of the four elements, reminding you that the Magician is incredible at operating complex systems. A lot may be going on at the moment, but you can manage all the nuances of your situation. Believe that reality fits together like an elegant puzzle and that you can connect the pieces.

If you're interested in spiritual practices, from manifestation to magic, this card suggests putting your gifts into practice to achieve your goals. The *lemniscate* (infinity sign) above the Magician's head implies that he draws upon an infinite, inexhaustible source to create his magic.

This card is also a sign favorable to any form of originality or innovation. Don't feel beholden to the tried-and-true ways; use your creativity to shake things up and move them in a new direction.

Reversed meaning: Here, you revert more fully to the earlier meaning of the Magician as a consummate performer. If you're not feeling entirely qualified for what you're trying to accomplish . . . fake it! If you're in any conflict, misdirect your opponent's attention elsewhere. This card may also be a warning to be on the lookout for hucksters and cheats.

II — The High Priestess

Keywords: Secrets, intuition, inner wisdom, observation

Divinatory meaning: This card has the most mysterious origins of any in the deck. Originally, the High Priestess probably either represented Pope Joan, a legendary woman disguised as a man to become pontiff, or Manfreda Visconti, leader of a heretical sect who believed women should lead the church. The card's modern meanings are appropriately elusive. The most maddening of them is simply, "You already know the answer to your question."

THE HIGH PRIESTESS

Pamela Colman Smith/Wikimedia Commons/ Public Domain

The High Priestess is the guardian of secrets, sitting before the veil of mysteries. If you look carefully, you see that behind the veil is a vast body of water. This is a powerful symbol of the unconscious mind, suggesting that the answer you seek can be hidden within you and not outside of yourself.

She sits between pillars representing extreme opposites, holding the sacred knowledge of truth. When people push you in different directions, you can quickly lose track of what you truly value. Let go of the surface concerns of your life and the day-to-day decisions that can seem so important. Shut all these voices out and take the time to go within. Be with yourself and listen to what your heart desires.

More simply, this card recommends trusting your intuition. Put the wisdom of that inner voice above rational, logical, strategic, and advisable points of view.

As the keeper of secrets, the High Priestess also suggests that you keep a tight lid on your own secrets for now.

Reversed meaning: When this card is inverted, something prevents your intuition from being a clear channel — possibly an excess of hope or fear. This position suggests that you look outside yourself for answers, checking in with people whose perspectives you trust. Inverted, she represents the revelation of secrets; if you're holding onto a secret, it may be time to let it out into the world.

III — The Empress

Keywords: Mothering, fertility, abundance, ease

Divinatory meaning: A royal woman lounges on a cushioned couch decorated with the symbol for Venus (also the symbol of womanhood) in a lovely and lively garden. The Empress is the epitome of the mother archetype. Not *your* mother in particular but the *idea* of a mother who provides the love, comfort, and attention you need to grow and thrive.

From the field of growing grain to the flourishing trees, all fed by a gentle stream, she is surrounded by all that's lush and alive. This is a fertile moment to plant the seeds of a new venture you want to develop. If you've kept things on hold, waiting for the opportune time, the soil is ready, and this is the moment.

Pamela Colman Smith/Wikimedia Commons/Public Domain

Like a doting mother, the Empress advises you to be good to yourself. This card is a reminder to stop ignoring health issues and address them directly.

With those fluffy pillows, this card permits you to take it easy. Don't be so hard on yourself. Are you feeling conflicted, disappointed, or uncertain? Pffffft! That sounds like far too much stress. Set aside cares and worries; for now, they aren't helping you.

This card also recommends reflecting all that care and compassion onto others in your life. Give people grace, space, and love; they may really need it.

As is often the case, some traditional meanings can be pretty literal, and this card can be connected to mothers and other maternal figures in your life. It's also a positive sign for anyone hoping to grow their family.

Reversed meaning: When this card is turned on its head, all that mothering goes too far and becomes smothering. Get off the couch, exit that park, and take action without waiting for anyone else to do it for you. If *you're* the one doing the smothering, give others space to grow by themselves.

IV — The Emperor

Keywords: Ambition, organization, command, rigidity

Divinatory meaning: A royal man sits on a throne high up in an arid mountain range. Beneath his robes he wears a full set of plate armor, and his throne is decorated with images of the aggressive Aries the ram.

Similar to the Empress in the preceding section, the Emperor epitomizes the father archetype. Not *your* father but the idea of a father who challenges you to measure up to his ideals and expectations. His love is challenging but can help you grow into your own power. He demands that you hold yourself to a high standard.

No surprise: The Emperor is a much less popular card than the Empress among readers. His energy can seem harsh and unyielding, but when he shows up, some force is likely needed to rein in things around this issue.

THE EMPEROR.

Pamela Colman Smith/Wikimedia Commons/ Public Domain

The Emperor prefers logic and reason over emotional decision-making and focuses on establishing and organizing useful systems that he and others can follow for their benefit. He's likely to advise you to, "Get it together."

The Emperor is an auspicious card if you want to take on a leadership role. Put yourself forward for consideration. Share your ideas openly, and others will be inspired.

Reversed meaning: When inverted, this card tips over into tyrant territory. That natural dominance turns toward cruelty or abuses of authority. It's a sign to step away from that type of leader if it's someone in your life. If you're heading in this direction, it's a call to calm down, chill out, and take things less seriously. Alternatively, it may suggest someone is acting in a territorial manner.

V — The Hierophant

Keywords: Tradition, learning, revealed wisdom, spiritual growth

Divinatory meaning: A figure dressed in a Catholic pope's traditional regalia holds his hands up to bless two monks. The keys of St. Peter, which open the gates of heaven, are crossed before him.

The Hierophant has been a part of the tarot from the beginning (originally named the Pope), but it's a tricky card because some readers are uncomfortable with traditional religious values or dogmas. Think of the Hierophant first and foremost as a spiritual teacher.

The name *hierophant* comes from Greek tradition and means "revealer of holy things." His role is to connect his flock with the divine, including the divine within themselves. This card can be a call to engage with whatever you personally find sacred. Your spiritual practices will be beneficial to you.

THE HIEROPHANT

Pamela Colman Smith/Wikimedia Commons/ Public Domain

This card is deeply connected with the most traditional ways of doing things. The tried-and-true methods are best currently; this is a time for common sense and conventional wisdom. In other words, don't reinvent the wheel.

The connection with traditions extends to the idea of systems and institutions. This is a good time to join the group or sign up to be a part of the team. Becoming a part of something bigger than yourself will reveal much to you.

The Hierophant is a teacher, and this card can be a call to learning. That can represent a more formal type of training or education or a moment to learn a new skill.

The hand gesture represents blessings (it appears elsewhere in the deck as well) and can simply indicate that you'll receive your own blessings imminently.

Reversed meaning: When upside down, the Hierophant indicates it's time for a bit of deviation. Forget the old way of doing things and forge a new path for yourself. This position suggests experimenting with new methods rather than sticking to the tried-and-true ones.

VI — The Lovers

Keywords: Union, choices, romance, attraction

Divinatory meaning: You see Adam and Eve from the Garden of Eden story, complete with trees of life and knowledge. But in this version, the angel blesses rather than expels the couple. The Lovers card has two major categories of meaning: union and choices.

First and foremost: Yes, having the Lovers card turn up when you're asking about romance *is* an excellent sign (depending, of course, on its position in the spread). When you're asking about love, this card suggests a powerful connection between the participants.

Of course, this card turns up for all kinds of nonromantic partnerships, where it suggests that you'll create something truly significant by joining with another in this endeavor. This partnership will elevate both of you. Form an alliance and stay faithful to your partner.

THE LOVERS.

Pamela Colman Smith/Wikimedia Commons/ Public Domain

When this card represents a choice, it suggests that you're at a significant moment of transition with the opportunity to commit yourself fully to a path that will either allow you to continue with what you've known or take you into unknown places. Unlike with the Fool, who just says yes to whatever, in this case you should thoughtfully weigh your options. It's a massive decision with lasting ramifications, but the wisest move is to follow your heart.

Some see the man as the rational mind gazing into the unconscious, which looks to the infinite in return. You may not understand why you're being called in this direction, but your soul longs to manifest *something,* and you need to go along for the ride.

Reversed meaning: When the card is reversed, the parties aren't so lucky in love or whatever partnership the reading addresses. Here, some form of discord between them keeps them from fully opening up to one another. They must address that issue, or a true union is unlikely. When considering a choice, this orientation of the card recommends sticking to what's familiar.

VII — The Chariot

Keywords: Achievement, triumph, travel, overcoming obstacles

Divinatory meaning: A charioteer in decorative armor and crowned by the stars rides in a cart drawn by two white-and-black sphinxes. The Chariot recalls the victory parades that gave the original *trionfi* deck (see Chapter 3) its name. It's a sign of outward success and riding forward with purpose. In short, whatever you're hoping to do, the tarot thinks you'll crush it.

Confidence is the key to success; the Chariot only rides forward — bringing all the lessons of cards 0 through VI forward, thanks to all the work done in preparation. Be assertive and uncompromising in your pursuit of your goal. This is no time to put on the brakes.

Pamela Colman Smith/Wikimedia Commons/Public Domain

The black-and-white sphinxes symbolize the opposing forces the charioteer needs to rein in to achieve forward momentum. Don't allow any chaos, conflict, or infighting to slow you down. Get everyone on the same page.

Similarly, the charioteer doesn't let anything get them down personally. Dwelling on hurt feelings or your dislike for others will only slow you down. Force yourself to rise above this sort of conflict in order to move forward.

The Chariot also has traditional meanings associated with travel. It can represent either a literal trip you'll take or a metaphorical move out of your comfort zone. This card rewards risk-taking and stretching your skills. It can also represent an actual vehicle, often a car, in a reading.

Reversed meaning: When reversed, this card indicates you may be revving your engine without managing to go anywhere. You may have an aggressive attitude, but not the skills to back it up. Hit the brakes for now. This position can also be a sign of vengeance, with those heightened emotions focused on addressing some past slight or wrong. The reversed Chariot can point to troubles with actual vehicles.

VIII — Strength

Keywords: Fortitude, self-mastery, determination, hunger

Divinatory meaning: A lovely maiden closes the hungry jaws of a ferocious lion. Her touch is gentle, and the chains she has to leash the beast are blooming flowers.

Where the Chariot symbolizes outer control and external victory, Strength represents your inner power to exert phenomenal levels of self-control. Instead of ruling over others, you must first learn to master yourself.

The lion symbolizes humans' most brutish tendencies: rage, hostility, insatiability, and so on. Left unchecked, you'd be consumed by its hunger. You can also think of the lion as the inner saboteur who seeks to wreck or undermine all the progress you make, causing you to get in your own way.

Pamela Colman Smith/Wikimedia Commons/Public Domain

A milder take on the lion is that it simply represents passion. Passion is a wonderful emotion, but it can overwhelm your other senses. Strength asks you to cool things down a bit and see the situation from a more sober point of view.

This card isn't an aggressive stance in which you go after others and bend them to your will. It's the stance that you won't be forced to bend to the will of another. You've set a path for yourself, and the only one who can defeat you is yourself.

As with the Magician, the lemniscate above her head suggests that the well of power she draws from is limitless. You may feel tested and pushed to the brink, but you have the inner fire to withstand this.

Reversed meaning: When the card is inverted, the slavering beast proves to be too much. You may give in to frustration, anger, or temptation. This position can also be a sign that letting your hair down and relaxing a bit is all right. Let your passions fly free for the moment.

IX — The Hermit

Keywords: Solitude, meditation, truth-seeking, austerity

Divinatory meaning: A wizened man stands atop a mountain peak, leaning on his staff. A star shines within his lantern. He's trekked into the heights to get the best possible view of the world.

In Christian tradition, hermits removed themselves from the broader culture, living in caves, forests, and generally uncomfortable places, to contemplate spiritual wisdom and find a closer connection with God. They were often sought out for advice, and in some old tales, they helped point wandering heroes in the right direction.

The Hermit card represents a search for the truth, and it's a sign that you need some time by yourself to contemplate what's important to you. Reflect

Pamela Colman Smith/Wikimedia Commons/ Public Domain

on what you want, separating it from the ideas and beliefs that others have placed on you. Keep your own counsel and ignore others' opinions (however well-meaning).

Some early versions of this card connected it with the hourglass-carrying god Saturn or Father Time. For this reason, the Hermit can represent things slowing down and taking longer than you'd have guessed.

This card has a loneliness to it, but it's a valuable period of solitude and being with your own thoughts when the card is upright. If you're asking about relationships or connections with others, the Hermit is a sign of a cool period with little contact.

More simply, the Hermit advises you to take a break from what you're focusing on to clear your head. Step away from the thick of things and get the perspective you need.

Reversed meaning: It's time to come down from the mountain and rejoin society. Here, the Hermit's aloofness keeps him apart from others unnecessarily. Solitude becomes painful loneliness. You'll be welcomed when you return to the fold. If referring to time, this may indicate that time is running out.

X — Wheel of Fortune

Keywords: Luck, cycles, opportunity, turnabouts

Divinatory meaning: A spinning wheel is surrounded by mythic creatures. They vary by deck, but in this one, a mysterious sphinx sits atop; Typhon, the serpent of destruction, follows the wheel as it descends; and Hermanubis (a fusion of the gods Hermes and Anubis, who both welcome souls to the afterlife) sends it back up again. The four figures with books come from the Vision of Ezekial and represent the four fixed zodiac signs (Taurus, Leo, Scorpio, and Aquarius, who also appear in the World later in this chapter).

WHEEL of FORTUNE.

Pamela Colman Smith/Wikimedia Commons/
Public Domain

The wheel itself is traditionally turned by the goddess Fortuna, patroness of luck. Despite all that mystical symbolism, the Wheel of Fortune is a remarkably straightforward card with a message about choices outside your control and the beginning and ending of cycles.

People often say "you can do anything you set your mind to," and though lovely and aspirational, that doesn't tell the whole story. Some larger forces affect your situation in ways that are indifferent to your desires, and you must account for them. You just need to hang in there for now.

Upright, this card can represent some good luck headed your way. It says things will go reasonably well.

The Wheel of Fortune is also auspicious for anyone anticipating a new beginning. The wheel spins, and your new cycle starts, allowing you to do things differently this time.

Reversed meaning: What goes up must come down. A cycle is coming in for a landing, and soon it'll be time to begin again. In this orientation, the card still brings luck, but it tends to be the bad variety. It's a sign that things won't go the way you'd prefer. That doesn't mean giving up; it just means having a Plan B ready and preparing to pivot.

XI — Justice

Keywords: Repercussions, balance, objectivity, decisive action

Divinatory meaning: The virtue of Justice is depicted as a crowned woman holding up a sword and a set of balanced scales. She isn't blind-folded (as images of Justice often are), suggesting she sees everything clearly and misses nothing.

Although the Hermit asks you to explore *your* truth (see the earlier section), Justice is concerned with discovering *the* truth. You may be asked to make a frank appraisal of your situation, despite how uncomfortable that may be. Leave no stone unturned in your pursuit.

You may be called to evaluate some of the relationships in your life. Honesty is the best policy with this card; speak forthrightly and encourage others to do the same.

Pamela Colman Smith/Wikimedia Commons/
Public Domain

This card also shows up when the fair thing will happen whether or not that's what you'd prefer. A decision will be made, usually by another person with authority, and you'll have to live with that decision.

This card may be a reminder that you only get out of a project what you put into it. The encouraging element here is that it suggests you'll reap rewards if you put in some effort. That's fair, after all. If you're trying to manifest something, this card asks, "Did you turn in the application?"

This card isn't especially receptive to any emotion-based decision-making. Don't place other people's comfort over reality.

Reversed meaning: When Justice is turned upside down, the card focuses on injustices. The fair thing won't happen; you probably won't get back what you're putting into the situation. This orientation can also suggest that now isn't the time for black-and-white appraisals of your situation, and you should consider various shades of gray.

XII — The Hanged Man

Keywords: Surrender, vulnerability, disempowerment, perspective

Divinatory meaning: A man hangs by one foot from a tree. This image originates from the Italian practice of hanging thieves or traitors up by their feet. If a traitor escaped, posters of them in this position may be distributed as a form of propaganda. Modern readers tend to eschew this origin and view this figure as submitting to an experience where restriction or a mock death precedes initiation or rebirth.

The Hanged Man points to a pause in activity. This is a time when you're unlikely to be able to make big moves or changes. You may be waiting for others to play their parts and (depending on what the other cards in the spread indicate), waiting for them rather than stepping in and taking over is best.

THE HANGED MAN.

Pamela Colman Smith/Wikimedia Commons/ Public Domain

You may be too invested in — dare I say hung up about? — the outcome of the situation. This card suggests releasing attachment to a result.

To allow yourself to be more vulnerable, enter this state of passivity willingly. With guard down, you can reveal the real you and improve your sense of connection with others.

Alternatively, you may be asked to hold a different point of view on your situation. See things from the perspective of the other side.

Do you want to slack off or procrastinate? The Hanged Man gives you permission to do so. Pausing in your work can improve the result if you use this time to think more expansively about a project or to rest and recharge.

Reversed meaning: When the upside-down card goes right side up, it's time to act again. In this position, waiting is an unnecessary delay rather than thoughtful contemplation. Fly free!

XIII — Death

Keywords: Endings, transformation, dispersion, minimalism

Divinatory meaning: A skeletal figure reaps people's lives from every station of society. This depiction of Death was quite common in the Renaissance, an era known for plague outbreaks and the upheaval they brought. A sun sets (or rises) between two pillars.

This card scares the bejeezus out of many people! In the earliest decks, when tarot was a game and not a fortune telling system, this card had no title because people worried that to write the word *death* out was to court destruction. And even its number, 13, makes many people uncomfortable.

This card rarely foretells the physical death of anyone. All card images are metaphorical, but it's worth spelling out in the case of Death. Having said that, its meaning is rarely pleasant or welcome.

Pamela Colman Smith/Wikimedia Commons/ Public Domain

Something is winding down. That means a new beginning is on its way, but you'll need to go through a transition period. The caterpillar's body must dissolve in its cocoon before it can emerge as a butterfly.

At its most mild, this card points to a transition from one phase to another. Things are progressing naturally, and soon you'll move onto the next stage. Graduations traditionally end the school days, and proposals move couples out of the dating stage. All good things come to an end.

And occasionally, Death means to trim down something that has become too complex and to take a more (here it comes) bare-bones approach.

Reversed meaning: When reversed, Death suggests that something that ought to come to an end lingers on. This situation tends to result in heavy, stagnant energy. If this card refers to something you're hoping will phase out naturally, the advice is to take the needed steps to formally bring an end yourself. Death reversed can also point to an extreme (but understandable) fear of letting go.

XIV — Temperance

Keywords: Moderation, blending, balance, compromise

Divinatory meaning: An angel with one foot on dry land and one foot in the water pours liquid between two cups at a rather improbable angle. A path behind the angel leads to the image of a golden crown. All elements are in a state of control and equilibrium.

Temperance is another card based on a Christian virtue. Some people confuse the idea of temperance with mere restriction and self-denial. But instead, this card asks you to take action — just in the proper way and the correct amount. In an age that values hyperbole and an all-or-nothing view of things, Temperance shows you how to find success by doing simply enough.

Pamela Colman Smith/Wikimedia Commons/Public Domain

In sword-making, steel is tempered by heating and cooling the metal, removing the brittleness and making the final creation stronger and more flexible. In this same way, you can find your "sweet spot" in life by finding the most constructive way to move forward with your situation.

Crucially, this card shows things being brought into a state of balance. With feet placed on both water and earth, you're encouraged to value both practical success and your emotional experience. Buddhists describe "the Middle Way" as an idealized path that avoids extremes of any kind.

If emotions are running hot, try to cool things down by taking a more peaceful view. This act can often require offering forgiveness and grace so that all parties can move forward together.

Reversed meaning: Oscar Wilde altered the phrase "everything in moderation" by ending it with "including moderation." When appearing in a position of advice, this card suggests you may benefit from letting loose, losing your cool, being too much, caring too little — you get the idea. In a predictive sense, this position can mean things are about to go sideways or that balance will be shaken.

XV — The Devil

Keyword: Domination, addiction, hedonism, reflection

Divinatory meaning: A winged devil perches atop a black stone with two humans (with demons' horns and tails) chained together. The card is a clear reference to the Lovers. Note how his torch points to the earth, suggesting he uses his considerable power for corrupt purposes.

When the Devil appears, something is exerting a dark influence over you. That may be in the form of compulsive or obsessive behavior or devoting too much of your time and attention to temporary pleasures. Reflect to decide whether anything has an unwelcome hold on you. The more you give yourself over to seeking these things, the tighter their grip on you.

Pamela Colman Smith/Wikimedia Commons/ Public Domain

His energy is particularly toxic, and the card can indicate someone in your sphere whose personality has a corrosive effect on your life. These types are often manipulative, which makes being free of them hard. Left unchecked, this behavior can become abusive.

In many decks, the chains that bind his prisoners are loose, reminding you that you can choose to cast off this malevolent force if you put your will toward doing so. You must love yourself more than you desire whatever force or person is dominating you.

Reversed meaning: In this orientation, chains slip away, and spirits are raised. A more positive look at the Devil comes when you compare him with the horned god Pan, who represents a lust for life, satisfying sexuality, and mortal pleasures. When other forces have no power over you, self-love and self-acceptance are likely to follow. In this light, the card suggests living on the wild side and letting the good times roll. Some readers who take issue with the idea of demonic figures make this lighter interpretation their upright meaning.

XVI — The Tower

Keywords: Upheaval, chaos, setbacks, breaking free

Divinatory meaning: A tall tower is struck by a bolt of lightning, knocking off its crown-shaped dome. Two figures fall or leap from the burning structure.

When the Tower appears, things tend to get turbulent. Plans get off to a rocky start or are derailed by unforeseen difficulties. A central theme with this card is the idea that the change happens without warning. The upset indicated here will likely sneak up on you.

Why might you miss the warning signs? The Tower may point to arrogant or overly confident attitudes that inadvertently set you up for failure. Humility and self-awareness can be a tonic for this sort of affliction.

Pamela Colman Smith/Wikimedia Commons/ Public Domain

You can't be sure what will happen to the falling figures, but it's certainly better than staying inside that tower. This card is a warning to make your exit from this situation. You're likely in a period when a speedy retreat is still possible. Cut losses, cut ties, and find someplace better to be.

Because of its terrifying imagery, this card is easy to over-read. Though it can refer to devastating accidents, lost jobs, and the like, in the average person's life these difficulties are less common than arguments, setbacks, technical snafus, or appliances needing repairs.

Some readers see this card as a sign that you'll be freed from something that imprisons you. This thing can be institutions, patterns, or relationships where the energy has become stuck or lackluster. Perhaps you wouldn't have escaped on your own, but the decision has been made for you thanks to some external force.

Reversed meaning: When the Tower is turned on its head, things could be worse. A crisis is averted. This orientation still indicates that things can get rough, but the situation is still salvageable. Hang tight and plan to do some speedy repairs. For some readers, this is the orientation associated with freedom from imprisonment.

XVII — The Star

Keywords: Hope, healing, repose, faith

Divinatory meaning: A nude figure pours out two jars of water, one on land and one into a pool. Bright stars illuminate the skies above her.

This card is one of the most uplifting in the deck, and it often serves as a guiding lamp during dark or troubling times, the proverbial bright light at the end of the tunnel. Upright, it signals genuine hope that you can rely on. It's a sign that present challenges can be resolved and that the process will likely be gentle and comfortable. You're right to pin your hopes on the solutions you've chosen.

The Star is an excellent sign that healing is on the way. This can refer to any needed form of heal-

Pamela Colman Smith/Wikimedia Commons/Public Domain

ing, whether physical, mental, emotional, or spiritual. This card's energy is restorative and is an indicator that self-care would be effective. Although that can certainly include massages and bubble baths, a more potent form is removing yourself from other people's dramas and negativity. Stepping away from stress and anxiety-inducing forces is a lasting cure.

Some see the figure as a traveler bathing in a pool or stream during a long journey. If you practice any form of energy cleansing or healing, this is a good time to use those skills.

On a similar note, the Star also suggests the power of faith. Having concrete proof to rely on would be great, but this card is a reminder that sometimes you must trust in your gut, the process, or the powers that be.

Reversed meaning: Alas, when inverted, the Star's hope may prove to be false. It can suggest you're holding out for something that won't arrive, at least not in time. It can also speak of faith being sorely tested.

XVIII — The Moon

Keywords: Illusion, visions, deception, subconscious messages

Divinatory meaning: A wolf and dog howl up at a shining moon on either side of a road that twists and winds between two pillars (you also see those pillars on the Death card). A crayfish emerges from a pool of water.

The Moon is a wild card with two very different interpretations in the modern era. Most traditionally, it's associated with illusions. This card may point to trickery in your situation or indicate that someone is hiding behind a false face. Look more carefully beneath the surface of things to find out just what's going on.

Where the sun's light is bright, direct, and projective, the moon reflects that light, creating lengthened shadows on eerie landscapes.

Pamela Colman Smith/Wikimedia Commons/Public Domain

Nothing is quite what it seems by moonlight. This may indicate that your mind is playing tricks on you. The crayfish is likely on this card because of the belief that they molt at the full moon. You may be more vulnerable than you realize and likely to arrive at the wrong conclusions out of fear.

A more popular recent meaning is that the Moon represents psychic information. It suggests that you trust your animal instincts as they communicate critical information on a deeper level. In particular, this card can recommend that you pay attention to dreams and nightmares, which carry a message from your unconscious self.

More simply, the Moon may just let you know that things are about to get pretty weird around here.

Reversed meaning: The reversed meaning really depends on what you see as the upright version of the card. If you follow the tradition of the moon as illusions, then the reverse is the sign of mystical clarity and revelation. If you see the upright card as the sign of psychic vision, then the reverse suggests self-deception and clouded insights.

XIX — The Sun

Keywords: Joy, optimism, clarity, reward

Divinatory meaning: A child rides a pony past a garden of sunflowers (somehow holding that flag aloft) as a dazzling sun fills the heavens. The overall energy of the card is open and uplifting.

The Sun is a welcome sign in your reading. It points to lightness, peace, and the time and space to enjoy all the good things you've worked for. You'll succeed in your endeavors.

Sunlight illuminates everything, and this card suggests greater clarity and certainty for you in the reading. Things you've long suspected may be revealed to be true.

This is the glorious dawn that follows any period of darkness. This card may urge you to fully accept

THE SUN.

Pamela Colman Smith/Wikimedia Commons/ Public Domain

that some problematic conditions have been overcome. You can allow yourself to believe in and accept a period of genuine happiness.

As the bright ball at the center of the solar system, everything revolves around the sun, which may indicate that you can focus more of your attention and energy on your needs. Feel free to be extra.

Reversed meaning: This card's energy is so bright that even when reversed it's a shining spot in a reading. Here, the Sun's light may dim a bit, but it'll still be a warm and wonderful time for you. That joy may fall slightly below what you were hoping for or be less readily apparent to you. Essentially, it means having a pretty good time rather than an amazing one. The reversed sun may show the effects of things being over the top. Think of the sunburn you may get after a lovely day at the beach.

XX — Judgement

Keywords: Destiny, awakening, fascination, release

Divinatory meaning: In a scene out of the Christian Book of Revelation, the archangel Gabriel blows a mighty note on his trumpet, causing tombs to open and the souls of the dead to arise and welcome their final reward.

A modern audience may look at this card with its apocalyptic scene, complete with rising corpses, and get the heebie-jeebies. For the original audience of the tarot, this card is the long-awaited moment when the universe is set right, and the forces of darkness are defeated forever. It's a *good* apocalypse.

Some folks find the title itself off-putting, so I want to be clear: Judgement has nothing to do with acting judgmental or feeling judged. This card

Pamela Colman Smith/Wikimedia Commons/ Public Domain

suggests that you may have been asleep, moving through life mechanically or without significant motivation. But the time has come for you to wake up.

You're being pulled toward something, possibly a grand adventure or a significant transformation. Judgement asks you to heed that call, to recognize what you've prepared yourself for, and to pursue it with all your might.

Pursuing this new path may require you to release unhelpful thought patterns or negative self-images that tie you to the past. Make peace with that self and let go of it just as a snake must shed its worn-out skin before showing off those bright new scales.

As a symbol of rebirth, Judgement may also indicate a time for second chances, do-overs, and fresh starts.

Reversed meaning: When Judgement is reversed, the call goes unanswered. A substantial opportunity presents itself, but you're not ready to go after it. More time in the chrysalis phase is required before you can emerge and flap your new wings. Alternatively, this position may indicate that an opportunity that may seem attractive just isn't right for you. Your moment will come — later.

XXI — The World

Keywords: Culmination, attainment, recognition, elevation

Divinatory meaning: A dancer performs at the center of a victory wreath. Around her, the images of the four fixed zodiac signs — Taurus, Leo, Scorpio, and Aquarius (also on the Wheel of Fortune; see the earlier section) — appear in the flesh. Their presence indicates that you'll experience this win across all areas of your life.

You did it! I don't know what "it" is, but you did it! At its core, this card shows the culmination of a journey and applauds your massive achievements. It also acknowledges how you've been magnified by absorbing the lessons of your journey. The triumph indicated here is more than arriving at your goal; it's also the tremendous growth that has earned you a new place in the universe.

Pamela Colman Smith/Wikimedia Commons/
Public Domain

The World completes the cycle of the Major Arcana. It suggests the full attainment of everything you've sought after across many personal challenges and transformations. As such, it points to your victory and the meaningful ways you've changed because of this process. Recognize and celebrate the new you, and allow this new you to call the shots.

At the end of Joseph Campbell's *The Hero's Journey,* the hero brings healing back to their community. Similarly, you may feel called to share the gift of the new you with your community.

All endings contain the seeds of a new beginning. Take a wider view of your life and consider where you want to go next.

Reversed meaning: When you're enjoying the journey, you may find yourself resisting arriving at the destination. If you're in a prolonged holding pattern, allow yourself to close this chapter so that something new can begin. Alternatively, the reversed World may simply say you're almost there and you need additional time and effort to complete what you set out to do.

Ace of Wands

Keywords: Excitement, potential energy, passion, confidence

Divinatory meaning: The aces herald a new beginning or opportunity, and with wands' focus on energy and passion, this card suggests that you're on the verge of a new adventure.

A hand holds up a massive wand sprouting fresh green leaves.

I sometimes think of the Ace of Wands as an elementary school kid sitting at their desk, knowing that in about 15 seconds, the bell will ring, and they can leap up and go to recess. Another analogy may be a battery, filled with energy ready to power your remote control. This card is a door that the universe is opening for you, and stepping through it is up to you.

Pamela Colman Smith/Wikimedia Commons/
Public Domain

With this card, you may experience an increase in your passion for the subject of the reading. Channel that vitality into creating the journey you desire.

Using this gift of energy requires you to ignore doubt, fear, and a need for certainty. You don't need to have every step of the way mapped out; beginning is more vital.

You see this theme across the wands, but boldness is very much a quality to cultivate and tap into when this card shows up for you.

In terms of love, this card is frequently a sign that physical chemistry will be present, and things will heat up quickly.

Reversed meaning: The reversed Ace of Wands is like a dormant volcano; the magma is boiling somewhere deep down, but it has no release. This position can indicate a delayed start or a warning from the cards that you're not quite ready for prime time. It may also indicate that you just don't have the energy necessary to move forward even if your heart wants to. Wait for the opportune moment.

Two of Wands

Keywords: Preparation, horizons, risks, wanderlust

Divinatory meaning: The twos show a desire for their suit's element, and with the passionate wands, that shows up as a need for action and excitement. This card is a green light to stoke your ambitions; you'll have a chance to go big or go home (but really, go big).

You see a figure standing high up at a castle parapet with a wand held in one hand and another bolted to the wall. His other hand holds a globe, and with his eyes looking out in the distance, you may imagine plans for an expedition or conquest.

This card holds a tension between the safety of staying where things are familiar and resting on your laurels or striking out and exploring

*Pamela Colman Smith/Wikimedia Commons/
Public Domain*

the unknown. It has a call to move out of your comfort zone but also a recommendation to have a plan in place. Where other cards say, "Leap and trust the universe," the Two of Wands says, "Check the map again." Take this moment to prepare yourself for the transformation you're making.

Twos also show their elements in balance and with fire that can indicate a struggle in relationships for dominance. The roses of passion are balanced with the lilies of innocence in this image, encouraging you to seek a way for both of you to get what you want.

Though this card shows a decision to make, it isn't whether you'll proceed with things; it's when and how you make your move.

Reversed meaning: When this card is reversed, it may not be time to take flight. Further preparation is needed. It may also urge you to worry less about interpersonal balance and choose to push for dominance in a struggle.

Three of Wands

Keywords: Commencement, motion, expansion, acceptance

Divinatory meaning: The threes bring their suit element into manifestation, and with the bold and fiery wands, that means real action is taking place.

A figure looks out to sea; on the water, the ships they've sent glide across the waves to the horizon. This person can do nothing more to control the voyage; they must trust the process, simply continuing their part of the plan and leaving the rest to others.

You've moved from wishing, debating, or planning into the doing of the thing. The Three of Wands suggests that your work will continue to grow, and that releasing doubts and continuing to follow through on your vision would be good.

Pamela Colman Smith/Wikimedia Commons/ Public Domain

Threes also nod toward expansion; you may be called to broaden your scope. Whether your question concerns a job, a love match, a spiritual journey, or anything else, keep an open mind to choices you hadn't considered before; they may surprise you.

On that note, expecting the unexpected means acquiring a talent for improvisation. That may leave you feeling like you've bitten off more than you can chew, but keep chewing. Doubling down may be necessary to maintain momentum. Taking on more can indicate a time to join forces with others. Partnership and cooperation boost the odds of success. Use your charisma to inspire them.

Some readers see those ships sailing out to sea and consider the virtues of making peace with the past. In this case, previous troubles aren't dealt with directly; you must find a way to move on enough to focus your attention on what's ahead of you.

Reversed meaning: Reversed, the opposite of expansion is contraction. Aim for smaller victories and bite-sized ambitions. Some progress is better than none; build more slowly and thoughtfully for now. In this orientation, all the ships you've sent out may not return to the harbor. It's not ideal, but it's also not a total loss.

Four of Wands

Keywords: Celebration, rites of passage, ceremony, revelry

Divinatory meaning: Fours bring stability, and for the ecstatic wands that results in an organized celebration. Expect a joyous occasion to arrive.

This card features four wands in an orderly pattern festooned with flowers as people in the background wave bouquets. Many readers see this decoration as the setup for a wedding, comparing the wands to a *chuppah* from Jewish tradition. The type of partying suggested by this card is less a case of wild debauchery and more of a ceremony where people gather for a shared celebration.

Pamela Colman Smith/Wikimedia Commons/ Public Domain

This is your time. If you've been in a dark place, this card is a sign that this darkness will recede and it's a moment to celebrate what you've created or achieved. Revel in joy and share that joy with those around you.

Because it tends to suggest major milestones like coming-of-age traditions and ceremonies, the Four of Wands may indicate growing up, coming into your own power, and recognizing that you now answer only to yourself.

Tarot card images are metaphors, so the wedding atmosphere here doesn't necessarily suggest that a relationship will end in marriage when you're reading about love. But it certainly suggests things are on the right track.

This card can also be a simple reminder to let your guard down a bit and try to have some fun.

Reversed meaning: Like many of the most positive cards, when reversed this one merely dims its light rather than heralds an upheaval. Someone (perhaps you) may want too much control to really be able to enjoy themselves. Alternatively, a problem at the party may be being ignored because things seem so good on the surface. Be on the lookout for details you still need to attend to before you can cut loose.

Five of Wands

Keywords: Competition, game-playing, infighting, training

Divinatory meaning: When you blend the chaos of the fives with the energy of the wands, you get an enthusiastic free-for-all where who'll come out on top is anyone's guess. Things may get messy for you very soon.

You see a group of combatants thwacking one another with wands (or a very inefficient method of putting up a tent). The message here is one of competition rather than genuine violence. This is no death match; they're all wielding sticks rather than swords, and the participants each wear different colored clothes. These aren't the members of two forces at war.

Pamela Colman Smith/Wikimedia Commons/Public Domain

The Five of Wands tends to show up when people play games or test one another. At its most positive, it suggests having different people in your group testing and debating their ideas to find the most effective method to move forward. On the other end of the spectrum are people stirring up turmoil and drama for the fun it brings them.

This card may signal a moment for you to make a challenge if you think you have a better idea. Or you may just need to try something to discover whether you like it. The battle of competing ideas suggested by this card can lead to bruised egos; remember that it's all in good fun and not to take anything too personally.

The Five of Wands is also an indicator of a need for training and putting your skills to the test in order to improve. Health goals require regular exercise, spiritual goals require daily practice, and so on.

Reversed meaning: When reversed, this card may indicate that the chaos you're experiencing will come to an end, making way for order and more forward movement. One idea emerges, and the rest may be set aside.

Six of Wands

Keywords: Success, recognition, progress, inspiration

Divinatory meaning: The sixes bring harmony to the energized wands, channeling all that passion toward accomplishing a desired goal. This card is a sign that victory is on the horizon.

The sixes also show hierarchy with someone above the others; in this case, one figure rides on horseback, whereas the others walk. The leader wears a laurel crown, symbolizing victory, and has a laurel wreath tied to his wand as a standard for the rest of the group to follow. This latter symbol is a reminder that the triumph is a shared one.

For hierarchies to work, you must have an engaging leader and enthusiastic followers. Consider your own situation to determine which role you're playing and whether everyone is moving in concert.

Pamela Colman Smith/Wikimedia Commons/ Public Domain

If you have a vision of what you want to manifest, this card is a sign to move ahead with your plan. This is no time to be small or be afraid of putting yourself and your name out there. Step into the spotlight.

In its simplest terms, this card answers the question "How will things go?" with "Successfully."

The Six of Wands can also indicate receiving recognition for your achievements and being raised up to your rightful place. You may finally feel truly seen by others and understood substantially.

If you find yourself as one of the followers in this situation, it's a healthy sign that leadership is making the right calls and can be trusted.

Reversed meaning: When this card is reversed, that forward and upward movement may grind to a halt. This orientation can be a sign of arrogance or egotism that may ultimately direct all this energy down the wrong path or before it's ready. Having everyone involved realign to get back on track would be good.

Seven of Wands

Keywords: Valor, defense, tenacity, advantage

Divinatory meaning: The sevens show a suit's sense of adaptability; for the fiery wands, that means pivoting to meet challenges head-on. Prepare to defend your position.

Pamela Colman Smith/Wikimedia Commons/Public Domain

You see one figure lifting his wand in response to six challengers coming at him simultaneously. Although the odds seem stacked against him, he maintains the high ground, a strategically advantageous position.

This card is a sign of confrontations ahead, and you need to be ready to meet them. What separates this card from other images of conflict (like the Five of Wands earlier in the chapter) is the single figure's position above their attackers. The suggestion is that you have what's necessary to withstand the incoming turbulence.

This card can also indicate the need for a leap of faith. Trust in your position and resolve. You may surprise yourself with how much you can accomplish when you put all your drive into it.

Some readers see a hidden significance in the fact that the character wears two different kinds of shoes. This discrepancy is most likely an illustrator error that wasn't caught in time, but if I were to see it as symbolic, I may think it means being ready to act at a moment's notice without any thought about which shoes you're wearing (or belts, for that matter).

At its simplest, you can see this card as "hang in there."

Reversed meaning: I like to keep things simple with this reversal. When upright, this card says you have a strong position; when reversed, you don't. That disadvantage doesn't mean defeat, but it suggests you can't succeed all by yourself. If the challenges ahead overwhelm you, remember that retreat is the better part of valor, and be ready to switch to Plan B.

Eight of Wands

Keywords: Velocity, focus, intensity, transit

Divinatory meaning: The eights deepen the fiery energy of the wands, making it unquenchable. Get ready to pick up the pace as you approach your destination.

Note the absolute lack of people or animals in this image. It merely has eight aerodynamic wands all in flight, headed in the same direction. The message is equally simple: go, go, go.

You have a need for speed; bring all your energy to bear when seeing things through to their conclusion. Just as the wands don't divert themselves at different angles, you probably want to avoid multitasking, branching out, side hustles, or anything else that causes you to take your foot off the gas. Let issues less critical to you sit on the back burner for now.

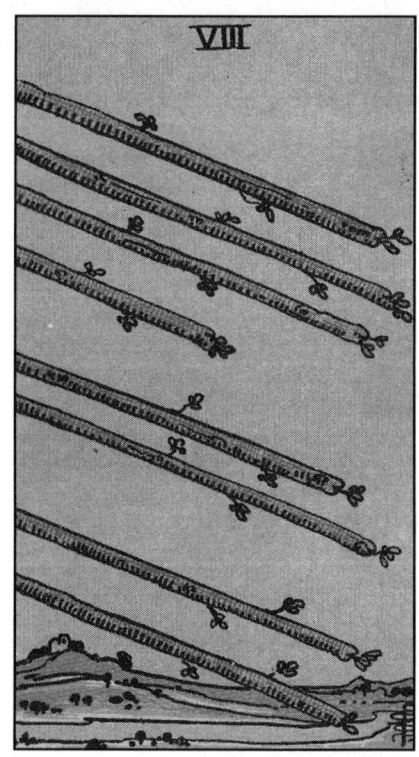

Pamela Colman Smith/Wikimedia Commons/Public Domain

Many see the downward slope of the wands as indicating that they're coming in for a swift landing. Similarly, you should direct your intention toward completing your endeavor rather than maintaining a holding pattern. It's time to land the plane.

This situation may need swift, direct communication. Say what you mean.

In the modern age, people sometimes relate this card to air travel. That may seem a little on the nose, but if any part of your question involves relocation or a temporary trip far away, this card is a sign to move in that direction.

Reversed meaning: Reversed, this card's wands no longer seem to arc toward the Earth. This position can indicate that what you pursue will take longer than expected. The sprint of the upright card becomes a marathon when inverted, and you need to slow your pace so you don't burn out. You'll still be moving (no rest just yet) but at a more sustainable clip.

Nine of Wands

Keywords: Resolve, defiance, vigilance, wear and tear

Divinatory meaning: The climactic quality of the nines becomes a fiery resolve in the wands. You need grit and conviction to see things through to their end.

A lone figure seems to be stationed as a guard by a fence of tall wands. The bandage on his head suggests he's recently participated in battle that wounded but didn't defeat him. You may feel similar, having endured bumps and bruises in pursuit of your goals. But still, you withstand the onslaught.

First and foremost, this is a card of endurance. Your courage will likely be tested, but you have good reason to remain firmly ensconced in your position.

Pamela Colman Smith/Wikimedia Commons/Public Domain

The determination in the figure's expression suggests an inner tenacity. Though he's been put through the wringer, it hasn't extinguished the fight within him. Imagine that all the challenges you've faced have been fuel for your fire, giving you the strength of an inferno. More simply: fire yourself up!

This can be a very challenging card when you're asking about anything relating to other people. A conflict may be at the heart of a relationship, withstanding attempts to resolve it. Tenacity's less pleasant nickname is stubbornness.

Reversed meaning: Reversed, all that persistence begins to look a bit like obstinacy. Question whether you're forcing yourself to suffer needlessly. Is this really what you want, or have you just wanted it too long to give up? If your pride can stand it, this may be the time to let go of the fight. Alternatively, this position may be a call to let others know about the struggles you're experiencing if you've been keeping quiet to avoid bringing others down with your problems.

Ten of Wands

Keywords: Burden, completion, weariness, perseverance

Divinatory meaning: The tens bring a cycle to its conclusion, and in the wands the fires have burnt up all but the last reserves of fuel. You'll carry a heavy load.

Can't you just feel the weight of those wands on your own shoulders? It must have taken an incredible amount of fortitude to haul them this far. The figure approaches a town in the distance. All the wand cards are on a grand adventure toward some glorious destination, and here you finally have that final objective in sight.

Readers tend to instruct you to lay down your troubles when they see this card, because why on Earth would anyone want to put them-

Pamela Colman Smith/Wikimedia Commons/Public Domain

selves through all of this? But with the end in sight, the upright version of this card suggests a final push (followed by plenty of self-care afterward). This advice depends on the position and question, of course.

You're taking on a lot. Doing a personal inventory to determine whether any small piece can be sacrificed to lighten the load even slightly is worthwhile.

For interpersonal interactions, this card may point to one person having to take on more than their fair share of supporting the relationship. Left unchecked, that arrangement can result in resentment. If you're taking on other people's troubles, who's left to manage yours?

Reversed meaning: Reversed, this card asks you to release yourself from this difficult burden. It's all too much, and if you continue to push yourself in this manner much longer, the strain may overcome you. Wands have a powerful, fiery drive, but that drive can debilitate body, mind, and spirit if it goes unchecked. Beware of martyr complexes; they never end well for the martyr.

Page of Wands

Keywords: Enthusiasm, messages, inspiration, exploration

Divinatory meaning: Pages embody curiosity as they begin to explore their suit element. The Page of Wands is a bright spark that can be kindled into a flame.

A young page grasps a wand that's slightly taller than him, seeming to gaze upon it with admiration.

This particular page is delighted by adventure. They learn best when they can get all fired up about or go all-in on a subject. Though they may have doubts or fears about what they're attempting, they don't let it hold them back.

Pages often point to new beginnings, and this one wants to go big. If you feel enthusiastic about something, this card

PAGE of WANDS.

Pamela Colman Smith/Wikimedia Commons/ Public Domain

is a green light for you to give it a chance. It also encourages you to follow through on any ambitions you're holding back on.

As a person, the Page of Wands is excitable and full of energy that can (hopefully) be directed toward something creative. They can also be fickle, discarding a pursuit just as quickly as they took it up if it doesn't hold their interest. Their spontaneity may be worrisome, but try not to get in their way. They're willing to make mistakes early and adapt.

An old tradition says this card represents a messenger or an important piece of communication (previously a letter, but these days almost certainly a quick digital exchange). This idea may indicate that someone will approach you soon with an impactful message, or something you hear will resonate profoundly and help resolve an issue.

Reversed meaning: When reversed, this page's natural tendency towards impetuous or insistent behaviors can get you in trouble. You want it *now* and aren't willing to wait. Here, the spontaneous behavior turns out to be senseless. Watch your words, which may get you in trouble. This orientation may also indicate that you're out of your depths, having bitten off more than you can chew.

Knight of Wands

Keywords: Courage, confidence, attention-seeking, playfulness

Divinatory meaning: A young knight rides his horse through the desert (complete with pyramids) to emphasize his fiery nature.

Knights are action-oriented, exploring their suit's element out in the world, taking risks and seeking direct experience. For the Knight of Wands, that means boldness, adventure, and excitement.

This knight wants something to do. This isn't a card for contemplating deep truths or spiritual wisdom. Live a little — actually, live a lot when this knight prances into your spread.

The whole wands court is loaded with charisma, and this knight expresses that as cocky and self-assured com-

KNIGHT of WANDS.

Pamela Colman Smith/Wikimedia Commons/ Public Domain

munication. They tend to do whatever they believe will bring them excitement. This card can indicate a need to be a bit of a daredevil. The depiction of the knights' horses tells you a lot about them. This horse rears up in the air, which is very impressive but isn't actually moving them forward. The Knight of Wands can be a bit of a showoff, eager to impress their audience.

Though this knight can be brash, they also have a heroic streak to their nature. They're willing to stand up for a person or a cause that's significant to them. You may be directed to channel your inner superhero into supporting something you value.

In recent years, this knight has earned a reputation for preferring hookups and brief whirlwind romances over anything long and protracted. If you want to keep your love life strictly physical for now, this may be the person you're looking for.

Reversed meaning: When you're this fiery, losing your cool is easy. The Knight of Wands can be exceedingly hot-headed and lose control of their temper if they feel challenged or disrespected. Their ego may cause them to center themselves too much in this situation.

Queen of Wands

Keywords: Charisma, bedazzlement, willingness, pizazz

Divinatory meaning: The queens represent an inner mastery of their suit element, making their actions instinctual and giving them a high degree of influence over others. The queens all care deeply about supporting the focus of their suits, and for the wands that means using their enthusiasm and infectious personality to break people out of their shells so that they too can shine.

The Queen of Wands sits confidently upon her throne in the desert — her faithful cat poised at her feet — and is a beacon of vitality, shining wherever she goes. With that vitality, she's easily the life of the party, elevating others' moods with words and attention.

Pamela Colman Smith/Wikimedia Commons/ Public Domain

Readers like to speculate about this queen's posture. Specifically, she's the only queen depicted with her legs apart (this dates back to the Tarot de Marseille; see Chapter 3), suggesting a confident demeanor and frank attitude toward sexuality. The cat supports this vibe and adds the idea that the Queen knows a thing or two about making magic. She doesn't back down when in pursuit of what she desires.

I see a sense of power in the pose, and power like that isn't something other people can give you. The Queen's confident she belongs wherever she goes and that her opinions and contributions are valued. You may need a boost in your own confidence. Believe that you deserve respect and admiration, and others will, too.

This card can also be a sign that you need some inspiration. Seek out art, media, or stories that light a fire within you.

Reversed meaning: With all that charisma and bravado, the wands court members have some issues with ego. For the Queen, shallowness, attention-seeking behavior, and self-absorption can lead to prioritizing popularity over authenticity. Reversed wands courts have fiery tempers; don't get on the Queen's bad side.

King of Wands

Keyword: Magnetism, politics, vision, encouragement

Divinatory meaning: Kings have achieved an outer mastery of their suit element, making them capable leaders with command over others. For this king, it's all about their undeniable charisma.

The King of Wands leans forward on his throne, gazing into the distance. At his feet sits a salamander, the alchemical symbol of fire.

As a person, the King of Wands is authoritative, confident, and perhaps a little ostentatious. They do well in the spotlight, captivating the attention of others. They appreciate someone who can show they have the guts to overcome difficult odds.

Pamela Colman Smith/Wikimedia Commons/Public Domain

The King has phenomenal political skills and knows how to raise the spirits of others and win them over. Think of a rousing speech by a heroic leader to the troops or to the masses in your favorite films. If this king shows up in your spread, it suggests a need to bring people into alignment through a shared vision.

If the cards push you to become more like a King of Wands type, you may need to be more skilled at wielding your power. They're a capable leader who is able to manage others, and you can be, too.

Confidence is very attractive. If that's an area you want to grow in, then this card suggests you begin by believing and reminding yourself you belong here (wherever here is) and that you're worthy of respect.

Reversed meaning: When the King of Wands is reversed, his big personality can fail to win others over. He may inadvertently come across as arrogant or self-centered, seeking only to feed his ego. Again, picture a rousing speech to the masses, but this time it's given by the villain. To take things in a different direction, I sometimes see the reversed card as a sign of imposter syndrome — convincing yourself that your success is an act.

Ace of Swords

Keywords: Clarity, pruning, insight, truth

Divinatory meaning: The aces all herald a new beginning or opportunity, and with swords' focus on intellect, this card suggests a clear plan will form to move forward.

A hand holds aloft a sword; it's encircled with a golden crown, suggesting that the realization of your ultimate victory comes down to the moves you make at the beginning of the journey. Time spent on thinking things through now will pay off greatly in the long run.

This particular sword cuts through doubt and illusion to reveal the naked truth. You can achieve greater clarity by not hanging onto any comfortable fantasies or half-truths you've become attached to. When you're honest with yourself about what's happening and what you want, you can move forward easily and gracefully.

Pamela Colman Smith/Wikimedia Commons/ Public Domain

This card also sweeps away all the clutter that has built up in your life. This can be a purge of any literal mementos from the past you may be holding onto, as well as habits, behaviors, and beliefs that no longer serve your greater good (perhaps they never did). Making new, healthy choices is easier if you're not weighing yourself down with old strategies and tactics.

Give yourself the gift of a fresh start.

When interacting with other people in your life, this card may suggest a need to clear the air. Be frank and direct to create a more open understanding between you.

Reversed meaning: Inverted aces often suggest delayed starts. Things aren't quite ready to begin. It may also indicate that you're sabotaging your chance at a new beginning by (consciously or not) clinging to the past. This orientation can also point to drawing the wrong conclusions from the data you're considering. Check your sources.

Two of Swords

Keywords: Balance, meditation, indecision, waiting

Divinatory meaning: The twos show the desire of the suit's element (in this case, air), and with intellectual swords, that's a hunger for knowledge. A major decision needs careful consideration.

A blindfolded woman sits on a bench, holding twin swords (one on either side). The sea stretches out behind her beneath the moon. The pervading feeling is one of stillness and peace.

The most common understanding of this card is indecision or contemplation of a choice. The two blades appear identical, and no information is yet available to help you choose effectively between them. Waiting until more is revealed before committing to a choice is best.

Pamela Colman Smith/Wikimedia Commons/ Public Domain

If you're thinking, "Indecision? But that's why I did a tarot reading about this!", I absolutely empathize. But a significant lesson of this card is waiting until the right moment to make a move. You must remain ready to act when the time is ripe.

Note that the woman is blindfolded. The Two of Swords urges you to avoid being swayed by preconceived notions or biases to make the best decision possible.

The moon is in its waxing crescent phase when the tide levels decrease. That indicates you have additional time to make your choice; the waves aren't going to come rolling in to carry you away. Whether the moon phase was intentional or an artistic choice is unknown; trust your intuition.

A more literal interpretation is to highlight the values of regular meditation practice. With a more detached mind, you may see your options more clearly.

Reversed meaning: It's time to choose. The thoughtful consideration of the upright meaning feels more like procrastination when inverted. Look to the rest of the reading for clues on which direction to move in.

Three of Swords

Keywords: Pain, betrayal, regret, trauma

Divinatory meaning: The threes show a suit's manifestation; in this case, the sword's connection with strife and sorrow is on full display. This card is a sign of palpable pain.

A heart is skewered by three swords as heavy clouds pour down rain. The swords are the least subtle of suits, and I can't really sugarcoat this image. This card is a relatively direct depiction of heartbreak and heartache.

I believe the most significant detail in this card is that the heart doesn't bleed. It's as if the swords have been left inside, and it has had to heal around them. This idea suggests a pain you hold onto long after the damage has been done. This sort of agony can become your identity if you can't find a way to release it.

Pamela Colman Smith/Wikimedia Commons/Public Domain

A hurt this severe is usually connected to a sense of betrayal, whether from someone you love or even a moment when you disappoint yourself. Compare people's words to their actions (including your own).

The cards are nuanced and varied and can mean many things, but I don't usually advise continuing down any path with the Three of Swords present in it.

At its most positive, this card can be an opportunity to fully address and process trauma you haven't dealt with.

Reversed meaning: When the heart turns upside down, I see those swords sliding out. This position is a sign that old wounds will be mended, and present pains will no longer have the same power over you. The rain clouds run out of rain. This card may presage a "good cry" that you've been aching to allow yourself. And it can be a sign of learning to trust again and letting others into your heart.

Four of Swords

Keywords: Peace, repose, stillness, convalescence

Divinatory meaning: The stability of the fours creates a balanced environment for the intellectual swords. A retreat is needed.

You see a knight's tomb with a lifelike image carved into the sarcophagus lid. With its stained-glass window and swords as decorations rather than weapons, the atmosphere seems tranquil — almost blissful. Although this setting may seem morbid, I see it as connected to legends of heroes like King Arthur who lie in wait for the moment when they're needed again.

If you look carefully at the halo over the head of the figure in the upper left in the RWS version, you can see the word PAX,

Pamela Colman Smith/Wikimedia Commons/ Public Domain

which is Latin for peace. This card strongly urges you to rest and relax your mind. It tends to appear when stress and anxiety are beginning to take charge of your psyche. You won't make your best decisions or have the most positive interactions with others if you're feeling overtaxed or overworked. You may need to step away from an issue to clear your thoughts and get a fresh perspective.

Ask yourself, "What will bring me peace of mind?" This may be time for a warm bath, a day trip, or a vacation — however much time you need to detach from the cares and concerns that threaten to overwhelm you.

In interpersonal interactions, this card may suggest spending time on your own to collect your thoughts. Be clear about communicating your needs to others (it's not you, it's me!) and enjoy some time spent in self-reflection.

Some cards speed things up and other cards slow things down — this is the latter. You may make mistakes if you try too hard to be nimble and reactive to your situation.

Reversed meaning: When the Four of Swords flips upside down, the vacation is over. It's time to return to the task at hand. This orientation can also indicate dwelling on intrusive thoughts, replaying them over and over in a way that heightens your anxiety.

Five of Swords

Keywords: Aggression, defeat, cruelty, ruthlessness

Divinatory meaning: The fives bring conflict and chaos to the strategic swords, resulting in a battle won by dominance rather than reason. This card indicates a difficult struggle ahead.

A man sneers at two dejected figures who are walking away; their swords have been cast down at his feet. He holds three swords (likely trophies from previous skirmishes), signaling the odds have been stacked to his advantage.

This card shows the swords in their most aggressive state. Here, the mind's gift for strategy and problem solving turns toward overpowering opposition. You may think of bullies and their behaviors or the issues that arise from over-competitiveness.

Pamela Colman Smith/Wikimedia Commons/Public Domain

The odds may be stacked against you, and defeat is imminent if you don't change your strategy. One tactic is to choose not to participate in interactions you find unfair. There's no shame in walking away from a fight you can't win.

Consider another view of this card: A practical lesson it teaches is to be comfortable with conflict and not always shy away from it. Diplomacy, cooperation, and negotiation are valuable approaches, but sometimes not everyone can agree to meet in the middle. In these moments, strive to be a strong advocate for your position and not make unhealthy concessions to others. When a spread places the Five of Swords in the position of recommended action, the deck may be telling you, "choose to win and don't hold back."

Reversed meaning: As is often the case with challenging cards, the reversed Five of Swords points to the possibility of healing. This position is an indication that you can reconcile with your difficulties or opponents. In this orientation the domineering blowhard has a hidden softer side and can be reasoned with.

Six of Swords

Keywords: Departure, journeying, learning, release

Divinatory meaning: The sixes bring harmony, and with the conflict-focused swords that can indicate a speedy retreat. Consider where you want to go next.

A ferryman guides a small craft onto the water with two figures huddling together in the boat. You see the first signs of land ahead of them. Some see the cloaked figure as the symbol of a refugee who must abandon what's familiar to them as a last resort. Others note the choppy water on the right and the smooth water ahead and to the left as a sign of passing out of difficult times.

The sixes feature figures at different heights, suggesting someone in need and someone else attending to that need. You'll know which you are in this case.

Pamela Colman Smith/Wikimedia Commons/Public Domain

This can be a card of literal travel, moving to some new location. A change of scenery or a change of pace may be what you need. This card tends to represent a one-way move rather than a temporary vacation.

More often the travel is metaphorical, and you're being asked to "move on" from the methods you're using to address some tricky issue that plagues or puzzles you. This shift may mean adopting a strategy or tactics you've resisted. It's time to try something new.

This card can also signify a transition to a new way of thinking. Digging your heels in and holding tight to your side of a debate is easy, but you may be surprised to find that you've changed your mind about a situation, seeing it more clearly from this novel perspective.

Reversed meaning: You still have some unfinished business to attend to before you can depart in peace. Things may not be as impossible as they seem. Consider what can be set in order to smooth the transition.

Seven of Swords

Keywords: Trickery, creativity, theft, partial victory

Divinatory meaning: The sevens show a suit's adaptability, meaning the smart swords get crafty and learn to work outside the rules.

A man slinks away from a few tents, carrying five swords and leaving two behind. In the background, you see the group being burgled — most likely an army. The card reminds you that there's more than one way to defeat an enemy: You can meet them on the field of battle on their terms or break the rules and change the game.

Many readers focus on this figure as a thief, seeing this card as one of lies and outright criminality. It can be a warning that someone isn't who they seem or may attempt to cheat you.

Pamela Colman Smith/Wikimedia Commons/Public Domain

However, you may also look at this figure as a creative problem-solver. The card may ask you why you must work within the confines that others set for you. That can mean breaking with tradition, taking an unexplored or unexpected path, and, yes, playing fast and loose with the truth if it helps your cause. I may get in trouble for saying this, but honesty isn't always the best policy.

Another interpretation of the card centers on the two swords left behind. They can be a sign of a partial victory, accomplishing much but falling short of everything you set out to do.

Reversed meaning: Fall in line, you rule breaker! The flip side of this card is learning to not be too clever for your own good. Color inside the lines for now. Alternatively, for clarity's sake, you may assign the upright version to creative thinking and the reversal to skullduggery and double-dealing.

Eight of Swords

Keywords: Imprisonment, helplessness, limitation, self-reliance

Divinatory meaning: The eights deepen a suit's energy; for swords, that can result in a preponderance of mental stress and other pressures that can seem like a trap.

Swords surround a bound and blindfolded woman. Although she has her feet free and space before her to escape, this isn't something she's aware of. She'll likely need to proceed carefully to escape her situation.

Because swords do the dual duty of representing both your mental abilities and difficulties and strife, this card's effects can manifest as anything from simple mental blocks to finding yourself stuck in an uncomfortable situation without a sense of how you can get yourself out.

Pamela Colman Smith/Wikimedia Commons/Public Domain

Where did the blindfold come from? The Eight of Swords can point to mental manipulation or conditioning. Consider whether your beliefs in this situation are your own or whether others have influenced you.

On the other hand, you may find that you're the one imposing imagined limitations on yourself or playing by secret rules no one else is aware of. Consider whether you're sabotaging your own efforts and growth by telling yourself you aren't ready or not good enough.

One of the most potent messages I've received from this card is "No one else is coming to save you." You may be tempted to see how long you can withstand a problematic situation until someone steps in to fix it. Don't wait for a referee, superhero, or other responsible adult to step in on your behalf.

Reversed meaning: Swords cards are often much lighter when upside down. This orientation is a sign of restrictions and limitations being lifted, granting you greater mobility and freedom.

Nine of Swords

Keywords: Despair, doubt, fear

Divinatory meaning: The climatic quality of the nines puts quite a strain on the swords' mental focus. This card often presages a period of heavy or overwhelming thoughts.

A figure sits up in bed holding her face in her hands as nine phantom blades hover above them in a dark room. She may be waking up from a terrible nightmare or, conversely, unable to sleep because of the difficulties that weigh on her.

Sometimes readers, intending to be helpful, point to the swords and say, "See, it's all in your head! Nothing for you to worry about." But this guidance completely ignores the real impact of stress and anxiety, which can compel you to make decisions out of fear.

Pamela Colman Smith/Wikimedia Commons/Public Domain

This is likely a time for you to prioritize mental health and wellness. This agony goes beyond what you can fix with a day off or a bubble bath. Let others in your circle know that you have a lot on your mind or contact professionals who can provide the specialized care and perspective you need.

More simply, this card can be a sign that you're overloading yourself with too many commitments or too much responsibility. If you're asking any form of "Should I . . .?", the tarot is likely replying, "Probably not."

When this card appears as a recommended action, consider scrutinizing the details and formulating backup plans.

Reversed meaning: Here the swords drift off, dissolved by the light of day, and a newfound sense of peace of mind is possible. With a reversed Nine of Swords, you're capable of separating genuine issues from unhealthy preoccupations.

Ten of Swords

Keywords: Defeat, debilitation, pressure, stress

Divinatory meaning: The tens bring a suit's cycle to its conclusion; for the swords, that results in a build-up of mental energy or difficulty that must end.

Hoo boy! A figure lies on the ground with ten swords stuck in their back. This is an alarming image; querents sometimes mistake it for the Death card. As always, the card images are metaphors, not literal previews; however, this is clearly not a pleasant moment.

When the Ten of Swords turns up in a reading, it's a sign that the current trajectory will lead to disaster without a concerted effort to change the course of events. It suggests you'll hit your limit with a situation, and

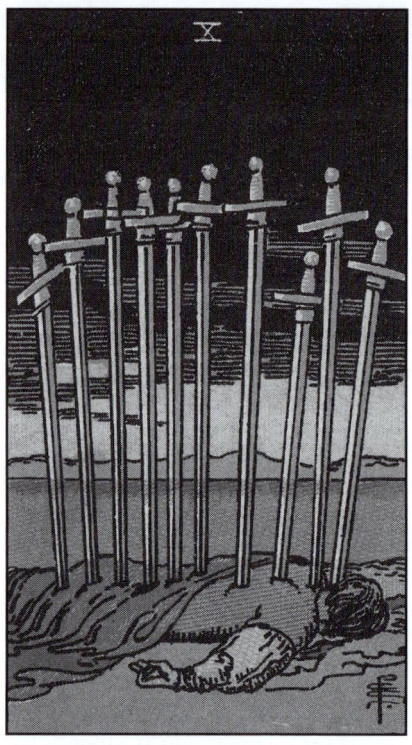

Pamela Colman Smith/Wikimedia Commons/Public Domain

it's time for a significant reset. Though other cards suggest slow, thoughtful change, this one recommends quickly pulling the plug on this situation.

In a word: Nope!

Swords are an intellectual suit, being connected to the element of air, but prolonged mental stress or trauma can affect the physical body. This card suggests you may see signs that your defense systems are working overtime to bring you into balance. Switch gears before you experience more significant burnout. This card can be a recommendation for bodywork like acupressure or acupuncture (you can see why).

Reversed meaning: If you're looking for solace (I am), the image has two parts to consider. One, black clouds fill the sky, but the golden light of a new dawn appears at their edge. Two, some interpret the hand sign made by the figure as a sign of blessing or surrender. Even reversed, this card doesn't mean everything is wonderful; rather, it suggests that although one door has closed, a new one is opening for you.

Page of Swords

Keywords: Investigation, observation, skill-building, stealth

Divinatory meaning: Pages embody curiosity, as they begin to explore their suit element. In the image, the Page wields a sword as clouds retreat in the background, which suggests opening your mind to new possibilities.

Because pages often represent learning and the swords suit focuses on the gifts of the mind, this page makes for quite the student. This card frequently signifies an opportunity to learn a new skill or start a new path or position where you'd be at square one. It can literally mean going to school or getting some formal training.

PAGE of SWORDS.

Pamela Colman Smith/Wikimedia Commons/
Public Domain

As a person, the Page of Swords is enthusiastic for more information. They may have a good head for solving puzzles or riddles, or they may appreciate a good mystery. They tend to listen more than they speak, taking note of all the details.

Their sword seems like it's cutting through those dense clouds to clear the skies ahead of them. I often associate the card with clarity after a period of confusion or doubt. The card may urge you to rely less on the opinions of others or even your own intuition and instead to seek out the cold hard facts themselves.

The Page of Swords has a stealthy quality to them; I sometimes think of them as the super sleuth of the tarot. This may be a good time for you to go into observation mode and scan for new information. It also means you don't need to broadcast everything you do; play your cards close to your chest until you're ready to make a move.

Reversed meaning: In this orientation, the studious page can become more like a spy, rummaging around in other people's business or going behind their backs. This position may be an indication that someone is talking about you or spreading false information. Or it may mean you don't need to learn this new skill you're considering.

Knight of Swords

Keywords: Eagerness, decisiveness, confrontation, action

Divinatory meaning: Knights are action-oriented, taking risks and seeking direct experience. For the Knight of Swords, this attribute means thinking quickly and making choices on the fly.

You can tell a lot about the knight by observing their horse. This one has no feet on the ground at all, almost flying across what seems to be a battlefield. This card indicates rapid movement without pausing to reflect on decisions. Look at the other cards in the spread to determine whether this approach will work.

As a person, the Knight of Swords tends to be self-assured and intense. They believe in what they're doing and prefer it if others can get on board with their goals. They're not afraid to put themselves forward for a task.

KNIGHT of SWORDS.

Pamela Colman Smith/Wikimedia Commons/Public Domain

Because the knight seems to be taking part in an active skirmish, this card can indicate that a conflict is fast approaching. If you're the knight in this situation, the card may urge you to speak your mind or to make the move, even though it may ruffle some feathers. If the knight is someone else in your orbit, be ready to go toe-to-toe with them.

More simply, the knight's tendency to act first and ask questions later may be urging you to make the move you've been considering. They move through life by trying things and seeing how they pan out.

Reversed meaning: Reversed, this card's swift action only brings trouble. The confidence and decisiveness are ill-advised bravado and thoughtlessness. You may want to slow down, hang back, or keep quiet. Don't take action just for the sake of taking action.

Queen of Swords

Keywords: Discernment, hard-won wisdom, wit, frankness

Divinatory meaning: The queens represent an inner mastery of their suit element, making their actions instinctual and giving them a high degree of influence over others. The Queen of Swords has a stunning mind, and very little escapes her notice.

She looks out on the world from her throne high up in the clouds. The Queen of Swords has a tricky reputation in the tarot with some traditional meanings, including *widow* and *unhappy woman*. This stems from how the Queen values achieving goals over maintaining interpersonal relationships and prizes truth and wisdom over the shallow comfort of others. This Queen isn't opposed to conflict if it'll improve a situation or cut to the heart of the matter.

QUEEN of SWORDS.

Pamela Colman Smith/Wikimedia Commons/Public Domain

The Queen of Swords has also learned much from the pains of the past and doesn't lie to herself or repeat her mistakes. When you're being called on to embody this card, giving yourself a frank reality check and being clear about what is and isn't working is essential. This card points to the value of thoughtful edits. Instead of losing time and energy to wishful thinking, this is a moment to assess what must be cut to move forward. This process can be painful but necessary.

As a person, this card represents someone clever and self-assured. They can be an excellent advisor, and you'd do well to heed their judgments. They'll "tell it like it is" more than any of the other court cards. They can be intimidating, but they have a quick wit and form strong bonds with people they respect.

Reversed meaning: When the card is reversed, some of this queen's more infamous attributes come to the forefront; for example, that sharp tongue can be a little too sharp. This orientation can indicate that what seems to you like a healthy sense of competition or friendly rivalry is actually viciousness and unneeded cruelty.

King of Swords

Keywords: Strategic thinking, discipline, emotional restraint, shrewdness

Divinatory meaning: Kings have achieved an outer mastery of their suit element, making them capable leaders with command over others. As a master of the mental suit of swords, the King uses their considerable intelligence to keep themselves in a favorable position. Of all the court cards, only the King of Swords looks directly at the viewer. His intense gaze feels like a challenge, especially with the sword casually held in his hand.

Like his mate, the Queen of Swords, this card has a challenging reputation among tarot readers, who see him as heartless and domineering. He prizes strategic thinking and logical facts-based conclusions (which conflict with intuitive

Pamela Colman Smith/Wikimedia Commons/ Public Domain

types). It's true that he can be shrewd, stern, and ruthless, and the card may mean you'll have a conflict with an authority figure. More simply, the King is a smart person with a methodical approach to life who, understanding the odds of the game, takes only calculated risks.

As a person, they've fought hard for success and likely bear the scars earned along the way. The card may indicate that you should take the wisdom of past failures and apply it here.

This card suggests that you'll find victory if you take a longer view of your situation. I'm reminded of master chess players who can perceive whole sequences of moves and countermoves in their minds. This card may require making sacrifices in the present moment to put yourself in a better position to achieve ultimate success. This card can also indicate that you'd benefit from having more structure. Consider the rules you may set for yourself or how you may better schedule your time or control your budget.

Reversed meaning: In this orientation, the King's approach to life is cerebral. They may value having their viewpoint proven right more than discovering the truth of a situation. Their dominant side can go too far, treating people like tools and making enemies. More simply, this position may indicate that you're overthinking things.

Ace of Cups

Keywords: Birth, openness, creative flow, healing

Divinatory meaning: The aces all herald a new beginning or opportunity; with cups' focus on emotional depth, this card suggests that something you care about very deeply is ready to start.

Just as the water flows freely from the chalice into the pond below, your life is brimming with possibility. This is a card of birth. That can occasionally be literal (in which case, congratulations!) but is most often the metaphorical birth of something vitally important to you. Similarly, the Ace of Cups can signify a significant rebirth. You may have an opportunity to begin anew, fresh and rejuvenated.

Pamela Colman Smith/Wikimedia Commons/Public Domain

Connected visually to the mysteries of the Holy Grail, the Ace of Cups points to the potential for profound healing, especially in the areas of emotional trauma, forgiveness, and self-love. Just as water can gently purify a surface, the tides are ready to sweep away the pains of the past, rejuvenating and restoring you. See yourself with fresh eyes.

Water is infinitely adaptable, and this card asks you to be open to your creative impulses, quelling doubts and going with the flow. Let your heart rule your head, and say yes to what pleases, interests, and amuses you instead of focusing on what's sensible or practical. This is an excellent time for makeovers, redecoration, and reinvention.

Reversed meaning: This card suggests that the long-awaited beginning will be delayed. Significant emotional issues or conflicts within may block forward movement, and you'll need to address them. When inverted, this card may suggest it's time to put the head back into the driver's seat and let the heart just enjoy the scenery for a while. This position may also advise against forgiving and forgetting a transgression.

Two of Cups

Keywords: Openheartedness, desire, tenderness, recognition

Divinatory meaning: The twos indicate a desire for the suit's element; in the case of cups, that's a desire for an emotional connection (platonic or romantic) with another. In the card, you see a man and woman offering one another a chalice. Their posture suggests an ease and connection already forming between the two of them.

Pamela Colman Smith/Wikimedia Commons/ Public Domain

Let me get this part out of the way: The Two of Cups is an excellent card for any matters related to love, friendship, and relationships of any kind. There's a sense of connection between the two, built on a foundation of trust and balance.

This card recommends a willingness to be vulnerable with others. You must risk your heart if you're going to let anyone in. This risk can create feelings of tension and anxiety as you put yourself in the hands of another, but the potential gain from taking such a risk is well worth it.

Whatever the subject of the reading is, emotional appeals rather than logical ones are recommended at this time. Sway someone by tugging on their heartstrings and demonstrating that you understand their desire.

The Two of Cups also recognizes the importance of feeling seen and heard by others. If you're being overlooked or misunderstood, this is the moment to speak your truth and demand that you be heard. In return, let others show you who they are.

Reversed meaning: When this card is reversed, something is getting in the way of the close connection suggested by this card. Someone may be hiding their true intentions or just not be ready to fully open themselves up to others. Look for opportunities to uncover what's causing turbulence. As a recommended action, this card may suggest that this isn't the time to completely open up and reveal your intentions. Play your cards closer to your chest.

Three of Cups

Keywords: Friendship, ease, levity, intoxication

Divinatory meaning: The threes bring their suit's element into manifestation, and with the emotional cups the result is pure pleasure and levity. It's high time to have a good time.

Three maidens make a toast amidst the fruits of a bountiful harvest, suggesting that your focus should be on satisfaction and gratitude for things just as they are rather than on pushing to improve them or create something from scratch. You've worked hard to create the life you have; be sure to enjoy it. So many cards speak of beginnings and transformation, but this one understands the value of "pretty good" or "good enough."

Pamela Colman Smith/Wikimedia Commons/Public Domain

More than any other card, the Three of Cups points to the power and value of friendship. Strengthen the bonds with those you love. This may be an opportunity to reconnect with anyone you've lost touch with.

In conflicts, this card urges you toward diplomacy and finding solutions that satisfy all parties. This is a good time to keep it light.

You may want to do something frivolous to destress or disconnect from life's toils. This act need not be dramatic — a day trip or evening out may be enough.

Reversed meaning: Reversed, this card can remind you of the consequences of too much of a good thing. This may be a time for seriousness instead of whimsy. This position can also indicate that something no longer provides the joy it once did, and you may want to consider what you're really getting out of it. Additionally, your circle of friends may be harboring unspoken problems that should be addressed.

Four of Cups

Keywords: Dissatisfaction, incompleteness, reservation, composure

Divinatory meaning: The fours bring a sense of strength and stability; with the watery cups, that stability can feel too rigid. Water can adapt to its container, but given its preference, it likes to flow freely.

With three cups arrayed before him, a young man dreams of one he does not yet possess — or perhaps it's being presented to him to complete the set. Maybe he doesn't care for that one, either; emotions can be hard to nail down precisely. This card recalls those times when you just can't shake the feeling that things don't feel quite right. An unease present within the card speaks of a longing for something more.

Pamela Colman Smith/Wikimedia Commons/Public Domain

You may find yourself rejecting what you've been told you're supposed to want. Perhaps someone has tried to place you in a box that reflects their ideas rather than yours. His crossed arms may indicate he has had more than enough of what others have handed him.

This card suggests a restlessness, an itch that longs to be scratched. You may need to step outside your comfort zone to satisfy this need.

The Four of Cups can also indicate good old-fashioned boredom. Something in your situation has lost its pizazz and now feels like a burden. Things may seem a little lackluster now, but this situation is often temporary.

Reversed meaning: Reversed, this card is in a much more comfortable state. In this orientation, the box is cozy and safe, and you'll do well staying put for the time being. Accept what's given; you'll likely enjoy it more than you'd think.

Five of Cups

Keywords: Regret, disappointment, loss, pining

Divinatory meaning: The fives bring both chaos and valuable lessons you can learn from that chaos. When this happens in the suit of the cups, you can expect emotional upheaval.

This is a heavy card, from the dark cloak to the bleak, gray sky. Interpretations of it center on the two sets of golden cups. Three cups have been knocked over, and their contents spill out on the ground, whereas two remain upright behind the mournful figure. Readers love to urge people to ignore the knocked-over cups, pick up the upright ones, and cross the bridge in the background. Essentially, they mean "Get over it." But the focus on the upright card is those toppled goblets.

Pamela Colman Smith/Wikimedia Commons/Public Domain

This card shows up when things fall short of your hopes and dreams. You may be underwhelmed by the results, find that the price you paid was too high, or find you're trapped by the thought of what could've been. Taking the time to process your experience is important; that may involve a period of shutting others out while you make sense of things.

This card can also signal an opportunity to avoid repeating a past mistake. If you can apply the wisdom from that moment to this one, then the pain will be worth it. Experience is what you get when you don't get what you want.

Reversed meaning: When the card is reversed, it *is* time to turn your attention to the two upright cups and find a way to move on. This sentiment isn't popular in spiritual circles, but you can find wisdom in lowering standards and expectations. Despite what you've been promised, you likely need to settle. This compromise doesn't need to be dire; it means accepting "fine" or "passable" to avoid getting stuck.

Six of Cups

Keywords: Gentleness, gifts, nostalgia, lightness

Divinatory meaning: The harmonious nature of the sixes creates delight and serenity in the emotional cups. Here, you see one of the most charming scenes in the tarot: one child offering flowers to another. You can almost hear the birds chirping.

The Six of Cups presents an idealized vision of childhood filled with sweetness and light, suggesting that you return to a simpler, more idyllic way of being. This card is strongly connected to nostalgia and fond feelings for the past. Does a core memory hold special meaning for your present situation?

A prominent feature of most people's memories of their childhoods is a lack of complexity and a sense

Pamela Colman Smith/Wikimedia Commons/Public Domain

that the world is a magical place (of course, this doesn't apply to everyone's childhood experiences). This card may recommend simplifying your situation and making things easier for yourself. Trust in the goodness of others and the possibility that things will work out.

Each of the sixes shows one figure above others; in this case, that highlights the dynamic of giving and receiving. In the cups, harmony is restored when you freely give the gift of kindness. The power of kind and uplifting words can't be underestimated. Make it clear to others just how you feel about them.

Reversed meaning: On the positive end of the spectrum, when reversed, this card can indicate that it's your turn to be on the receiving end of kindness instead of being the one doling out kindness to others. In this case, the card urges you to ask for (and expect) compassion and patience. Conversely, the reversed card may suggest a sense of naivete. You may be a little too trusting of others at this moment and may benefit from taking a closer look at the finer details.

Seven of Cups

Keywords: Possibilities, daydreams, delusion, identity

Divinatory meaning: The sevens demonstrate a suit's adaptability, which is an area where cups excel. Their extreme fluidity results in both the blessing and curse of having choices.

A figure looks at a dreamlike vision of cups holding strange objects ranging from appealing things like jewels and a castle to the potentially intimidating dragon and snake (depending on how you personally feel about both dragons and snakes).

The Seven of Cups asks questions like "Who do you want to be today? What if you get to decide? What if you could change your mind?" This card is a call to consider alternate options you want to take and transformations you want to make.

Pamela Colman Smith/Wikimedia Commons/
Public Domain

This card is an opportunity to expand in a direction you want rather than one expected of you. Don't let anyone pin you down. And wherever you're going, you may want to take the scenic route and see the sights along the way to your destination.

While contemplating your path, this card also suggests that some goals may be illusions, and you should consider carefully what lies behind them. Notice the skull symbol hidden on the chalice holding the laurel wreath. Performing a crossroads spread (see Chapter 6) to consider the long-term prospects of your decisions may be wise.

The trick here is to eventually move beyond the consideration stage. This energy can be overwhelming, and that can lead to shutting down and deciding not to decide. This feeling is keenest when the card is reversed.

Reversed meaning: When reversed, this card indicates it's time to get your head out of the clouds, stop dillydallying, and make up your mind. Here the imaginative qualities of the card are fleeting daydreams, and returning to inside-the-box thinking is best. As the Seven of Cups can suggest illusions, its reversal may mean that you learn what's hiding beneath the mask.

Eight of Cups

Keywords: Reevaluation, reversal, releasing attachment, detours

Divinatory meaning: The eights tend to deepen the energy of the suit. In the cups, the result is greater emotional awareness that can have challenging consequences.

Here you see a figure turning away from the lovely arrangement of cups and walking up a rocky hillside. Every aspect of this card shows a heaviness, from the figure's posture to the terrain and the moon eclipsing the sun in a gray sky. The decision to turn away wasn't easily made.

This card tends to turn up when you no longer feel confident that you're following the correct path. At this time, your best bet is to listen to that voice and turn back. Let go of any sunk-cost fallacies that say you must keep going because of how

Pamela Colman Smith/Wikimedia Commons/Public Domain

much of yourself you've already invested in this. Why continue waiting outside the door that never opened?

This can be an exceptionally painful card to turn over in a reading because you tend to ask the tarot about pursuits that are near and dear to your heart. As heartbreaking as the "no" suggested by the Eight of Cups can be, remember the incredible value in turning your vital time and energy toward goals that have more hope of working out.

On a simpler level, this may be a time for you to take a break and step away for a short while to avoid emotional burnout. Things are likely to feel clearer when you give yourself this space.

Reversed meaning: Reversed, this card has more hope to offer you. In this position, the Eight of Cups suggests some value in continuing this path despite how rocky and rugged the journey has been. Keep on keepin' on.

Nine of Cups

Keywords: Contentment, wishes fulfilled, pride, self-focus

Divinatory meaning: The climactic energy of the nines reaches a beautiful crescendo for the emotional cups, resulting in a sense of contentment and ease.

For many readers, the figure on the Nine of Cups recalls the feeling you have after finishing a very satisfying meal. You don't really notice the absence of the hunger you felt in the lead-up to this moment as you bask in bliss.

This is an overwhelmingly positive card because it suggests both attaining what you set out for and feeling genuinely pleased with the result.

Sometimes when things are going your way, you may find yourself waiting to discover the catch.

Pamela Colman Smith/Wikimedia Commons/Public Domain

Though no state of being is permanent, this card asks you to take it easy and allow yourself to enjoy the good things in life.

An old tradition designates the Nine of Cups as the "wish card" because it tends to signify getting your heart's desire. When some readers turn it over, they take a moment to make a wish. Try it and see how you feel.

The cups depicted here are elevated or displayed in such a way that they seem to be trophies of past victories. When upright, this arrangement is a reminder to take pride in your accomplishments and speak well of yourself.

It also suggests that it's time to put your emotional well-being at the top of your priority list. A healthy amount of self-focus is warranted.

Reversed meaning: On the other hand, when reversed this card suggests you may be engaging in a little too much self-focus. This imbalance can result in ignoring significant problems in your quest for happiness and overindulging to cover for unhappiness. The reversal can indicate selfishness that causes you to miss out on the needs of other people in your life.

Ten of Cups

Keywords: Attainment, delight, home, happily ever after

Divinatory meaning: The tens bring the suit element into a state of resolution, and for the cups that means a profound happiness that future successes can be built upon. A cycle ends, but the rich rewards of tranquility you've earned remain.

Just look at how happy everything seems on this card. With the rainbow, the posing, and the dancing, it's a bit like watching the final song in a musical from behind the stage. Don't get cynical, though (well, not until the reversal); attaining this enduring sense of ease and contentment is actually possible. Across the cups suit, you see highs and lows, but the Ten suggests more stability in your happiness.

Pamela Colman Smith/Wikimedia Commons/ Public Domain

Cups are all about that interpersonal connection. In the Two you see a passionate first meeting with all its intensity. In the Ten, you see what happens when two crazy lovebirds prove they have what it takes to make things work. Whether you're asking about romance, business, or any other field, this card asks you to prioritize the long-term health of the various relationships involved. It means giving and taking and working through the difficult times so that everyone wins.

This card is great for any creative pursuits. It suggests your work will be elevated and appreciated as more than the sum of its parts.

Reversed meaning: Reversed, this card may make you question whether the outer expression of happiness is just a façade. Maybe you're seeing your life through rose-colored glasses because you don't want to acknowledge pain. It can also represent putting up a brave front for others because you don't want to burden them with your struggle. If that's the case, let down your guard and let people know what you're going through.

Page of Cups

Keywords: Imagination, artistic expression, sensitivity, self-exploration

Divinatory meaning: Pages embody curiosity as they begin to explore their suit element. For the emotional suit of cups, that means discovering how to see with their heart.

A young person smiles at a fish peeking out of a chalice. Tarot readers have had a lot of conversations about that fish in the page's cup. Though some see it as esoteric (obscure), I prefer to think of it as simply unlikely. The scene has a dreamlike quality, suggesting that you keep an open mind about what's real for you.

As a person, the Page of Cups is creative, excitable, and sensitive, feeling things very deeply. They're likely to take the most innovative approach to accomplishing a goal — the scenic

Pamela Colman Smith/Wikimedia Commons/
Public Domain

route or the long way home. They excel at changing the energy in a tense situation but need guidance when coloring within the lines is necessary.

Pages are celebrated for their artistic gifts. This card may be a call for you to exercise your own creative muscles. Make art; write a poem; sketch out what you want to have happen in your life.

The cups court is particularly sensitive. The Page is attuned to the subtle needs of others, and this card may encourage you to display more empathy and kindness. That may also include psychic sensitivity, which recommends that you learn the basics of your gift. (Hey, you're reading this book, so you're ahead of the curve.)

Reversed meaning: When stood on their head, the page's sensitivity can trend toward hypersensitivity. This imbalance comes from centering their own feelings above the needs of others in a situation. Be on the lookout for someone having an outsized emotional response to their predicament. The reversed Page of Cups may also be a directive from the cards to stop doodling in the margins and address the challenges you face directly.

Knight of Cups

Keywords: Romantic overtures, soul searching, devotion, spiritual journeys

Divinatory meaning: Knights are action-oriented, exploring their suit's element out in the world, taking risks, and seeking direct experience. The emotional cups will look far and wide for what will fulfill their desires.

A questing knight holds a chalice before him. The Knight of Cups is a romantic, and when the card is upright, you can see them as a hopeful romantic. They're happy to wear their heart on their sleeve, letting others know their true feelings on the matter.

As a person, they're charming, considerate, and complex. They have a charitable nature, giving of themselves because the act is its own reward. They

KNIGHT of CUPS.

Pamela Colman Smith/Wikimedia Commons/ Public Domain

may have appeared in the reading because they're willing to help you out.

The knights' horses speak volumes. This knight's steed seems to move forward at a comfortable pace. This knight is willing to take their time on a journey, pausing to reflect on the next move, never rushing.

Because I keep saying *romantic,* I should note that the Knight of Cups is the sort of person a lot of folks want to show up in a love reading. They may be that Prince or Princess Charming you've been pining for. If the knight in the reading represents you, this is an opportune time to express your attraction to your intended.

With that golden chalice held aloft, the knight recalls the stories about King Arthur and the quest for the Holy Grail and spiritual enlightenment. This card may be a sign to set aside more worldly concerns to deepen your spiritual practice.

Reversed meaning: Here you find the romantic sans hope; what they seek just isn't available right now. All knights are prone to excesses, and for the Knight of Cups that can mean allowing emotional wounds to overcome them. This card also has a history of signifying drunkenness and debauchery — party till you feel good, not till you feel bad.

Queen of Cups

Keywords: Emotional wisdom, listening, care, empathy

Divinatory meaning: The queens represent an inner mastery of their suit element, making their actions instinctual and giving them a high degree of influence over others. This queen, seated on a throne festooned with images of mermaids and water sprites, is adept at soothing hurt feelings or frayed emotions. She gazes intently at an ornate chalice, which calls to mind the Holy Grail from Christian tradition or a *monstrance* (a container for the eucharist in Catholic churches), suggesting that the queen herself is a holy vessel.

Pamela Colman Smith/Wikimedia Commons/ Public Domain

As a person, the Queen of Cups is someone gentle and loving. They're nonjudgmental and not afraid of going deep; you can confide your secrets to them and expect to receive understanding. If you're the queen in the reading, this may be an opportunity for you to be there for someone who is struggling. You may serve as a guide or mentor for them, but mostly the Queen of Cups heals by listening and holding space so others can reflect on their feelings. The Queen can represent the healing that you can achieve when you give voice to your pain or fears.

The Queen of Cups embodies the benefits of vulnerability. By acknowledging any difficult experiences or reactions within themselves, they can face those and give them the time and attention they deserve. The Queen's empathy and understanding nature extend to people that they find very challenging. In conflict, do your utmost to comprehend the other side of the issue. Imagine what you'd want in the other person's place. Even if you can't side with an opponent, understanding their mind is helpful.

In tarot, water symbolizes emotion and this is the wateriest of all the water cards; the Queen represents the vast depths of the subconscious and your psychic nature. This may be a moment to engage in forms of energy healing.

Reversed meaning: Whenever the lovely, sensitive cups are upended, their emotions tend to get the better of them. Here, the Queen's natural talent for feeling things intensely can turn into wallowing and excessive self-pity. This orientation may be a sign you're not being allowed to express your feelings.

King of Cups

Keyword: Tranquility, therapy, composure, diplomacy

Divinatory meaning: Kings have achieved an outer mastery of their suit element, making them capable leaders with command over others. For the emotional cups, the king brings a framework for exploring your inner workings.

In the midst of a turbulent sea, a king sits on a simple throne of gray stone set on a solid block of stone. The blending of flowy, expressive wateriness with a king's penchant for command isn't an easy one. He has control over his emotions, which can be both beneficial and restricting.

As a person, the King of Cups is calm, cool, and collected. Although other kings rule by will or domination, this one leads with their compassion and

Pamela Colman Smith/Wikimedia Commons/ Public Domain

their impeccable character. People want to follow them because they believe the King respects them.

With the King's more cerebral take on the emotional realm, they've often been compared with a therapist, and their presence in a spread may indicate this is a time to seek professional counseling services.

The King has a peaceful nature and can use their skills to be an effective peacemaker. This card may urge you to find a way to smooth over a conflict you're experiencing. First, steady your own psyche, and then, when ready, extend an opportunity for harmonious reconciliation with others. Let the turbulence subside for now; it can be addressed in the future.

On a similar note, this card can indicate the benefits of etiquette. This may be a time to take a more formal and cordial approach to your interactions.

Reversed meaning: A mentor once described the reversed King of Cups as a person everyone likes but no one respects. In this orientation, they're too soft to be an effective leader. Conversely, this position may indicate that someone is going too far in restraining their emotions and needs to be allowed to feel and express themselves.

Ace of Pentacles

Keywords: Foundation, investment, prosperity, manifestation

Divinatory meaning: Aces begin a new cycle, and for the pentacles that means a first careful step to form the future. A solid opportunity is on the way.

This suit was originally named coins in the first tarot deck. The symbol here resembles a massive golden coin, and that's no accident; it suggests an initial expenditure of your time, energy, or money that will grow. You also see a garden gate and a lush lawn filled with flowers — signs of prosperity and good fortune to come. The card displays an appreciation for the finer things in life.

The Ace of Pentacles reminds me of the expression "The oak is in the acorn." A significant and successful undertaking can sprout from

Pamela Colman Smith/Wikimedia Commons/ Public Domain

very humble beginnings, and you have a chance to make a small but decisive move with great long-term potential. Of course, just about everything with the pentacles suit is long-term.

Where some other suits concern themselves with the ethereal, pentacles focus on solid results. What's the first material step that will move this situation out of the hypothetical and manifest it in the world? This endeavor can take the form of a new job, a new home, or a special gift — in other words, something exciting that also requires your attention and care.

This ace favors the most grounded and stable way forward.

Reversed meaning: At best, reversed aces tend to mean delayed beginnings, requiring extra patience. At worst, the seed you hope to plant in this situation will never take root or flourish.

Two of Pentacles

Keywords: Multitasking, balance, managing, precariousness

Divinatory meaning: Twos show a desire for the suit element, which for the pentacles suggests a longing for certainty and stability. You may find yourself in a rocky state, attending to multiple tasks.

A juggler poised on one foot while dancing on sand tosses pentacles from hand to hand, their arc depicted as a lemniscate. In the background you see ships sailing over rolling waves. The whole effect is topsy-turvy (imagine being a passenger on those ships), suggesting a hectic time when your attention will be divided.

Sometimes, you're asked to choose between *A* or *B*, and your answer is "Both." In theory, it'd be lovely to only ever focus on one matter at

Pamela Colman Smith/Wikimedia Commons/
Public Domain

a time, but this card reflects the reality that you must often stretch yourself to cover several things at once. That can include family, friends, career, romance, and so on. Here, you see a person who can work their magic while maintaining their equilibrium.

The trick for jugglers is that they must also make the act look effortless. You're likely feeling tested, but this is your time to shine. When upright, this card says, "You've got this." Devote just enough of your time to each area and avoid getting buried in too many details.

You don't want to always be in this state, but currently you'll likely be able to stretch and make it work. As precarious as things look for those ships, their sails are full and they're above water.

Reversed meaning: Sometimes the juggler misses a throw, and things come crashing down. In this orientation, you're advised not to take on too much for the moment. Imposing reasonable limits on how much is being asked of you is a good idea. Something has to give; it's up to you to decide what goes on hiatus.

Three of Pentacles

Keywords: Cohesion, masterpiece, skill-fulness, collaboration

Divinatory meaning: The threes bring their element into manifestation; for diligent pentacles, the result is superb work elevated by meaningful collaboration.

A sculptor works on the fine details of a cathedral observed by an architect holding a set of plans and a member of the church who has sponsored this project. Each person has their area of expertise, which is required for this masterwork to be built.

When I see the beautifully aligned pentacles at the top of the scene, I can't help but think of a set of gears turning together in perfect time to power a machine. This card indicates that collaboration will improve your situation. Teamwork makes the dream work.

Pamela Colman Smith/Wikimedia Commons/ Public Domain

Just as each figure in the card has unique skills, you're wise to seek help or perspective from people who have the expertise you don't, and then (this is the tricky part) actually listen to them. Trusting expertise will advance your knowledge.

Speaking of your skills, this card suggests that you have what it takes to stretch your muscles and demonstrate what incredible work you're capable of. No need to be humdrum.

More simply, this card suggests that you focus on what you do best. Stay in your lane and trust your instincts; you've earned them from a life of trial and error.

This card is also a positive sign that what you're focusing on will be especially significant, and you'll be pleased with your results.

Reversed meaning: In this position, those perfectly aligned gears get out of sync, and the whole machine grinds to a halt. This orientation suggests that cooperation may have broken down between team members and they'll need to come back together to move forward. Some elements of the situation could be causing a problem for the whole. It can also indicate that you aren't doing your best work in this situation.

Four of Pentacles

Keywords: Guardedness, greed, conservation, barriers

Divinatory meaning: The fours bring stability, and for the cautious and conservative pentacles that can create an unscalable and unshakable wall around your life.

A man wearing a crown holds a golden pentacle tightly in his arms, with two more pentacles trapped beneath his feet and a fourth perched on his head. He is some distance away from a large and prosperous city.

You can interpret this card in two directions in its upright position; they boil down to too much or too little. People usually see the figure on the card as a miser caring only for wealth. So a straightforward

*Pamela Colman Smith/Wikimedia Commons/
Public Domain*

interpretation is a warning against the excesses of greed and selfishness. This attitude goes beyond money to include a general fear of vulnerability that causes you to erect walls to keep others out and at a distance. What's the good of gold pentacles if you keep them trapped beneath your feet?

The other side of the coin (pun intended) is the sensible policy of guarding your resources of time, energy, and money. People may ask for more than you can or want to give, and the Four of Pentacles points to the value of healthy boundaries in those moments. Don't feel compelled to give beyond your means (or desire).

To determine which interpretation is right, look to see whether other cards in the spread support a strategy of insularity and self-focus or urge you to let your guard down.

Reversed meaning: In this orientation the walls come down, and you can connect deeply and without fear. This position may be an opportunity to address any insecurities causing you to doubt yourself or hold yourself back from the world. This reversal may be an invitation to release attachment to things and devote your attention to the relationships that matter to you. Conversely, this card could point to a waste of precious resources. Look to the other cards in the spread to see if that interpretation is indicated.

Five of Pentacles

Keywords: Despondency, destitution, struggle, endurance

Divinatory meaning: The fives bring chaos, shaking the comfort and security of the pentacles to their core. Prepare for hard times. Two figures in tattered clothes, one limping along on crutches, trudge through a freezing snowstorm past a church whose stained-glass window is lit from within.

The fives all have difficult lessons to teach (spiritual people like to call disasters "lessons"), and this one explores what happens when you're cut off from the necessary resources represented by the pentacles. This signals a time of having to make do with less or to work only with what you have at your disposal.

Pamela Colman Smith/Wikimedia Commons/Public Domain

Some speculate that the figure on the left has a leper bell around his neck, warning people to flee from them. You may draw strength from the card's sense of being cut off from others, as well as help from people or institutions who are supposed to be there for you. Note that it shows a church wall and not a door.

This is a moment to focus on necessities. Don't go over the top; just do enough to keep the lights on and the trains running on time.

Though no one else is there to help them, these two figures have one another. Powerful bonds form between people overcoming adversity together. Find strength in those in your circle and do your best to offer one another as much support as you can manage.

Reversed meaning: Turned on its head, this card suggests that the trying times you're experiencing will come to an end. In particular, readers advise turning the corner and finding the door of that proverbial church so that you can step inside and find the warmth and comfort you need. Badly needed resources and support will become available.

Six of Pentacles

Keywords: Charity, gratitude, rebalancing, adjustment

Divinatory meaning: The sixes bring harmony to the suit; with the practical concerns of the pentacles, the result is a restoration of vital resources.

A gentleman who seems to be well off (check the fancy hat) drops coins into the hands of a beggar. He holds a set of scales that rest in a state of equilibrium. The fingers of his right hand make the blessing sign seen on the Hierophant (see the earlier section). The sixes all point to hierarchies with one person raised above the others.

The world doesn't exist in a state of perfect balance. From the moment of birth, genetics and economics divide people from one another in just about every imaginable cat-

*Pamela Colman Smith/Wikimedia Commons/
Public Domain*

egory. But throughout their lives they experience moments of restitution where the inequities are healed even just a little. The Six of Pentacles suggests a need for such a rebalancing.

A key to understanding this card is to figure out which person you are in this card: the giver or the receiver? If you're in a position of plenty, you may be called to share your resources (such as time, energy, or money) with someone who's in need. If you're always the one who gives more than you get back, this is a call to accept (or even request) help from others.

A simpler take is that the upright card highlights the value of charity and suggests that someone needs your assistance. If you don't read reversals, use your intuition to determine whether you're the one in need.

Reversed meaning: If you take the more straightforward approach, the reversed card suggests that you're in the position to receive. Ask for what you need. Alternatively, if you see the upright as "give," the reversal may simply be "don't give."

Seven of Pentacles

Keywords: Respite, waiting, plateaus, appraisal

Divinatory meaning: Sevens show the suit's ability to adapt, and with the driven and hard-working pentacles that represents the patience to stop tinkering and evaluate progress.

A farmer or gardener looks at his thriving plant. His mysterious expression has divided readers on some aspects of this card's meaning, and you should consider whether it seems bored, proud, or even sad to you. The answer will push you in a useful direction.

This card is a reminder that so much you can't see is happening beneath the surface. If you're feeling restless or frustrated with how long something takes to manifest, know that you've played your part and set things in motion. It's up to the universe and others to take it from here.

Pamela Colman Smith/Wikimedia Commons/
Public Domain

Wanting to stay active and keep pushing things along until you have the desired result is natural. But this card may be a call to take a more passive role and truly observe your progress. After you have a stronger sense of how things are transpiring, make more effective choices.

This metaphor becomes especially tricky around relationships. You may feel you've put in the effort but aren't seeing the return from another person. Or you may need a break from someone or you may realize they need their space right now.

Where other cards show the need to rest your mind or your spirit, this one may push for you to rest your body, giving it the nourishment it needs.

Reversed meaning: Here you may need to adjust your expectations. You've done what you can, but you may need to tolerate some imperfections if possible. Alternatively, this position can announce that it's finally time to harvest what you've worked so diligently to create. Pour yourself back into the work and get things over the finish line.

Eight of Pentacles

Keywords: Labor, boredom, repetition, systems

Divinatory meaning: The eights deepen the suit's energy, and for hard-working pentacles that results in a flood of industriousness.

Pamela Colman Smith/Wikimedia Commons/
Public Domain

An artisan at his workbench uses a hammer and chisel to put the finishing touches on a golden pentacle, the latest in a series. Where the Three of Pentacles shows a masterwork (see the earlier section), here you see the more simple, day-to-day sort of effort.

The Eight of Pentacles demonstrates the value of plain (often hard) work. The indication here is to apply yourself to the task at hand. Begin at step one, proceed to step two, and so on and so forth, without taking any shortcuts. There's no need to reinvent the wheel.

Alternatively, this card ties into the idea that sometimes you learn best by doing. Try your hand at a new skill or process.

This metaphor extends to the hard work of relationships, where you must show patience and tenacity, accepting another's flaws and earning their respect as they learn to accept and earn yours.

When showing a progression, the Eight of Pentacles suggests things will develop slowly and a little bit at a time. This meaning has connected the card to the idea of boredom (not an uncommon theme in the pentacles).

Reversed meaning: Here the card may suggest a sense of overwork or overcommitment. Similarly, you may become too focused on small, inconsequential details and lose sight of the broader picture. This orientation can also be a sign you're doing the same thing repeatedly and hoping for different results. Or it may be an opportunity to be less of a worker bee and think more for yourself.

Nine of Pentacles

IX

Pamela Colman Smith/Wikimedia Commons/
Public Domain

Keyword: Productivity, independence, focus, acumen

Divinatory meaning: The climatic energy of the nines results in a bountiful harvest thanks to the thoughtful investments and careful work of the pentacles. Follow your internal compass, and you'll flourish.

A lady of means stands in an opulent garden where the vines are heavy with both grapes and pentacles. One hand gently rests on the harvest, suggesting a satisfaction born from seeing careful plans come to fruition. You see a sense of ownership and pride in this enterprise.

Readers focus on two animal symbols in this card. First is the hooded falcon (an accessory for a true aristocrat). The hood is used to calm and restrict the bird, which ties into this card's theme of self-discipline as a path to success. Hold yourself to a high standard, always doing your level best, and you'll achieve greatness. Challenge yourself, support yourself, and enjoy the results.

The other symbol is the snail, which can retreat into its shell when it needs to shut out the world. Note that the lady is in a walled garden, pointing to the singularity of her vision. Following your own path can set you apart from others; you can feel great pressure to conform to their visions, but what you create will truly be yours from concept to creation.

To put it more simply: Get comfortable doing your own thing.

The nines usually carry a sense of "you're almost there." This card can indicate that your methods are paying off and you're on the verge of receiving the rich rewards of your labors.

Reversed meaning: In this orientation, question whether you're truly enjoying the life you've created. Paradoxically, you may be sacrificing too much to "have it all." You may be focusing more on pleasing or impressing others.

Ten of Pentacles

Keywords: Accomplishment, harvest, wealth, legacy

Divinatory meaning: The tens bring a suit to its resolution; for the worldly pentacles, that means an established foundation on which to build future dreams. You'll achieve great success.

Pamela Colman Smith/Wikimedia Commons/ Public Domain

Several generations gather in a well-appointed courtyard with an arched gateway, suggesting that the wealth built here is passed down to others for their benefit. An architect can tell you that, despite their fragile and elegant appearance, arches are very strong and can support a great deal of mass placed on them.

When a ten appears, you're often encouraged to finish what you started so that a new, worthwhile venture can begin. But if you want to take things further, you can build on your earlier success.

This card suggests that you've created something substantial that's worth more than the sum of its parts. Shaping it has changed you by teaching you new skills and demonstrating them for others to see. Very little is temporary about this card when upright.

This card is also connected with the idea of blessings and living a blessed existence. It suggests a refreshing time of security and stability when you concern yourself less with day-to-day issues and focus more on ideas of expansion and seeking out new opportunities.

Reversed meaning: On the surface, you seem to have accomplished what you set out to do. But if you look carefully, you may find cracks in the foundation, and your empire may be on shaky ground. You may find some intergenerational conflict in play (however that applies to your situation). Or possibly you want to break free from the constraints of your past and do something entirely new.

Page of Pentacles

Keywords: Attention to detail, assistance, reliability, practicality

Divinatory meaning: Pages embody curiosity, as they begin to explore their suit element. Thanks to the earthy nature of pentacles, this one has a keen sense of the details.

The young page scrutinizes his golden pentacle intently. As a person, the Page of Pentacles is loyal, considerate, and eager to try their hand at something new. Thoroughly dependable, they can be relied on to do what they say they'll do.

Leaders who concern themselves with grand strategies require others to actually attend to all the tactics needed to execute those plans. This page has strong intern energy, taking direction from their superiors and following the process.

Pamela Colman Smith/Wikimedia Commons/ Public Domain

People who learn best by engaging in hands-on activities and touching and moving things are called *kinesthetic learners.* If you're overwhelmed by high-minded theoretical approaches, this card may indicate that you need to put the book down and get your hands dirty by trying the task yourself.

Where other courts like to be innovative or unconventional, the Page of Pentacles takes a more straightforward, practical approach. They're the type to ask whether you've read the instructions all the way through. Well, have you?

Conscientious, reliable people may not always be entertaining to be around, but if you allow the page to nerd out on the minutia, you may be impressed.

If you're considering a career change, this is an auspicious card, suggesting that soon you'll learn the ropes in a new position.

Reversed meaning: When this page engrosses themselves too thoroughly in the details, they can lose sight of the bigger picture — missing the forest for the trees. They may focus too much on practical matters and miss out on the human aspects of a situation. Sometimes, this reversed page may indicate that you're bored with it all and need some distraction.

Knight of Pentacles

Keywords: Dedication, stability, progress, grit

Divinatory meaning: Knights are action-oriented, exploring their suit's element out in the world, taking risks, and seeking direct experience. The pentacles' practicality makes this knight a staunch ally.

This armored knight, sitting atop his standing horse, looks through his helmet's visor at a golden pentacle. As a person, the Knight of Pentacles is serious, patient, and hard-working. They're earnest and steadfast in their approach to a task and level-headed in the face of adversity.

Pamela Colman Smith/Wikimedia Commons/
Public Domain

I find that the knights' horses tell you a lot about their characters. This one has all four of its hooves on the ground, which is very stable but means that both horse and rider aren't going anywhere at the moment. Pentacles' careful and steady approach to life can be an uncomfortable fit for knights who want to prove themselves and their skills. The Knight of Pentacles will pursue their quest . . . cautiously.

When I see the Knight of Pentacles, I think of the expression "The only way out is through." You may feel yourself resisting what needs to be done, hoping the task will vanish if you put it off. But the knight encourages you to complete the first step, the second, and so on. Ordeals won't end until you cross the finish line.

Knights usually crave adventures and novelty, but the Knight of Pentacles does better with routines. You may want to develop a schedule for yourself so that you fall into and follow a steady rhythm.

Similarly, the knight's presence in a reading suggests a need for a strong commitment to your path.

Reversed meaning: When this knight gets too comfortable with their way of doing things, they can find themselves in a rut. This orientation may indicate a need for flexibility or a pivot ahead. It can also speak to the problem of perfectionism. The perfect is the enemy of the good, and this knight can get too hung up on a flawless finish.

Queen of Pentacles

Keywords: Caretaking, nurturing, hospitality, generosity

Divinatory meaning: The queens represent an inner mastery of their suit element, making their actions instinctual and giving them a high degree of influence over others. This queen has cultivated an appreciation for the finer things in life.

This queen has set her ornate throne in a lush garden. She lovingly cradles a golden pentacle in her arms. As a person, the Queen of Pentacles is warm, wise, and sensual. Their attentive and nurturing nature allows them to put people at ease.

The Queen of Pentacles is keenly aware of the delicate relationship between body, mind, and spirit. They understand that each of these needs to

Pamela Colman Smith/Wikimedia Commons/ Public Domain

be nourished. Consider how you're treating your body, how you're challenging your mind, and what you're feeding your spirit.

When she turns up in a reading, someone likely needs comfort, and that someone may be you. This queen is uninterested in self-denial and will urge you to give yourself what you need right now to be happy. They're generous and may remind you to be generous with others in your life, too. You may be called to pause your own journey to use your resources of time, energy, and money to benefit another.

Where the other pentacles court cards can lose themselves in tedious details, the queen appreciates the bigger picture and how each piece plays a part in creating a more meaningful whole, like notes coming together in a symphony. They ask you to clearly visualize what you're ultimately trying to accomplish and then determine whether your actions serve to materialize that goal.

Reversed meaning: When this queen gets carried away, they can devote themselves exclusively to attending to the needs of others. Watch out for becoming a people-pleaser. At this angle, the Queen can be somewhat superficial, caring more about the surface and perceived status something provides. Be careful not to become too attached to things.

King of Pentacles

Keywords: Bounty, opulence, management, achievement, stewardship

Divinatory meaning: Kings have achieved an outer mastery of their suit element, making them capable leaders with command over others. Practical pentacles make for a steady, results-oriented leader.

This king sits in a prosperous vineyard on a throne decorated with bulls, the symbol of earthy Taurus. As a person, the King of Pentacles is resourceful, driven, and successful. They may be an authority figure in your life who can offer you some much-needed support. They can also be the sort to push you to excel when they know you can do better.

Pamela Colman Smith/Wikimedia Commons/
Public Domain

They're advanced in terms of self-discipline and may urge you to not shirk your commitments or find a way to let yourself off the hook. The pentacles suit itself indicates what you must endure to create something worthwhile and, in the King, you see the result of that effort. This card can indicate that you'll achieve great things if you stick with the program.

In particular, this is a fortunate card for any questions about wealth or career. It shows a return on investment and the greatness you can attain if you go above and beyond.

The King of Pentacles is plainspoken and prefers the direct approach when relating to others. They've worked hard for what they have attained and will generally encourage that capacity in others. The card may urge you to be more straightforward with people.

This king prizes "stuff" as a physical testament to their achievements. When it becomes too important to them, it can lead to miserliness and hoarding.

Reversed meaning: You may be working too hard. When reversed, the King spends too much time striving for more and doesn't get to make use of what they've created. This orientation may indicate dissatisfaction with your achievements, finding them unfulfilling after all that build-up.

4

Embracing Oracle Cards

Get an overview of the growing field of oracle card decks, from historical traditions to modern innovations. Think through the approach you want to take in exploring your deck and reading the cards.

Go beyond the guidebook, using your insights and intuition to glean a deeper understanding of the cards.

Maximize your experience with one-card readings and consider a few spreads specially designed for use with oracle cards.

Chapter **11**

Approaching Oracle Systems

This chapter shifts the focus to tarot's younger sibling: oracle cards. As I discuss in Chapter 1, oracle cards are a slightly ambiguous category.

The number of decks available has grown exponentially since I started as a reader. In this chapter, you explore their strengths as a system, figure out which decks you want to work with, and consider two different approaches to consulting your cards.

Meeting the Mysterious Oracle Cards

Oracle decks have been in production for a few hundred years (and I touch on a few of the older systems later in this chapter). At the end of the 1900s, there was a marked rise in new divination decks all emblazoned with the word "oracle."

Defining divining

When you hear the word *oracle*, you may generally think of a person, for example the Oracle of Delphi in ancient Greece, whom people go to in order to hear about their future. But the word can also refer to any system of divination, such as bone oracles, dice oracles, and card oracles. Just as the priestess at Delphi is the means by which the divine speaks to the querent, so too does an oracle deck speak to you in its own way.

Tarot is *technically* a kind of oracle deck but when readers use the term today, they mean something different. Most often, an oracle deck is a pack of cards organized around a specific theme. Each card in that deck depicts one facet of this theme. For example, an animal oracle deck may contain cards that feature a horse, an eagle, a dolphin, and so on. Each card is assigned a meaning that communicates a meaningful message to the reader.

Here's the crucial bit: These modern oracle decks are each a unique system containing whichever figures or symbols the author has chosen. While every tarot deck has a Three of Cups, not every oracle deck contains a Horse card. Since there's no official structure in place, every card included in the deck is there at the discretion of the author. Does that mean they're all just made up? Yes, but that's true of every other divination system on the planet. In fact, in Chapter 12, I show you how you can design your own.

Understanding the anatomy of an oracle deck

While each deck is unique, you'll find these features across the board:

>> **Artwork:** This is what draws most people to these decks. Each card centers on a large image illustrating a single aspect of the deck's theme. A few decks out there have only words on them, but for the most part you're drawn to the deck by its attractive artwork.

>> **Title:** This communicates the name of the card. It can be as simple and straightforward as "Horse" or more evocative in a way that communicates some of its meaning to you, such as "Faithful Steed."

>> **Keywords:** Many decks add a single keyword alongside or beneath the card's title to further suggest the meaning of the card. This keyword may spark an immediate intuitive hit for you, and you won't need to look anything up.

>> **Guidebook:** The companion book for any deck contains all the information you need to read with it. Each card has its own entry and these tend to include a few common elements:

● **A description:** This gives you some needed background information on the card's subject. The entry for a Horse card may tell you what the animal is and some of its chief qualities. What the author focuses on here goes a long way toward giving your answer.

● **A divinatory meaning:** This should spell out exactly what the author intends for you to take away from the reading. In most cases, this includes advice for what you should do regarding your question.

● **Affirmations, activities, and rituals:** Some decks take things further by providing ideas for ways you can embody the energy of the card such as an affirmation to recite or meditate on.

Appreciating the Approachability

The community of card readers is a little divided on oracle cards. In the following sections, I take a moment to consider both sides of the same coin.

Acknowledging their foibles

Like many people, I like to say (and have elsewhere in this book) that a person's greatest weakness is their greatest strength pushed too far. This saying can be applied to oracle cards, which have earned a reputation for being a little lightweight for the following reasons:

>> **Their simplistic structure:** Where tarot cards are known for their elemental correspondences, astrological assignments, and mysterious images, oracle cards are much less complex. They're usually ordered alphabetically; if not, they'll have an accompanying number for easy look-up. Some oracle decks have suits but most aren't subdivided into suits or other groupings.

>> **Their dewy-eyed optimism:** In the late 1990s and early 2000s, certain popular talk show hosts were known for featuring new age thinkers and teachers who had a shared message for the world: "You can do anything." Similarly, oracle cards are famous for their emphatically positive messages. But don't you sometimes not get the things you've worked and hoped for? If a deck only knows how to say *yes,* how can it prepare you for *no?*

>> **Their straightforward operation:** You pull a card, you read a single prompt, and you're done! These decks provide a fairly on-rails experience, making the reader a more passive participant in the process.

REMEMBER

This isn't always the case, however. Some decks offer affirmations, rituals, journal prompts, and more to empower you to take the message further. Chapter 12 has more advanced techniques for working with your cards.

Marveling at their strengths

While in college, I worked at a new age bookstore that had a huge set of shelves dedicated to tarot decks and a much smaller space displaying a handful of oracle card decks, mostly featuring angels, fairies, and animals. Yet we sold *way* more oracle cards than we did tarot (I'm not kidding). What made those decks so much more popular? Here are a few reasons:

>> **Bypassing predictions:** I love using cards for prediction, but some days you'd rather not know all the details. If you're about to have an important job interview, would you rather

   a. Hear whether you'll do well or crash and burn?

   b. Receive some encouragement or advice for the conversation?

If you prefer Option b, reach for an oracle deck rather than the tarot.

>> **Providing uplifting messages:** The language most oracle decks use is noticeably gentle and empathetic. One person's dewy-eyed optimism (see the preceding section) is another person's desperately needed reassurance. You may see this approach as naive, but it may also be exactly the thing you need when you're feeling blue. I just think oracle cards have a better bedside manner than tarot some days.

>> **Encouraging a proactive perspective:** Across the board, the message of oracle decks is "This is what you can do." Even when a card centers on conflict or chaos, that information comes packaged with meaningful actions or spiritual practices that you can use to address the issue. They don't leave a reader feeling helpless.

>> **Being less terrifying:** There have been, to date, no horror films in which a mysterious fortune teller lays out cards from an angel inspiration deck to tell the hero they're fated to die or suffer cruel torments. And you won't find many grim reapers or stabbed hearts in oracle decks. Today's culture has, rather unfairly, connected card-reading to messages of doom and gloom.

Oracle cards aren't seen as overtly occult, so they also seem to cause less friction with people's religious beliefs. Many people who may be put off by a Devil card are enchanted by a deck filled with angels.

>> **Having better giftability:** Some of my favorite customers at the new age bookstore where I worked were the cool aunts and uncles who liked supporting their nieces' and nephews' mystical interests while still flying under the parents' radar. I've heard many stories of tarot decks being confiscated by alarmed parents and none about animal oracles getting the boot. These decks are largely considered safe and fun.

>> **Serving as a complete system in a box:** An oracle deck requires no previous knowledge to make it work. In most cases, the system is self-contained. That's both a blessing and a curse, as I explore throughout the chapter, but generally speaking, oracle decks don't have much in the way of hidden or esoteric symbolism for you to uncover.

Selecting Your Oracle Deck(s)

A seemingly infinite variety of oracle decks are on the market today. To be clear, the oracle decks I address are the popular and widely available variety organized around a single theme in which each card is unique. These decks don't belong to any formal tradition or system. Very often, their titles are simply The _____ Oracle.

NOTING A FEW HISTORICAL ORACLES

A few styles of oracle decks out there *do* have very formal systems, like the Lenormand, Kipper, and others. Gaming companies in Europe and the United States developed these systems in the 1700s and 1800s, when they served as a popular pastime in the parlor where friends told each other's fortunes for fun.

These decks have experienced quite the renaissance in the 2000s, largely because of their reputation for making accurate predictions. This comeback came as prediction seemed to have fallen out of favor in the tarot community, which had shifted its focus to psychological interpretations. I credit the revived popularity of these oracle decks for prediction with playing a significant role in renewing the enthusiasm for prediction in tarot.

These systems are lots of fun, but they have their own venerable traditions that don't fit within the scope of this book.

Considering your options

With the tarot, it's easy to say, "Get a Rider-Waite-Smith or a deck that closely follows its structure." (You can read more about the RWS deck in Chapter 2.) No corresponding oracle deck serves as a foundation for hundreds of other decks. For that reason, I can't endorse a single deck for you to use, but I cover some of your options here:

>> **Animals:** Who doesn't love animals? These decks either feature a broad swath of critters on the cards or dive deep with one species (especially cats and dogs). They occasionally draw inspiration from specific cultural traditions but mostly focus on animals' physical traits to derive their meanings. These decks are a great choice for animal lovers and people who want to stay away from anything too mystical.

>> **Spiritual and mythological beings:** The first oracle decks I ever encountered were based on angels and fairies, and they're still wildly popular. To this category, card makers have added deities, dragons, unicorns, and so forth. These cards either depict specific individuals, like Archangel Michael, or characters aligned with a keyword, such as Angel

of Serenity. With their superhuman characters, these decks are wonderfully aspirational and great for anyone wanting to explore their mystical side.

>> **Religious and spiritual traditions:** These decks take inspiration from the symbols and teachings of various religions, including Christianity, Buddhism, and Wicca, as well as broader spiritual practices like light working, Reiki, and so on. These cards may feature actual passages from sacred texts or depictions of sacred objects, holidays, and festivals. They're a great choice for anyone of those faiths or a reader interested in interfaith explorations.

>> **Nature-based (non-animal):** This group encompasses crystals, flowers, herbs, biospheres, celestial bodies, and so on. These decks form an interesting subset of oracles that don't feature people or creatures on them. This aspect makes them a little more challenging to relate to but also more neutral in tone. They're great for the crystal lover, kitchen witch, or any outdoorsy types.

>> **Fiction and entertainment:** Oracle decks have become a popular form of merchandise that celebrates books, films, games, and television series. Officially licensed versions are produced in connection with the creators of those franchises, and fan-made projects abound. Your existing knowledge of and affinity for the characters means that you'll have an easier time deciphering the meanings.

TIP

If you can imagine the deck, then it probably exists. Try a quick Internet search for whatever theme you have in mind. You'll likely find either examples of the exact deck you imagine or conversations in the community about what sorts of decks go well with a particular theme or need.

Choosing your deck(s)

Because of the huge variety in oracle deck themes (which you can read about in the preceding section), narrowing down which deck you want to take home can be tricky. Here's my advice if you haven't gotten an oracle deck yet:

>> **If you have a metaphysical shop in your area, it's likely to have demo copies of its decks for you to try out.** Ask each deck the same question and buy the one whose guidebook

resonates the most with you. The staff members there also likely have their own favorite decks to recommend.

>> **Pick a deck whose art you really love.** If you find the images inspiring, you'll be excited to read with the cards as often as possible.

>> **Limit your categories.** If you're still unsure, pick a deck from one of these three categories: angels, animals, and gods and goddesses. Whichever of those beings you relate to most strongly is the one you should focus on.

TIP

When you're on the fence about a particular oracle deck based on its cover and description, check online. More than likely, you can find one or more videos that provide a review and flip-through of the cards. Additionally, some decks are available as mobile apps, allowing you to explore them thoroughly on your own before purchasing a physical deck.

Creating an Oracle Card Library

This section is the part where I encourage wanton materialism. Each oracle deck has its own particular "voice." Undoubtedly, so do themed tarot decks, but oracle cards — which have longer, more direct messages — give a distinct sense that certain decks are good fits for certain questions and situations.

REMEMBER

You don't need to assemble an entire library of oracle decks before you start. The intention here is to open your mind to the types of decks that may fit into your practice. You can acquire them one at a time, giving you the opportunity to dig in with your latest deck. Oracle decks are also very tradable among your reader friends.

Here are a few categories for which you may want to have a deck:

>> **Seasonal decks:** These decks are either specifically associated with each of the four seasons or just have a "springtime" or "perfect for a summer day at the beach" vibe.

>> **Love-themed decks:** Love questions are second only to "What message do you have for me today?"; therefore, you may want to have a deck or two that fits this category. These options can be decks explicitly created for love topics, erotic decks, or simply decks whose characters you find especially attractive.

>> **Spooky decks:** These decks are for the moments when you're feeling particularly witchy, it's midnight during a thunderstorm, or you want to perform readings concerning the dearly departed. *Remember:* The art for these cards can range from trick-or-treat to truly terrifying.

>> **Decks for healing:** Spiritual and emotional healing are areas where oracle decks excel. These decks have softer imagery and especially gentle guidance in the book.

>> **Heartwarming decks:** This group is similar to the healing category, but these decks emphasize cozy, encouraging energy, not unlike a greeting card. They're a good fit for those tough moments when you're really going through it and need to have your spirit uplifted.

Getting Comfortable Working with Oracle Cards

Despite being so user-friendly and working as intended right out of the box, oracle cards are deceptively challenging to master. One reason is that each deck is completely unique unto itself. Tarot (and the older oracle systems I discuss in the "Noting a few historical oracles" sidebar earlier in this chapter) have a set structure shared across most decks, so plenty of books have been written that deeply explore the cards' meanings. The only resource for oracle decks, however, is the guidebook that comes with the deck. But this is just the beginning.

You've got your deck in hand and you're ready to begin. The following sections outline two different approaches to learning to read with the cards.

Diving deep with your deck

With this approach, you fully explore the ins and outs of a single deck. This task is a big commitment, and you need to focus your attention and energy on just that deck so you can develop a strong bond and learn all your deck's shades and nuances.

Exploring your deck's point of view

Every deck has a voice; some lean noticeably in certain directions. This isn't a weakness! If you think about friends and family members you may go to for advice, you can probably already guess the tone and type of suggestions they'll give. However, knowing this bias is helpful as you work with your deck.

Instead of just opening the guidebook to the passage for a single card, make a point to spend an evening or two reading it from cover to cover. As you read, consider what you're learning about your deck's voice with these questions:

>> What values does it advocate for?

>> What themes or even phrases come up multiple times?

>> Do any cards give opposite meanings?

IT'S IN THE CARDS

If you want to dive deep into your deck, go through it card by card and note the keywords assigned to each in your journal. I grabbed a goddess oracle I enjoy and did this exact exercise.

Inspiration	Kindness	Boundaries
Mothering	Releasing Stress	Energy
Overcoming Self-Doubt	Sexuality	Love and Beauty
Change	Self-Esteem	Intuition
Laughter	Female Empowerment	Abundance
Environmentalism	Home	Health and Healing
Sensuality	Choices	Courage
Death and Rebirth	Inner Peace	Independence
Anger Management	Pleasure	Integrity and Responsibility
Growth	Beliefs	Inner Peace

As you can see, this deck has a strong theme of personal empowerment. That position in its guidebook is crystal clear, so this information isn't a surprise.

With your complete list in front of you, think about which messages are emphasized in the deck, which messages appear infrequently, and which messages don't appear at all. In my optimistic Goddess oracle, I see the following:

>> **Lots of cards encourage you to believe in and accept yourself.** Many cards emphasize the message "Do what you want!"

>> **A very small number of cards challenge the reader.** A few suggest it's time to move on or to channel your energy in a different direction.

>> **No cards suggest that the reader has the wrong idea about a situation.** None of them ask the reader to compromise and give way to another. And none of the cards recommend leading or managing other people or holding back information.

All in all, it's a fairly balanced oracle deck, with a few cards willing to tell you something you don't want to hear; most of the time, however, this deck seeks to encourage and empower you. Oracle decks don't have to be everything to everyone — most people don't go to a steakhouse when they're hungry for a shrimp platter. But it's important for you to know your deck's point of view.

The deck I use in my example can handle most situations, but if I'm genuinely concerned that I may have the wrong idea about something I'll turn to a different one.

Getting your reps in

If your goal is to fully master a particular deck, you should go beyond doing a single card pull for daily wisdom to spend more time with each of the cards in action. Most oracle decks have somewhere between 36 and 52 cards, so you'd need a couple of months before you encountered each of them even once.

TIP

To help find more opportunities to work with the cards, consider turning to the oracle with even the smallest of decisions. You may also let those in your inner circle know you're available to do consultations for them.

If you enjoy the tabloid reading exercise in Chapter 4, it works equally well for Oracle cards. In brief, acquire a tabloid magazine with celebrity gossip and imagine you're reading for the stars being written about. Pull a card and think through how you'd apply its wisdom to the new project, relationship, or breakup in the magazine.

Becoming a "page"-of-all-trades, master of . . . all!

An alternative to becoming a field expert with a particular oracle deck is to release attachment to expertise altogether and embrace the multitude of messages you can gain from an extensive library of oracle decks (and beyond). In this way you benefit from the wisdom of many of perspectives.

This take isn't just an excuse to binge on buying decks, however. This point of view opens you up to receiving information from all corners of the universe. If you follow it, you may find that just about everything around you begins to speak to you.

For more on various deck categories you may want in a broader collection, head to the earlier section "Creating an Oracle Card Library."

Rotating the roster

A key component of this point of view is getting a little taste of so many options. If you pull a card a day or use the activities in Chapter 12, consider limiting each oracle to a week or so of focused use so you become familiar with its style, and then setting it aside to learn from another.

Or let your intuition lead you to a different deck for each question you ask. As you can imagine, this approach is ideal for the person with a stack of oracle decks they haven't yet played with.

Putting decks in conversation with each other

I get into blending systems in Chapter 12, but a great way to begin is to introduce your decks to each other. Some decks have an instant rapport because they follow a similar theme (two nature-based decks, for example), whereas others may combine in an interesting way because of their stark contrasts.

Take two decks that have different tones or points of view — for example, an "animal deck" and a "people deck" or a "light deck" and a "dark deck." Pose the same question to both and lay out one card from each side by side. Consult the meanings in each guidebook and then pause to consider the message between them at the center of the Venn diagram. If you combined these two answers into one, what would it be in a few sentences? The answer may surprise you.

Chapter **12**

Divining with Oracle Cards

'm skeptical when I hear someone assert that something happens 90 percent of the time, but I'm pretty sure that when someone performs an oracle card reading, 90 percent of the time it goes like this:

1. They mix their oracle cards.

2. They pull one card.

3. They read the text from the accompanying guidebook. The End.

You couldn't ask for a simpler process! All the interpretations have been done for you, and the guidebook gives you a nice, compact message. (Head to Chapter 11 for an introduction to oracle cards.) But I believe this simplicity is a trap that can lead to shallow, unmemorable readings that don't amount to much beyond the few minutes you spend with the cards.

The chief issue is how passive the process can be, reading out a set answer with very generalized language. In this chapter, I show you how to take a more active role in this practice, turbocharging your readings by using your intuition and a few innovative techniques.

Doing Your First Oracle Reading

IT'S IN THE CARDS

Try starting your oracle journey by engaging directly with the cards. Grab your favorite deck; ask, "What do I need to be aware of when reading oracle cards?", and then draw a card. Spend a few moments looking at the card and contemplating any keywords written on it before turning to the guidebook. I pulled a card from a Greek mythology deck. I got the goddess Hera, queen of Olympus and long-suffering wife of Zeus. Based on what I already knew about the goddess coupled with the very dignified image of her on the card, I suspected that she had a strong opinion about my commitment to the craft. And here's what I further discovered:

>> The guidebook confirmed that Hera is the patroness of committed relationships of all kinds, especially marriages. This information supported my initial reaction to the card. To deepen my oracle card skills, I must dedicate myself to the practice instead of treating them as a fun sidepiece to the tarot.

>> I also considered how Hera's stories often center on issues of fidelity and monogamy. For me to go far at this point in my path, I'll benefit from deepening my relationship with a single deck rather than trying out multiples. If I'd drawn Zeus instead, that would indicate having fun with as many decks as I can lay my hands on.

Spend a moment with the card you pulled and consider the message it has for you.

Cultivating an Oracular Mindset

When practicing any form of divination, you find the greatest success by balancing these two factors:

>> The rules of the system

>> Your intuitive response

The system's rules create a foundation for you to begin with, but if you don't add in your personal knack for understanding the message, the system will be hollow. On one hand, an oracle deck's "system" is a unique set of cards and official interpretations for them written in the guidebook. But really, the "system" here is deciding to listen to the messages coming to you from the universe, whether that's a divine consciousness or the miracle that is your human consciousness.

The guidebook entry will begin your journey by providing the first part of the answer to your question. By making a connection between that meaning, your unique situation, and the choices available to you, you'll arrive at the answer to your specific question.

Here's an example: Suppose you asked your animal deck about a conflict in your family and the card you pull is the Dog. The guidebook may focus on how canines are faithful friends, and that may feel like a perfect match for your situation. But when you look at the card, you may start thinking that dogs are good at sniffing out problems. You may then conclude that something about your situation isn't passing a smell test and you may suspect you're not being told the truth.

Opening to information

Whether divination works by transmitting mystical information or through the resourcefulness of your clever brain (or both), the process works best if you can reset your usual mode of thinking and become aware of other possibilities.

Beginning with the art

Start by spending a quiet moment taking in all the visual details the artist has provided. How does the image make you feel? Excited? Nervous? Encouraged? This first reaction will tell you a lot about your hopes and fears around the question.

Turning to the text

In this chapter I cover techniques that empower you to go beyond the guidebook, but the guidebook remains an essential component. When you rely purely on intuition, your preconceived notions, biases, hopes, and fears clamor for the steering wheel. Let the wheels of your mind be still for a moment, and read the entry from beginning to end. Notice when any of the words in the passage sparks your interest. Performing this part of the process sets up a gameboard for your intuition, intellect, and emotions to play with.

TIP

The oracle priests and priestesses of the ancient world were known for their dramatic pronouncements of destiny. Don't underestimate the power of the spoken word in this process.

Oracle card guidebooks tend to feature lengthy, densely written blocks of tiny text for each card; busy diviner that you are, you're likely to skim through that text and pull out the juiciest words. Reading this passage aloud forces you to pay attention to every word.

TIP

An even better technique is to have someone else read the guidebook text to you, giving you the opportunity to separate speaker from listener and fully absorb the passage. It also lets your friends and family get a shot at playing diviner.

Listening with intention

A key component to accepting that this little deck of cards can answer your question is accepting that *something* can meaningfully answer your question. Divination requires an inner response to an outer stimulus. Deepen your capacity for receiving wisdom by allowing the world itself to be your oracle.

IT'S IN THE CARDS

As a diviner, you can choose to receive messages from just about anywhere. So that's a good place to start: anywhere. Take a quick trip to a nearby place that's bustling with people and activity (a park, a mall, a coffee shop, or whatever). If possible, put on some headphones and listen to music of your choice when you arrive. Make your way to the center of activity and remove your headphones when the moment feels right. One of the next clearly spoken sentences you hear has a useful message for you. If you feel comfortable pulling an oracle card right there, do so and combine the deck's message with the sentence the universe gifted you. If you don't want to pull cards in public, do this step before you make your trip.

Need more information? Decide that when you leave this place and make your way home, an animal you see will have an extra clue for you, whether it's in the type of animal or its behavior. If it's all still feeling a bit screwy, just write down the experience in your oracle journal (see the following section) and be open to having the message become clearer in the next few days.

Keeping the omens on file

Sometimes an oracle card reading or any other message you receive doesn't resonate right away. You don't need to try to force a square peg into a round hole and turn the message that doesn't add up into an acceptable common-sense answer. Instead, note the reading in your journal and be open to the idea that at some future point, it will click into place when you need it most.

Your oracle journal can be paper or digital, and it can undoubtedly be the same one you keep for your tarot readings (which I explain in Chapter 4) if you're not a notebook-collecting maniac like I am. All you need to note is the following:

>> The date

>> Your question (if you had one)

>> The name of the deck and the card you pulled

>> A couple of sentences in which you reflect on how the message shows up in your life and whether there's any action you plan to take

And that's it! You *don't* need to write out the entire passage from the book; having the card written down means you can return to read it whenever you like. Future-you will benefit from a few concise thoughts about the reading and how you think it applies to this moment.

REMEMBER

Journaling isn't just important so that you'll have a record for later. The process itself forces you to take the fully articulated oracle guidebook answer and distill it down to a message for how the reading applies to your life. You don't need to regularly review your entries to benefit from this process.

Speaking of that journal . . .

I happen to be an excellent tarot journal user. For all the reasons I outline in Chapter 4, I've made a point to write down my readings so I can noodle over their meanings, make predictions, and return to them later for further reflection. I've amassed more than a dozen such journals, and that doesn't include all the readings I've recorded in my notetaking app. In preparation for this chapter, I scanned through them to get insights into my oracle practice.

Tumbleweeds.

I rarely wrote the oracle card readings down because the little guidebook would give me its sermon and I'd nod my head and say, "Ah, yes, that makes sense." And put the oracles back in the box. I'm a divinatory failure! In response to this alarming discovery, I quickly started a spreadsheet to keep track, and it's encouraged me to make oracle card readings a daily practice in the same way tarot has been.

Guarding the gates of your psyche

I once heard a spiritual teacher say, "Your mind is like an oven; if the door's always left open, everything will come out half-baked."

A key element in the exercise in the earlier "Listening with intention" section is that you're *choosing* to be open to receiving a message with a particular intention or question in mind. The gate opens, the information comes through, and the gate closes (with gratitude from the diviner).

WARNING

If you imagine that every conversation you hear and every animal you meet is an omen of vital importance, you'll have a hard time getting through your day. In fact, this sort of thinking can lead to paranoia. A wall covered in papers connected by red strings may not be far behind.

TIP

That's why marrying the exercise to your oracle card readings is helpful. It allows you to be specific about when and why you're becoming aware of omens around you.

Gleaning insights from the process of creating oracle cards

As someone who has had the good fortune to co-create several oracle card decks, I want to share a few insights into that process that may help you make more sense of your readings. Here are two methods publishers use:

1. The author dreams up a new deck, imagining the scene that will appear on each card to convey a meaning they have in mind. If they're not illustrating the cards themselves (they usually aren't), they collaborate with an artist to create the deck card by card together.

2. The guidebook author receives a PDF file from the publisher with all the images for a new deck. The author's job is to name each card, decide what each means, and write out the entries for the guidebook.

I've used both methods, and the existence of that second process tells you two things:

>> **Just like with tarot, oracle cards don't necessarily have a single correct, intended answer.** The artist was making an interesting image that the guidebook writer responded to.

>> **Your resourceful guidebook writer used some techniques to arrive at the meaning of the card.** You can use those same techniques to wring further wisdom out of the image.

These strategies are like those used to interrogate a tarot card but without the added benefit of suits, numbers, and more than 200 years of tradition.

Select a card you find a little challenging from your oracle deck (or pick one at random) and consider each of the techniques in the following sections.

Taking things literally

Begin by considering the image from a purely literal standpoint. You're not allowed to infer anything not made explicit in the image. For instance, if your oracle deck used the famous painting *Washington Crossing the Delaware,* you'd note the design of the boat; the number, dress, and actions of the various men in the picture; and the presence of a flag. What *isn't* literal about this image is the identity of the man standing in the middle of the boat, the name of the body of water, the reason these men are in the boat in the first place, the war they're fighting, and so on.

REMEMBER

By cataloging only the elements you can see on the card itself, you notice so many more small details in the piece. Is every single one of these details intentionally placed there by the artist to convey meaning? No. The butterfly hovering over the bush in the background of the picture may be there because the artist thought it'd be pretty. But if "butterfly" sparks an idea for you that relates to your question, this element can be meaningful in this reading.

Finally, considering these literal elements reveals how many assumptions you're making about the picture. If you see a character holding a key, your brain may naturally leap to the conclusion that they're about to unlock something. But they may just as easily be locking something away, passing the key to another person, or checking out a key they just found on the floor. Think about why you arrived at the conclusion you did.

Homing in on the title or keywords

The titles and keywords do a lot of heavy lifting in an oracle deck. If the title is simply the name of the character, animal, or object on the card, then the accompanying keywords are going to help narrow down your focus with this card. An animal oracle with a Spider card can go in so many directions; if the author chose "artistic weaver," that tells you the vibe they want you to be in when you look at the card.

IT'S IN THE CARDS

If a card's meaning doesn't seem to resonate, or if you want to consider a card more broadly, one method is to give it a new title. The Spider card can also be "Skilled Huntress," "Threshold Guardian," "Venomous Bite," "The Watcher," "Unexpected Visitor" — you get the idea.

Consider the card you chose from your oracle deck. What other titles can you bestow upon it? Think of how you can take the card in a completely different direction with new names or keywords. You're not tossing out the original; you're adding to its scope. This exercise opens up a range of possibilities for what the card can mean in your reading.

Considering the minute differences

One of the most challenging aspects of writing a guidebook meaning for an oracle card is that sometimes other cards in the deck seem almost identical. This situation is very common in a deck where all the figures share a common theme (witches, mermaids, dragons, or whatever).

For example, if you're working on the guidebook for a deck that features both a Hawk card and a Falcon card, you may find yourself perplexed. But these minor differences add a ton of meaning to the card. Doing a quick bit of research, I learned that hawks glide over their prey, and falcons use powerful wingbeats to make high-speed dives. Thus, the cards both indicate pursuing your goal, but one recommends a graceful or elegant approach and the other suggests much more aggressive maneuvers.

IT'S IN THE CARDS

Set the card you're considering on the table and then look through your deck for any other cards that seem very similar to it in tone or nature. Arrange them around your card and think about all the ways it stands apart from the rest. For each of these differences, think of one way that would change your answer to a question if you pulled the different card instead.

Asking yourself questions

Whether you're the oracle card reader or the guidebook writer, you sometimes find yourself staring down at a card and trying to make heads or tails of its meaning. In those moments, a very effective method to uncover layers of meaning is to allow yourself to start to wonder about the card.

Effectively, this process is the opposite of the literal scan I discuss in the earlier section "Taking things literally." It's entirely subjective, and you can follow any aspect of the image that catches your interest.

If the card features a character, you may wonder

>> What happened to them yesterday?

>> What do they seem to want?

>> What will happen if they do or don't get it?

>> What would it feel like to be them for a day?

>> What would they say to me if I were with them now?

For a card that has an object instead, you may ask questions like these:

>> Who created this object?

>> What would holding it feel like?

>> What would I do with it?

>> Who might I give it to, and why?

These questions don't need to result in immediate revelation. If the answer doesn't spark your curiosity further, let it float away and move onto the next one.

Finding Unexpected Ways to Work with Oracle Cards

The more you read oracle cards, the more their hidden versatility will start to reveal itself to you, and you'll find yourself taking them beyond card-of-the-day inspiration. In this section, I show you unique ways to weave them into your practice.

Blending oracle cards with tarot

As close cousins, the tarot and oracle cards get along swimmingly. As a team, their individual strengths complement each other, and their structural differences allow them to play different roles in a reading.

Picking an oracle significator

Rather than searching through the court cards for a significator (which is the card that represents you in the reading), consider drawing one from an oracle deck. This card describes your perspective when entering into the reading. Note how the vibes of the tarot cards compare or contrast with the significator.

TIP

In practice, tarot and oracle decks that share a similar mood or theme go especially well together. For example, maybe you pair an animal oracle with a nature themed tarot or put your spookiest deck in each category in conversation with one another.

Complementing a troublesome tarot card

In practice, pulling clarifying cards in a tarot reading can feel like just trying to replace a card you don't like with a new one. But if you find yourself puzzling over a tarot card, ask an oracle deck, "How can I best make use of this wisdom?", and then let its naturally proactive message give you additional guidance.

Serving as a chaser to a tarot reading

When I work as a tarot reader at a party or other event, I keep an oracle deck on the table. If a reading is particularly profound or revealing, the air sometimes holds a slight tension afterward, with the querent unsure of what they're supposed to do next. To keep things flowing, you just ask them to pull a single oracle card for some parting wisdom. This move always relieves that tension and conveys to the querent that the reading has ended.

Because you're not going to have time to read entire passages from a guidebook, be sure to use an oracle deck you're intimately familiar with for this exercise so you can condense the message down to a couple of sentences.

Enhancing interactions

Because oracle decks are so user-friendly, they fit easily into group settings where people who aren't experienced readers can get in touch with their mystical side by pulling a card.

Elevating check-ins

If you have a spiritual group, book club, or any other gathering that begins with people checking in on what they've been up to, have each of them pull an oracle card. Let the person seated to their right turn to the appropriate page in the guidebook and read out the entry for that card. The querent then reflects on how the card matches their check-in and what's been going on with them.

I suggest removing any intense or potentially confronting cards from the deck before you begin. People are already in the spotlight during these moments, and keeping the cards lighter helps make that situation less nerve-wracking.

Offering DIY fortune-telling at your next soiree

If you leave a deck of tarot cards out on a table at a party, your guests rarely give them a whirl because they "don't know how to use them." Conversely, a fan of oracle cards on a table with the accompanying guidebook is more approachable, and you may notice your guests trying them out individually or in small groups. I recommend posting a small sign saying "Pick a Card, Read Your Fortune" on the table.

Gifting wisdom

If you acquire a second copy of one of your favorite oracle decks, you can offer individual cards from it to friends and family as a simple guidepost they can take home and display prominently where it will continue to inspire them.

For this idea to work, choose an oracle deck that features a prominent keyword they can reflect on. Mini-decks are especially useful here because they often have their meanings written on the back rather than in a booklet.

Creating Your Own Oracle Cards

Sure, hundreds of oracle decks are already available, but why not one more? If you wish someone would make a deck about [insert your topic here], why can't you be that someone? If I can do it, you can do it!

The focus in this section is on creating a unique tool for your own use, and I consider how to utilize existing images if you don't have the artistic skills to illustrate them yourself.

WARNING

If you do decide that you want to publish your deck, don't use any images you don't have the rights to or create a deck based on a copyrighted property, like a show or film series, that you'd need to license to avoid legal dilemmas.

Thinking about your theme

You'll have the best success if you create your oracle system around something you're intimately familiar with. Doing so allows you to have enough cards in your system for it to have meaningful distinctions. Your theme is the connecting current that runs through the entirety of your deck. When choosing a theme, you have two options:

>> **Going broad:** This approach involves creating cards that represent many individual characters of a type, like all the heroes and villains from a particular superhero comic universe. Each of these cards would feature a different character, and the interpretation would center on what makes them stand out in their category.

>> **Going deep:** This angle entails creating cards that represent the many facets or aspects of a theme. For example, if you wanted to make a bee oracle, your cards would depict many scenes from bees' lives with objects like hives, honey, and flowers, as well as cards showing the various members of a bee colony and their life cycles.

Either works if you have enough to say about your theme to fill a deck with unique cards that give different pieces of advice. No rule dictates a set number of cards an oracle deck needs to have, but most seem to run between 36 and 52 cards.

Something you need to consider is the pervasive vibe of your theme and the impact it has on the images. When I created a just-for-fun oracle deck from a set of Star Wars trading cards, I quickly realized that a huge number of the images showed people in peril, fighting, or trying to escape. That vibe creates a wonderful tension for the films, but it meant that a lot of the cards were speaking to conflict.

This observation paid off years later when I was asked to write the guidebook for a deck based on Homer's *The Odyssey*. Once again, most of the images showed scenes of danger, combat, and sailing. I had to find a way to reframe the action of the cards to scenarios that are more common for mere mortals.

Assembling the images

If you're an illustrator, you can create the exact images you want for your cards. If you're not skilled at drawing, you need to get scrappy and crafty.

If cards for the theme you have in mind are already available (like the Star Wars trading cards from my example in the preceding section), you're in luck; most of the work has been done for you. However, note that this tactic does restrict you to using only the characters and images on those cards.

If cards don't exist yet, a very easy method to create your deck is to find images online and resize them to the dimensions of a poker deck. You can then print the images and glue them to an inexpensive pack of playing cards so that you have a nice, uniform deck that's easy to shuffle. Blank tarot decks are also commercially available if you want a taller image.

Companies that make collectible card games sell sets of plastic sleeves to protect your valuable cards when you play with them. These are available at most game stores and come with opaque backs in an array of colors or with fun imagery. They're a great way to make your DIY deck easier to shuffle.

If you want to add titles or keywords to your cards, an electronic label maker will be your friend.

Printing professionally

If the idea of cutting out images and gluing them together doesn't get you excited, you can turn to the pros for help instead. On the Internet, you can find a few companies that specialize in creating and printing custom playing cards in small batches. These sites offer templates you can use to size your images and add titles. If you're interested in going the professional printing route, keep a few things in mind:

>> **To create a high-quality product, these services may require you to upload large, high-resolution images.** If you're illustrating them yourself, be sure you know the necessary dimensions for the images. If you're using found images, you may need to work harder to source larger files.

>> **If your deck is based on a copyrighted or trademarked theme, the printer may reject your project.** Be sure you know that *before* you've made 50 cards with that printer's template.

>> **The cost to print per deck will be higher if you're ordering a small number of them.** Order at least two copies just in case a card gets lost or damaged.

Assigning meanings

Assuming that you aren't planning to publish your deck, you don't need to write out a full guidebook for it because only you and your friends will be using it. Still, you want to spend some time with your full set of cards so that you can think through what each of them will mean in a reading.

A very straightforward template to follow is to look at each card and think through these questions:

>> What does it mean to be more like _____?

>> How would _____ solve problems?

>> What does _____ usually do, and what would they never do?

>> When am I most like and most unlike _____?

Taking your deck for a spin

After you've assembled your amazing little oracle deck, have some fun with it by giving readings to yourself as well as your friends and family.

If they share your affinity for your deck's theme, you can discover new insights by letting them drive the reading and sharing what the cards say to them. Getting this outside perspective is a handy way to keep your personal preferences and biases from making every card sound like the type of advice you prefer to give.

REMEMBER

Because this is your system, you can always add more cards to it or ditch the ones that didn't feel particularly meaningful when they came up.

Chapter **13**

Selecting an Oracle Spread

The bread-and-butter oracle card experience is pulling a single card to answer your question. Most guidebooks are written with this assumption, so they're wordy and direct with their advice.

But why should tarot have all the fun with fancy layouts? In this chapter, I show you how to beef up your one-card readings and find a few fun spreads designed specifically for oracle cards.

Maximizing Your One-Card Pulls

Spreads are great, but they aren't the only way to take your oracle practice to the next level. In the following sections, I spend a moment with the humble one-card reading and consider how to kick it up a notch.

Beginning your day with divination

Have you noticed how so many people are obsessed with creating the perfect morning regimen? On top of the usual showering and teeth brushing, it often involves exercising, engaging with an array of skincare products, and feeding a preferred caffeine addiction. Some people add spiritual reflection to their a.m. rituals.

Oracle cards are a perfect addition to your morning habits because they offer gentle guidance that may sustain you throughout the day.

Drawing cards at dawn

A very useful practice is making your oracle card pull the very first thing you do when you wake up. If you keep the deck you're working with on your nightstand, you can draw a card for the day's wisdom. Bonus: Doing so means you get a couple of extra minutes under the covers as you read through the guidebook entry for your card.

Pulling the card first allows you to mull over its meaning as you hop in the shower or enjoy your cup of coffee. It's likely to be a less taxing subject to keep top of mind than any stressful items on your agenda that may otherwise dominate your daily prep time.

TIP

You can keep your oracle card central to your morning experience by using a place card or photo folder clip to display it prominently next to your mirror or wherever you spend your time getting ready. If you do use this method, just be sure that the style of clip doesn't damage your card and that you keep the card out of the splash zone if it's in your bathroom. If the card can follow you to your work in some way and continue to serve as a source of inspiration, then so much the better.

Supporting other spiritual habits

Some folks already carve out extra time in their mornings for reflective practices like meditation and bullet journaling. Your daily oracle card can serve as a handy prompt for those activities, either by being the focus for them or by helping spark another idea about what to focus on.

Making today special

Perhaps you've occasionally felt like your days are a humdrum routine, with each day consisting of the same unremarkable tasks as the one before. Pulling an oracle card banishes that sense of monotony by declaring that today isn't the same as yesterday; it's Compassion, Healing, Cleverness, Facing Fear, Union, or whatever else your card's keyword indicated.

In the evening, the card you pulled can provide one more opportunity for reflection as you think back on the day's events and wonder where that card surfaced in your experience.

Like any spiritual habit, a card-of-the-day practice doesn't live or die by a perfect track record. No one who forgets to brush their teeth because they're rushing concludes, "Well, that's it: Oral hygiene just isn't for me." If you miss a day, just pick it up again tomorrow.

Embodying the archetype

Another way to enhance your one-card pulls is to use a bit of creative visualization to *become* the card you draw, whether it features a person, an object, or an ideal. This approach works whether you're turning to the deck to answer a question or just to receive wisdom.

Identifying with the oracle

When you pull a card, take a moment to verbalize everything you see in the image as if it were you. For example, if your oracle card depicts the Statue of Liberty, you may say things like these:

>> I wear a crown and robe.

>> I hold up a blazing torch.

>> I look out on the vast ocean.

>> I welcome people to my shores.

>> I'm a sign of hope and possibility.

As you make each of these statements, take a moment to feel them within your body and mind. Hold up that torch, and receive that gratitude or adulation from the people below.

When you're suffused with this alternate sense of yourself, think about the question you asked (if applicable) and consider what actions this other you may take.

To continue the example, you may wonder

>> How would Lady Liberty help my friend?

>> How would Lady Liberty find the love of her life?

>> What would Lady Liberty never do when in conflict with my mother?

Crafting effective affirmations

A really great way to take the wisdom you receive from your oracle card and create genuine change in your situation is to compose a simple affirmation that you can recite whenever your mind turns to the subject of the reading.

Affirmations are easy to assemble, and your oracle guidebook may even offer one you can use or modify slightly to fit your situation. When you're crafting affirmations, keep a few simple rules in mind. For these affirmations, I use the Statue of Liberty example from the preceding section and center specifically on the value of liberty:

>> **Begin with *I*.** To make your statement an affirmation and not a wise aphorism, always start off by personalizing it with *I*.

>> **Use present tense language.** Saying "I will be free" means this affirmation is true for some future version of yourself. Saying "I am free" means it's true of you today.

>> **Stick to positive language.** If you say "I have no chains on me," you're going to picture chains. "I do as I please" doesn't conjure up those restrictions.

>> **Make them exciting.** You're allowed to be larger than life with your affirmations and use bold words that energize you. "I am powerful and create a remarkable life filled with the things that bring me joy and vitality."

>> **Keep them short.** Less is more, and less is memorable.

Exploring New Layouts

This section dives into the higher math of working with oracle card spreads. In theory, you can use the same tarot card spreads in Chapters 7 and 9 with your oracle decks, but a few key differences between the systems mean you get more mileage out of spreads designed with oracle cards in mind.

Here are a few distinctions you may notice:

>> **Oracle cards don't tend to emphasize prediction.** For this reason, you don't find too many positions like "forces outside of your control" or "the ultimate outcome."

>> **Oracle cards are action-oriented.** Given the more direct, advice-centered (ahem, occasionally preachy) nature of oracle cards, most positions focus on what you and others can do right now.

>> **Oracle spreads are shorter.** Asking an oracle deck a question is like asking a friend for their opinion or advice. Think about what it's like to ask too many of your friends to weigh in on a situation. I keep the spreads in the following sections limited to three or four cards at most.

The Body, Mind, and Spirit spread

This spread examines three of your "selves" separately to check in on what each of them needs. Imagine that these three different parts of your being have an opportunity to speak with you, advocating on their behalf through the cards (see Figure 13-1):

1. **Body:** Your physical needs and anything that will promote your continued health and vital energy

2. **Mind:** Your psychological needs and thoughtful strategies for mental health and well-being

3. **Spirit:** Your soul's needs, your connection with your experience of the divine, and advice to promote spiritual growth

The placement of the cards intentionally mirrors *Maslow's Hierarchy of Needs*, a psychological theory that explains how people prioritize needs. Although spiritual types are often most excited for what's indicated in position 3, you have to remember your body's needs. When you manage to support your body, you can focus your time and attention on having your mind in tip-top shape. *Then* you'll have the freedom to focus on spirit.

IT'S IN THE CARDS

This spread is a perfect opportunity to try out a more mystical form of shuffling and choosing the cards. Shuffle your cards and fan them out on the table before you. Now rub your palms together as quickly as possible for about 30 seconds, causing them to generate a small amount of static.

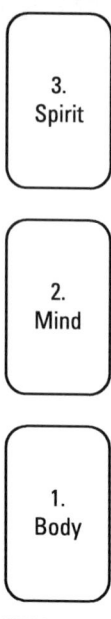

FIGURE 13-1: Explore your whole self with the Body, Mind, and Spirit spread.

Slowly wave your nondominant hand (if you're right-handed, that means your left hand) over the fan of cards and feel the static waver between you and the deck. Use this feeling to select three cards:

>> A card that seems to make your hand heavier and draw it down toward the deck is the card for Body.

>> A card that seems to oscillate between gently pulling your hand down and pushing it up is the card for Mind.

>> A card that seems to make your hand rise above the table is the card for Spirit.

You may need to rub your hands together between cards to recreate the feeling of static electricity.

The Heart to Heart spread

This layout is an ideal spread for anyone looking for insights into improving a relationship. You'll most likely use it for romantic readings, but of course you can apply it to any interpersonal relationships. It calls for three cards (see Figure 13-2):

1. **Your needs:** This card speaks to how to achieve your desires within the relationship. It shows what may be best for you specifically.

2. **Their needs:** This card indicates what would be most helpful for your partner at this time and would help them achieve their goals.

3. **The relationship's needs:** This position imagines the relationship itself to be a third entity and describes the perspectives and actions that will help it to thrive (and that require the participation of both of you together).

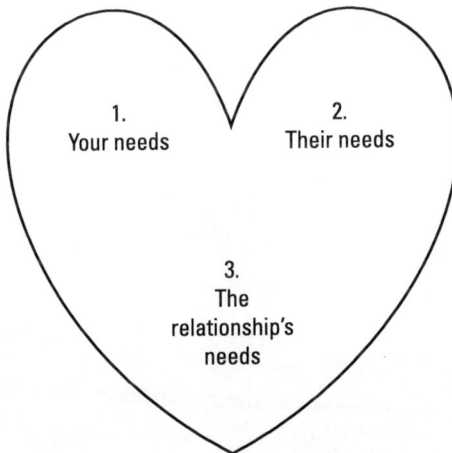

FIGURE 13-2: The Heart to Heart spread is ideal for exploring all types of relationships.

Having a couple perform a relationship spread together with the tarot takes courage because that system has images of hearts stabbed with swords and despondent people crying over spilled cups. Oracle cards are, for the most part, much more positive or encouraging in tone, so you're less likely to regret performing this reading with your special someone. To choose the third card, let one person shuffle and the other cut the deck. This reading can make for an intimate ritual on your next date night; you can follow it up by sharing a meal together, during which you discuss each of your cards and how you can both support the vision suggested by the final card.

TIP

If you're performing this reading for more than two people, in theory you can draw additional cards to represent the various connections between each pair of people. But given how chatty oracle guidebooks tend to be, that may take all night to get through. Let that last card speak to the entire group.

The Do's and Don'ts spread

This one is exactly the same as the Do's and Don'ts spread featured in Chapter 9. You can't beat a classic! This one requires just two cards (obviously; see Figure 13-3):

1. **Do:** Take this approach.

2. **Don't:** Avoid this approach. As you read from the guidebook, you can audibly insert a "don't" at the beginning of the sentences.

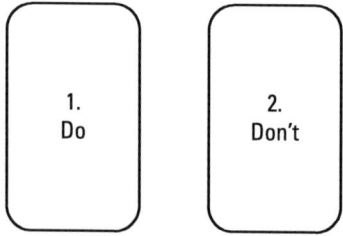

FIGURE 13-3: The Do's and Don'ts spread — simple but effective.

REMEMBER

You may be asking, "Why do I need the second card if the first one tells me what to do?" The key here is to identify the actions to avoid *while* you're pursuing the path outlined by Do. These are the things you may do in tandem (possibly without noticing) that can undermine your success.

The Dialectical Reasoning spread

Dialectical reasoning is a way of comparing and contrasting two opposing ideas (the *thesis* and *antithesis*) toward reconciling them into one solution (the *synthesis*). This spread is great for getting a complete 360-degree view of a subject. In a way, using this one is a bit like combining the Heart to Heart spread with the Do's and Don'ts spread. Combining spreads together is how baby oracle spreads are made. These are the positions (see Figure 13-4):

1. **Thesis:** This piece speaks to the strategy for success that seems most ideal for you.

2. **Antithesis:** This card suggests a viewpoint in opposition to the Thesis. After reading the guidebook entry, consider how the first two cards most clash or differ.

3. **Synthesis:** This position suggests an alternative view or path that can marry the best parts of the first two cards together.

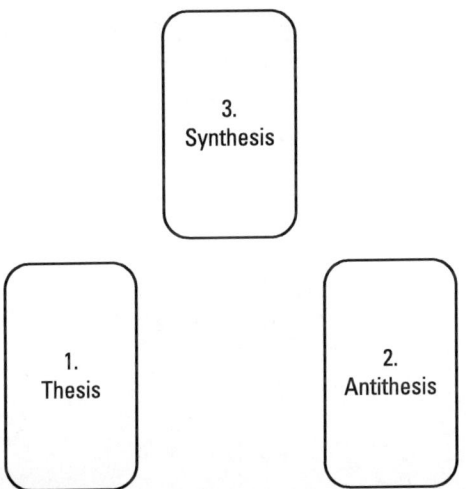

FIGURE 13-4: Take a 360-degree view of a subject with the Dialectical Reasoning spread.

The Messages from the Four Directions spread

This spread taps into the elemental correspondences of the four suits of the tarot, as well as some folklore associated with the directions themselves. (Head to Chapter 3 for details on the tarot suits and their elements.)

The goal of the spread (shown in Figure 13-5) is to support a life in balance. If you want, you can make a small ritual of this reading by moving around your table as you draw each card so you can face that direction:

1. **Wisdom of the East:** This position suggests the steps you can take to create a new beginning in your life and how to

release attachment to aspects of your past that no longer serve you.

2. **Wisdom of the South:** This position indicates what you can do to fuel your passion. It may show you how to achieve ambitions you've suppressed out of fear.

3. **Wisdom of the West:** This position signifies the community of people in your life that love and support you and how to deepen those relationships.

4. **Wisdom of the North:** This last position makes you aware of how you can prepare for unseen adversity you'll encounter in your journey. Symbolically, it's concerned with what must be done to prepare for the harshness of winter.

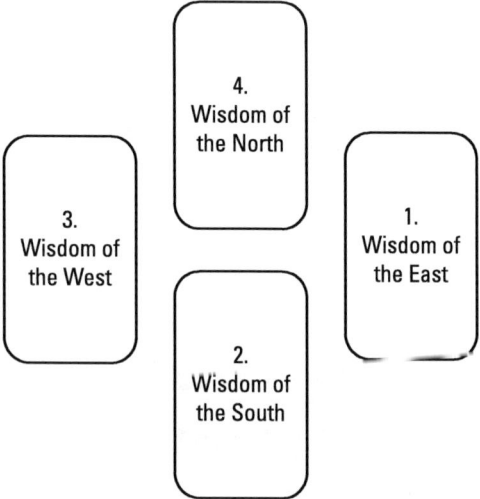

FIGURE 13-5: Tap into the elements with the Messages from the Four Directions spread.

You may be tempted to place a fifth card in the center of the spread. Don't do it! You're already at the center of the reading (especially if you've faced the four directions throughout the reading). A central card may steal too much focus from the other four because it seems to be the most important. Also, remember the wisdom of not asking too many different people for advice.

The Metamorphosis spread

This spread may look suspiciously like the tarot past-present-future Three-Card spread from Chapter 7. It *is* similar, but the key difference is that while the tarot spread focuses on events that have happened or will happen to you, this spread considers the personal transformations you've made in your journey. It takes you from your time as a pupa to the transitional chrysalis you find yourself in to the beautiful butterfly or moth that will soon emerge.

Saying each position name out loud will deepen the personal connection you feel with the cards (see Figure 13-6).

1. **I have been:** This card shows key aspects of yourself that have contributed to creating the life you now have. It can show lost parts of you that you miss and may want to recover.

2. **I am:** This card acknowledges the moment you're in and the challenges you now face. It points to what needs to be resolved to clear the way for growth.

3. **I am becoming:** This card gives a preview of what lies ahead for you on your current trajectory. It will most likely be aspirational and provide you with a guiding star to move toward. If it seems like a warning from the Ghost of Christmas Yet to Come instead, consider the messages from cards 1 and 2 to find a way to alter that journey.

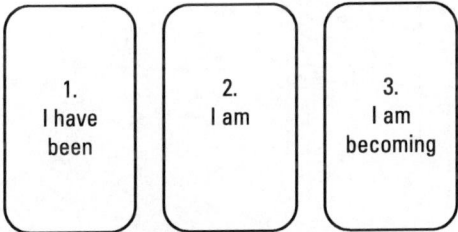

FIGURE 13-6: Reflect on personal transformation with the Metamorphosis spread.

The Sacred Gifts spread

This cozy reading lets you explore your relationship with yourself and others and what you contribute through your words, deeds, and beliefs. The Sacred Gifts spread, shown in Figure 13-7, is a lovely spread to use around the holidays, your birthday, or other moments of major transition. It can also be a great way to help another person recognize their significance in the world. Let them pull the cards and then, holding as much eye contact as is comfortable for you both, describe the difference they make:

1. **My gift to myself:** This position gives insights into how your actions are contributing to your current life and what needs you may be ignoring. It's an especially important card for people who tend to put their focus on others before they think of themselves.

2. **My gift to my circle:** This explores your connection with the people you interact with directly. It affirms the impact you make on your friends and family and may also highlight hidden needs that others aren't voicing.

3. **My gift to the world:** This card speaks to the difference you make to the people you don't necessarily know. It can show the mark you're making on the world and the legacy you're meant to leave. It may also indicate your more superhuman qualities.

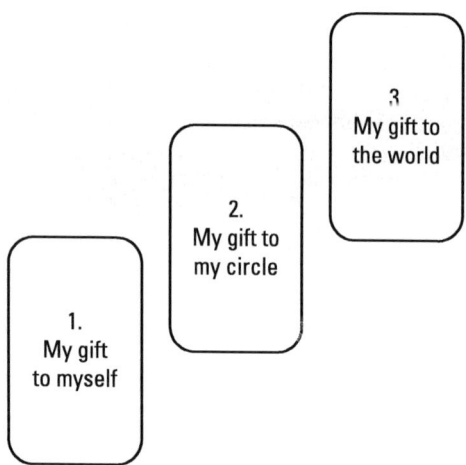

FIGURE 13-7: Use the Sacred Gifts spread to recognize your unique gifts.

5

The Part of Tens

IN THIS PART . . .

Understand the beliefs and habits that can impede your progress as a reader.

Get insights from real-world experience in the card reading space.

Chapter **14**

(More Than) Ten Behaviors That Limit New Readers

L earning *cartomancy* (card reading) is a challenging — but rewarding — undertaking! Beginners get in their own ways sometimes and can sabotage their experiences. In this chapter, I provide a quick list of tendencies that can stunt your growth.

Expecting Clairvoyance

In the movies and late-night psychic hotline commercials, readers have absolute certainty. They just need one glance at the cards to see your whole future in HD. Compared with their example, a very strong hunch seems pedestrian. When you start out, though, a strong hunch is plenty.

Heeding Unhelpful Taboos

Be suspicious of the words *always* and *never.* You can add any layers of ritual or mystery to your practice if they're genuinely meaningful to you. Still, you can also read for yourself during a lunar eclipse with a deck you purchased and haven't kept wrapped in black silk. For more unhelpful myths, see Chapter 2.

Giving Your Deck Human Feelings

You'll form energetic bonds with decks you use very often, and they may become sacred tools. But they don't have petty human responses. In other words, no, your deck isn't mad at you or trying to trick you/teach you a lesson.

Disqualifying the Reading

Perhaps you shuffled incorrectly, or your mind was on something else. *That* must be why this reading can't possibly be right!

REMEMBER

You asked for an answer and got one. If you toss it back because you don't like it, all you're left with is doubt. You can't do much with doubt.

This holds true for *clarifying cards,* a term for extra cards that readers pull when they're confused about a card's meaning. Most often they're pulled because you wanted a different answer. You don't often end up with more clarity.

Overreading a Card

The cards have a multitude of complex meanings, and some of them have dramatic artwork. But their meanings usually manifest in simple, straightforward ways. It's *possible* that the King of Swords refers to a ruthless tactician who plays four-dimensional chess with their opponents, has become a renowned expert in their field, and is also a Libra. They may just be a smart leader, though.

Not Engaging with the Querent

You may feel a lot of pressure to say astoundingly accurate things that will impress your querent. You might worry that asking the querent questions during the reading will make you seem like a con artist or an inept reader. I made the mistake many times of being certain of a particular meaning or narrative and running with it, getting all the way to the end, and finding out it didn't apply to the querent's situation.

REMEMBER

When you make a statement about the meaning of a card, especially at the beginning of a reading, it's okay to ask if that resonates with their situation before moving on. And if they tell you that you're heading down the wrong path, you learn more from the experience by taking their word for it and backing up a step than by insisting you know better. Sometimes they just don't want to hear the truth, but usually they're trying to help you.

Engaging with Unkind Skeptics

Skepticism is healthy and warranted. Rudeness isn't. If someone is insisting that divination is a scam and you're either a fraud or a simpleton for reading cards, there's really no point in continuing to engage with them. They usually aren't won over by demo readings. It's their loss.

This type of querent — who I often call the Mythbuster — is part of my rogues' gallery that I discuss in Chapter 5.

Reading without a Spread

Single card pulls are great, but when you have a line of cards in front of you with no rhyme or reason, you're working too hard. Spreads provide you with structure and give you the language to formulate an answer to your question. I cover working with spreads in Chapter 7.

Turning to Others for Answers Too Quickly

You'll find a lot of posts in online cartomancy groups that consist of a picture of five or so cards accompanied by the statement "Help, I don't know what this means!" Groups often require that posts include a good faith attempt at interpretation because you'll never learn if you always ask others to figure it out for you. When in doubt, try the "If you did know the answer, what would you say?" exercise from Chapter 8.

Buying Too Many Decks Right Away

Tarot and oracle decks are amazing works of art, and it's great to collect the ones you like whether you plan to read with them or not. Excitement for your new craft and some extra pressure from social media might encourage you to buy lots of them right away. But when you're starting out, it's useful to hone your skills with just a few decks that you'll become intimately familiar with. This builds the muscles that enable you to read with dozens of decks later on.

Growing Too Fast

Thanks to the popularity of video-based social media platforms, an alarming number of readers are going from purchasing their first decks to becoming professional readers in a few weeks. Give yourself time to develop your practice.

Going It Alone

The card reading community is a welcoming group of people. Encountering other readers and sharing your skills with them will open your eyes to a world of possibilities. Online groups connect you to readers around the world as well as in-person gatherings and conferences. Find your people.

Major tarot conferences you might want to check out in the United States include Reader's Studio in New York, New York; the Northwest Tarot Symposium in Portland, Oregon; and StaarCon in Palm Beach, Florida.

In the United Kingdom, the Tarot Association of British and International members (TABI) holds multiple gatherings for readers.

Chapter **15**

Ten Lessons I Learned at the Table

've had the good fortune to read cards professionally in a range of different settings, from private readings to Renaissance fairs to large corporate parties. This chapter offers ten things I learned along the way that no books had prepared me for. Even if you don't plan to go pro or charge for readings, you may find something useful in this list.

If You Read It, They Will Come

A lot of people who'd never seek out and pay for readings get curious when they happen upon you and your cards unexpectedly. When I've started shuffling a deck or mentioned that I'm a reader, I've gotten a line of people in cafes, bars, campuses, online role-playing games, dating apps, workplaces, public transportation, and everywhere else. Be fearless, and you'll get to practice your craft. (And even if you don't charge for the reading, you may get free drinks!)

They'll Ask You Anything

I'd done readings about finding love, career growth, and the future in general, but nothing prepared me for many questions querents asked me. I didn't imagine being asked about selling businesses, running for office, fertility issues, deceased relatives, past lives, otherworldly contacts, sports championships, and so much more.

REMEMBER

You can absolutely refuse to take any question you feel is inappropriate. Still, most days, I prefer to be of service to the person sitting across from me. Even with health readings — the trickiest of the bunch — remember you aren't being asked for a diagnosis. People have diverse teams of advice-givers, from medical professionals to fellow patients to friends and family. You're one member of their team telling them what they can do for their highest good.

Stay Nimble

When you read at large parties or other events with a long line of querents, you need to deliver readings quickly. The gold standard is five minutes per reading. I'm not kidding — five minutes. As you hone your skills to meet this time limit, you'll discover that delivering direct and succinct answers makes your readings more confident and more memorable. Here are a few pro tips for trimming down the process in these settings:

>> Shuffle the cards yourself as they ask their question and let them pick from a fan of cards.

>> Use either the Foresight and Action spread (see Chapter 7) or the Do's and Don'ts spread (see Chapter 9).

>> If the querent doesn't immediately have a question, just say, "Let's see what comes up," and give a general reading. They'll quickly understand what it relates to.

You Can't Control What People Hear

I've occasionally had a querent tell a friend that I gave them an amazing reading . . . but the reading they describe isn't what I told them. Sometimes it's the opposite! Everything you say goes through the querent's many internal filters and biases. Your job is to deliver the message you get; they can do with it what they will.

All Your Knowledge Comes into Play

You may think the path to expertise is to read increasingly more complex books on *cartomancy* (card reading). But your answers to questions will come from the vast database of information and wisdom you've accumulated throughout your life.

The cards spark inspiration and point in certain directions, but the things you've learned about business strategy, psychology, dating advice, and pretty much everything in the self-help section are what provide you with the vocabulary your querent needs to actually make use of the insights the cards offer. You'll turn over a card, and something you learned from a TED Talk, your kindergarten teacher, or a magazine quiz will pop into your mind.

So all you need to do is become an expert on everything. Good luck!

Some People Have Tarot Trauma

They got a reading once from someone less skilled or less ethical than you — perhaps an overzealous teenager or a scam reader. That reader told them something upsetting that still haunts them. As a good ambassador for card readers everywhere, you have the opportunity to correct this issue and show them what a helpful reading looks like. Having a trusty oracle deck on hand is a great, gentle approach for these folks and for any curious types who are wigged out by tarot.

They'll Show You Things You've Never Seen Before

A card reader is always learning, and a significant source of knowledge comes from the querents themselves. They see symbols on the cards you've somehow missed. They make connections in the meanings that you never considered. The new meanings that arise from these readings get added to the "mulch" that is your collective knowledge of the cards. For this reason, never be afraid to ask your querent, "What do you see in the card?"

Sometimes, They Just Want to Talk to Someone

In most sessions, you'll lead the conversation, but occasionally you'll get someone chatty (the Chatterbox from Chapter 5's rogues' gallery). They may be talkative by nature, they may be very nervous or enthusiastic about the topic they asked you about, they may just want to kvetch, or they may be lonely. Let them talk! While they're speaking, mentally figure out the most streamlined interpretation you can give so you're not trapped all day.

Your Readings Have Value

When I first started doing professional readings, I had a lot of anxiety about the financial aspect. Were my readings really worth actual money? Isn't this just for fun? I quickly learned that people at every level of society go to readers when they have real-life decisions to make, and the insights that surface in these readings empower querents to move forward with confidence and creativity. Like any other service provider, you have a crucial role on your querents' "team of experts."

It's Very Rewarding

Card reading can make you popular at parties, but sometimes the universe (or whoever) puts you where someone needs you to be. Your words can help people heal their wounds, lift themselves up, and navigate their way out of dark places. They may express that to you in the moment or contact you years later to tell you how things worked out for them.

REMEMBER

From the days of the Oracle of Delphi (see Chapter 4) all the way down to you at this moment, divination is about being of service and finding the necessary answers — often for yourself but also for those who find their way to your table.

Just don't let it go to your head.

Index

About the Author

Charles Harrington has been reading, teaching, and loving tarot for more than 25 years. He's the author of a number of deck guidebooks, including *The Tarot of the Vampires, The Dante's Inferno Oracle, The Murder of Crows Tarot, The Ferenc Pinter Tarot, The Odyssey Oracle, Tarot V,* and *The Incubus Tarot* (all published by Llewellyn Publications) and others. An active member of the cartomancy community, he has given keynotes and workshops at conferences, hosted podcasts, and led meetups in the San Francisco Bay Area. In his free time, he loves to find new and strange ways to use the cards in pursuit of wisdom, fun, and the occasional free cocktail.

Dedication

For Dale and Nancy Harrington, who always encouraged my fascination with the cards; for Barbara Moore, my fellow wild mystic; and for Mitchell, my future.

Author's Acknowledgments

I would like to express my deepest gratitude to the entire team at Wiley for their insights, encouragement, and patience throughout the writing of his book. In particular, I want to thank Nicole Sholly, Megan Knoll, and Alicia Sparrow, whose kindness and enthusiasm kept me fired up each step of the way.

You can't ask for a more qualified expert editor in this field than Barbara Moore. I'm incredibly thankful for her ability to refine and challenge any text so that it will be of the greatest value to the reader.

Heartfelt thanks to all Bay Area cartomancy community members for their wisdom, guidance, and the many fun oracular adventures we've shared along the way. Special thanks goes out to Rodney W. Carter, Mary K. Greer, Anastasia Haysler, Mari Hoshizaki, HiC Luttmers, SallyRose Robinson, Debra Rosenthal, Thalassa Therese, and Benebell Wen.

I'm eternally indebted to my spiritual family in the Order of the Sacred Grove for our many years of magic together.

Publisher's Acknowledgments

Associate Acquisitions Editor:
  Alicia Sparrow

Development Editor: Nicole Sholly

Copy Editor: Megan Knoll

Technical Editor: Barbara Moore

Managing Editor: Murari Mukundan

Production Editor:
  Tamilmani Varadharaj

Cover Image:
  © Adam/stock.adobe.com